If you like *Leadership Coaching*, try...

The Calling Journey

Filled with examples from the lives of biblical and contemporary leaders and overflowing with insight on how God works through our circumstances, *The Calling Journey* provides a powerful perspective on your own journey and a great set of tools to work with those you coach. By mapping out the progression of stages and transitions God moves us through on the road to our call, the reader will gain an understanding of the unique agenda of each growth stage and how to coach each stage differently to line up with what God is doing in that season.

Coaching Questions

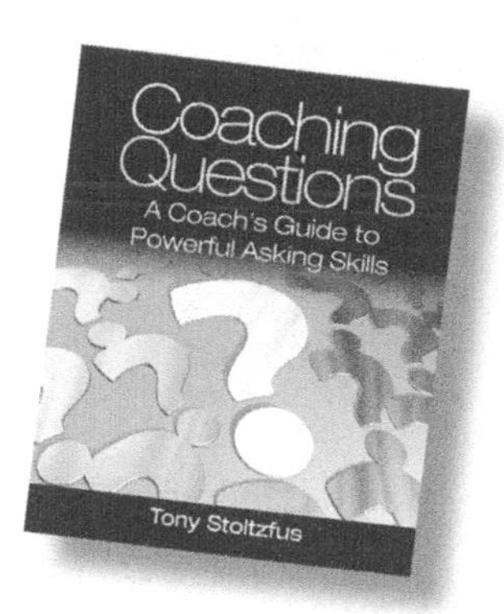

This best-selling coaching reference combines dozens of practical asking tools with over 1,000 examples of powerful coaching questions. Each major area of the coaching conversation is illustrated with multiple approaches. Covering everything from options and actions to decision-making strategies and reframing techniques, this book can help everyone from experienced coaches to trainers improve their asking proficiency.

The Christian Life Coaching Handbook

This sequel to the acclaimed book *Leadership Coaching* is the presentation of a thorough, practical toolkit for coaching Christian leaders to discover their destiny. Divided into two major sections, the first section opens with an in-depth treatment of the foundations of life coaching based on the premise that the models we use to understand purpose must fit with the record of Jesus' life we find in the Gospels. The second section presents a model of life purpose discovery based on the five themes of allegiance, design, passion, preparation and calling, each explored using case studies and coaching dialogs interspersed with biblical examples and descriptions of powerful coaching techniques.

For more information or to purchase the above coaching resources from Tony Stoltzfus, go to www.Coach22.com.

Praise for Leadership Coaching

"This is a great book for those who want to not only learn about coaching but also want to improve their coaching skills. Coaching is a core skill for cell church planters and leaders. They will find Leadership Coaching an invaluable tool for improving their own coaching and for training others in the art of coaching."

Jeannette Buller
Professional Coach and author of *The Cell Church Planter's Guide*

"They have read four chapters and they absolutely love the book! The story approach and practical lessons were really hitting home with everyone. It was definitely the best choice for a text that I could have made for the [coaching] class."

Brian Simon
President, iCoachnet.com

"It is a must read for all coaches, but especially those who coach Christians. Perhaps even more significantly, this book will change the lives of those who have no aspirations to coach. This book should be considered a basic handbook in human relations."

Dr. Jerry Graham
Professional Coach and Coach Trainer

"...it is nearly impossible to find a book to read that is actually worth your time. Leadership Coaching is one of those rare finds. Whether a cell church pastor or cell member, cell coach or cell leader, whether mature in the faith or brand new in the Lord, if you deal at all with people, Leadership Coaching is a 'must read'... I strongly recommend it be read, and applied, by cell church leadership everywhere."

Dr. Les Brickman
President, Strategic Cell Ministry International

"Tony was my personal coach and coach trainer for many years. I experienced the coaching paradigm and process with Tony first by my heart—and now I get it by my head after reading this book. It is an honor for me to endorse the power of Tony's book and message. This book will serve many Korean leaders, inspiring them to become coaches and provide a road map for their practice. Thank you for the excellent work."

Paul Jeong
President, NCD Korea

"Tony Stoltzfus and the Transformational Leadership Coaching (TLC) process radically revolutionized my life and ministry. Tony's authentic guidance and support coupled with the TLC process enabled me to clarify God's direction and purpose for this season...

Tony is truly an experienced and uniquely gifted coach. I most strongly recommend his services to anyone seeking to soar into their God-given destiny and purpose. He will coach you to your 'true greatness.'

Dr. R. Earl Brown
President, Giving People Hope International Ministries
Author, Coach and Coach Trainer

Leadership
COACHING
The Disciplines, Skills and Heart of a Christian Coach
TONY STOLTZFUS

ISBN 1-4196-1050-3

Cover Design by Mark Neubauer

Some of the anecdotal illustrations in this book are true to life, and are included with the permission of the persons involved. All other illustrations are composites of real situations, and any resemblance to persons living or dead is coincidental.

For additional copies of this book and other coaching and coach training materials, visit our web site at:

www.Coach22.com

Table of Contents

INTRODUCTION

Introduction

The Future is Coaching

"In the future, people who are not coaches will not be promoted." Jack Welch

In our generation, a seismic change is occurring in the way that leaders are trained and developed. The way we lead and the way we learn to lead is already quite different than it was a few decades ago. Top-down systems are giving way to team models that empower more people to lead, in a much wider variety of roles. This shift toward teamwork and empowerment puts a premium on having great interpersonal skills. Much more than in the past, ministry leadership means influencing and empowering rather than ordering—working together with others instead of telling them what to do or simply doing the work yourself. In short, to be an effective leader means being a coach.

Leadership Coaching is the discipline of using relational influence to develop and empower adult leaders. By contrast, the old familiar tools we've used to work with people one-on-one center more around imparting than empowering. A mentor imparts wisdom and opportunities to a junior; a counselor diagnoses a problem and suggests solutions; a discipler communicates the basics of Christian living and helps keep a new believer on track. While these are effective methods, the weakness of impartation is that it is better at creating followers than at developing leaders. When you offer a diagnosis, solution or plan of action, the person you offer it to will tend to *follow* your counsel instead of *leading* with their own ideas. To develop adult leaders, we need a method of working with people that pushes them to take responsibility and lead, not follow. That, in a nutshell, is coaching.

Do you have a systematic method for developing the leaders God has given you to steward? Coaching can give you that system.

> **Stories and Illustrations**
>
> Most of the stories in this book are real, and come directly from client interviews or my own experiences. When I'm training coaches, we always practice with real situations from the lives of the trainees. There is nothing like seeing a real change in someone's life.
>
> When the coach's name is mentioned, it is the real name of a real coach. So if you'd like to be coached by someone mentioned in this book, give him or her a call! In other stories, dialog has been reconstructed where memory fails, or names and details have been changed so the gist of the story remains but individual clients cannot be identified.

Purpose

This book has two objectives. The first is to help you understand how the coaching approach develops leaders and how it fits in with the broader purposes of God. In essence, it's laying out a coherent biblical ***Coaching Paradigm***. Part I of this book examines what coaching is, the heart and perspective of a coach, the value system that undergirds coaching, and how the coaching approach is uniquely suited to leadership development.

The second objective is to provide local church leaders with a practical how-to guide to the ***Coaching Process***. In Part II, I'll be sharing some of the principles and practices I've used to train hundreds of professional Christian coaches worldwide. We'll start by looking at the underlying context of coaching: it is client-centered, relationship based and goal-driven. Then we'll build on that foundation by examining the four key skill areas in the coaching conversation: listening, asking, acting and supporting.

Finally, Part III talks about ***Getting Into Coaching*** by furthering your coach training or getting involved with what God is doing with coaching around the globe. It includes several appendices of coaching resource materials.

This book is written for:

- Those who want to become more effective at walking with other leaders
- Local church leaders who want to learn to coach
- Christian coaches who want to sharpen their skills and develop a more coherent biblical coaching philosophy
- Coach trainers who want a text for offering basic Christian coach training to others

Getting the Most from this Book

Years ago, I spoke to a leader who had trained every one of the small group leaders in his church in a certain leadership skill. The training involved teaching and demonstration, but didn't include any practice time. A year later he went back and surveyed that group of trainees and made a surprising discovery: only one in seven of the leaders he'd trained had even *attempted* to use the new skill they'd been taught. It was a sobering lesson for him on the weakness of teaching skills without including practice.

While the statistics vary, one study I've seen found that learners who practiced a skill retained *700% more* than those who simply read about it. Reading or teaching can give us the conceptual knowledge to use a skill, but only practice and feedback provide the confidence most of us need to apply it in real life.

Because practice is so important to skill development, the "how-to" section of the book contains application exercises that let you try out what you're learning on friends, relatives or yourself. Part II also includes many practical "Master Class" chapters, which use plenty of exercises, examples and transcriptions of coaching conversations to demonstrate the core coaching techniques in action. If you'd like to get 700% more out of this book, take time to do the application exercises in these chapters!

To further enhance your learning experience, an audio CD set called "*Leadership Coaching Live*" was created specifically to complement this book. Filled with coaching demos, actual coaching appointments, and live training sessions, this CD set will bring the concepts you're reading about to life. To purchase a copy, visit www.Coach22.com.

Leadership Coaching gives you the basics you need to begin coaching or start using coaching skills in your leadership role. However, this book is *not* a substitute for a professional coach training program. If you plan to coach for an income, the coaching industry provides professional training and certification that will prepare you to do so. The interaction and practice you'll receive by working with a coach trainer will take you much farther than you can go with a book alone.

Coaching Everywhere

This book describes how to set up and maintain formal coaching relationships with a "client," using a covenant, regular appointments, etc. However, the same techniques can be used in one-time coaching sessions or even in informal conversations. For example, this past Sunday I had a powerful coaching encounter at church between services. I found myself talking to a woman who was at a transition point in her life, so I asked a coaching question: "What have you always dreamed about doing?" She had a dream but had gotten stuck and didn't know how to pursue it. Just those ten minutes helped get her re-energized about pursuing her destiny.

Coaching skills can make every conversation you have transformational. I use coaching questions every day, with my kids (they're great with teenagers), in supermarket checkout lines, on airplanes—every conversation is an opportunity to coach. Learning these skills can improve your performance as a leader, take your relational skills from good to great and give you the tools you need to develop the leaders around you. So, join me as we explore how the disciplines, skills and heart of a coach can radically transform your influence and ability as a leader.

The Coaching Paradigm

The Disciplines, Skills and Heart of a Coach

At its heart, leadership coaching is about helping people solve their own problems, not telling them what to do. One of the most difficult changes beginning coaches must make is learning to ask questions instead of giving advice. As they struggle to get used to this new approach, the following kinds of questions invariably come out:

- *"Would it help if you'd keep track of how much time you're spending on that project?"*
- *"Could you just come right out and say something to her about the problem?"*
- *"Do you think you should talk to your pastor about that?"*

To see what's really going on, simply cross out the first several words of each question, like this:

- *"~~Would it help if you'd~~ Keep track of how much time you're spending on that project."*
- *"~~Could you~~ Just come right out and say something to her about the problem."*
- *"~~Do you think~~ You should talk to your pastor about that."*

Oops! What we thought were good coaching queries turn out to be statements instead. The coach is dutifully attempting to ask questions, but what actually comes out are pieces of advice with question marks stuck on the end.

These statements are what I call *solution-oriented questions:* advice-giving masquerading as coaching. While the coach is working diligently at the technique of asking, the change is only skin-deep. The coach is still the one identifying and solving the problem, then trying to lead the client to a certain solution. On the surface it looks like coaching, but the underlying advice-giving paradigm hasn't changed.

Solution-oriented questions are a great illustration of what it looks like to try to change what you *do* without changing who you *are*. Jesus discussed this age-old problem when He stated, "Out of the abundance of the heart the mouth speaks" (Matt. 12:34). In other words, what you do and say comes out of who you are—your "being". What you say won't change until *you* change. According to Jesus, to fundamentally alter the way you function, you have to be transformed at the "being" level (values, identity, paradigms and worldview) and not just in your "doing" (skills and techniques).

If you approach leadership coaching as a set of tools and techniques to add on to your existing ministry paradigm, you'll never be a coach. I can't emphasize this enough: *leadership coaching is a whole new discipline,* with an underlying philosophy and value set that most likely is far different than what you are used to. Becoming a great coach is a major remodeling project that will alter your values, the way you look at people and the conversational habits of a lifetime. Becoming a transformational coach starts with being transformed.

Disciplines, Skills and Heart

As a former Director of Training for a Christian coaching school, I've worked with hundreds of aspiring coaches around the world. In the process, I've developed a training philosophy based on the idea of *disciplines, skills and heart.* While all three are needed for maximum effectiveness, the heart of a coach is the foundation. When you begin to think like a coach, believe in the coaching values and see others through the eyes of a coach, the coaching skills come naturally to you. Simply put, coaching is a radical belief

Coaching from the Heart

I once sat in on a coach training role-play where the trainee was floundering badly. She interrupted the client, gave unwanted advice, and asked solution-oriented questions—it was painful to watch. During the debriefing time following the session, I struggled to find anything positive in her performance to affirm.

Later that afternoon, I came around to her table and watched her coach again. The difference between her first and second attempts was like night and day—she listened intently, asked excellent questions and helped the client develop his own great solution. Afterward, I complimented her profusely, then inquired, "You did so well this time—what changed from the first session?" After thinking it over for a moment, she replied, "Well...I guess I was just so interested in what this person had to say that I really wanted to listen." It was a great demonstration of the principle: *When you have the heart of a coach, the techniques come naturally.*

in people, practiced in a consistent, disciplined way in order to help others grow. Understanding and embracing the heart of the coaching paradigm is vital to coaching success.

When you start with the heart of a coach, the coaching skills take on a greater significance. They are not practiced as stand-alone techniques, but as *the disciplines of believing in people.* Coaches don't listen because listening is a good technique, because it is effective, or even because people like to be listened to. A coach listens because to listen is to believe in you. It's a conscious imitation of the way Christ treats others. Listening is one of the most powerful, compelling ways to say, "You are a great person—I have confidence in you!"

When I practice a technique as a discipline, an important by-product is that it changes me as well. For example, when I pray regularly, my ability to tune into God increases, I see more clearly how God is at work in my life and I come to value prayer even more. In the same way, when I listen habitually, my ability to tune into others increases, I see more clearly how God is sovereignly at work in them and I come to value what they have to say even more.

Practicing the coaching techniques (listening, asking, goal-setting, and taking responsibility) in a disciplined, consistent way is living the lifestyle of a coach. It's when you believe enough in the coaching paradigm to reorder your own life around it that you'll truly be great at coaching others.

Your Biggest Obstacle

The biggest obstacle faced by the Christian coaching revolution is the get-skills-quick mentality we bring to leadership development. Everybody wants to go to a one-day workshop and then come out magically transformed into a coach. It doesn't work that way. That approach treats coaching as a set of techniques, not a lifestyle. Practicing techniques on people just to get a certain result ultimately fails: technique without heart is manipulation. Sooner or later, people will realize that you are more interested in the results than you are in them.

Reading a book in a few hours won't make you a coach either. Beyond what's in this book, the things you'll most need to coach well are:

1. To have your own heart genuinely and radically transformed by the coaching values;
2. Lots of practice;
3. Interaction with a professional coach trainer.

But, ultimately, everything comes back to your heart. If you have the heart of a coach, you can make every technique mistake in the book and you'll still transform people's lives. My prayer for you is that this book makes you hunger to discover and passionately live the lifestyle of a coach.

Chapter 1

What is Coaching?

"I've been through counseling and all kinds of training in business and in church, but I've never had anything like this before, that combines the business world and the church and what is going on inside me... I'm just growing so much."
Christian Entrepreneur

My first coaching appointment of the morning was 15 minutes away. The client, Doug Jefferson, was a church planter from a Midwestern metro area. We'd met at a workshop the year before, and, several weeks after the workshop, he called to explore what a coaching relationship might look like. After a 30-minute "test drive" session, Doug was charged up and eager to be coached.

Up to this point, Doug's gregariousness, character and work ethic had served him well in his church plant. In only two years, without a whole lot of support ("My supervisor just rented a building one day and told me, 'Here's where you start—your first service is this Sunday!'") he and his wife had built the congregation up to 125 people. While Doug was a naturally high-energy guy, two years of working flat out had taken a toll on him, and he realized he needed to refocus and give attention to other priorities.

My first step in getting ready for the coaching session was to review the client's change goal and my notes from our last meeting.

Doug's goal was to "Make the transition in my schedule and time management from start-up church-planter mode to a sustainable, long-term lifestyle by the end of the year." So far, we'd worked on developing a plan to raise up leaders for several key teams, and on finding time in his schedule to visit the gym and work out three times a week.

Glancing back through my notes reminded me that Doug's progress had been outstanding. Each time we'd talked about his action steps, I'd found that he'd met his exercise target for that week and he was on track with the deadline he'd set for himself to get new team leaders in place. In our last appointment, Doug had identified the need to reduce his workload by an additional eight hours per week, so we spent most of the session brainstorming about different options. Doug settled on several responsibilities he could delegate or let go of all together and wrote them down as his action steps for the next week. I was looking forward to hearing back from Doug about his progress on this latest set of steps.

I settled down in my black leather "coaching recliner," plugged the headset into my cordless phone and spent a little time in prayer for Doug as I waited for his call. A few moments later he was on the line.

What is Coaching?

Like most people who have discovered leadership coaching, Doug signed on with a coach to help him reach goals that he had a hard time accomplishing on his own. He knew what he wanted to do, but he also knew enough about himself to realize that a demanding job made taking control of his schedule a big task. Change always takes energy. Having a change expert to walk with while he pursued this important goal kept Doug focused and reduced the energy he had to expend—and that made it possible for him to tackle bigger changes at a faster pace than he could on his own.

Simply stated, *coaches are change experts who help leaders take responsibility for their lives and act to maximize their own potential.* Learning to coach is learning to set up relationships that provide the exact kind of support a leader needs to radically pursue his or her God-given destiny. A coach is a true friend and a close confidant on the path of life, someone who often hears, "I've never told this to anyone before, but..." A coach is someone who sees

Definitions of Coaching

"Coaches are change experts who help leaders take responsibility and act to maximize their own potential."

"Coaching is like having a personal trainer for every area of your life."

"Coaching is a dialogue, not a monologue."

Joseph Umidi

"Coaching is practicing the disciplines of believing in people in order to empower them to change." Tony Stoltzfus

"Coaching is unlocking a person's potential to maximize their growth." John Whitmore

"Coaching is the art and practice of guiding a person or group from where they are toward the greater competence and fulfillment that they desire." Gary Collins

"Mentoring is imparting to you what God has given me; coaching is drawing out of you what God has put in you."

Dale Stoll

you as made in the image of God and tells you the truth about who you really are. A coach pushes you to think, to stretch yourself, to take responsibility for your life and get done what you know you need to do. A coach is also someone who will hold you accountable, challenge you to live out your values or occasionally give you a swift kick in the pants when you need it.

Coaches are many things, but the essence of coaching is *believing in people.* Nothing is more empowering, nothing causes us to reach higher and accomplish greater things than having people in our lives that love us for who we are and believe unconditionally in what we can become. That is what Jesus does for us—He sees in us who we were made to be and loves us for who we are. Coaching is a conscious imitation of the way that Christ looks at us and the way that God develops leaders. It's a relationship centered on helping people discover and fulfill their destiny, which uses goals and action steps to move strategically toward that end. In summary, coaching is *Relationship-Based, Goal-Driven* and *Client-Centered.*

All that being said, trying to give a description of coaching that makes sense the first time around is a tough row to hoe. It's when I *show* a group what coaching is (usually by pulling a volunteer from the audience and coaching them in front of the group) that the lights really start to come on. So, in this chapter, we're going to examine a typical coaching conversation to highlight several key principles that make coaching work.

Exercise 1.1: Who Sets the Agenda?

Let's start by returning to the narrative about Doug at the beginning of this chapter. Flip back to that story and underline each time a goal, objective or action step is mentioned. Then, at each place you marked, note whether the *coach* or the *client* came up with that goal or step. By the time you are done you'll have discovered the first of our key coaching principles:

"The ______________ sets the agenda."

If you've skipped down to this paragraph to find the right answer without doing the exercise, you won't see it here—and there's a good reason for that omission. Coaching is about pushing you to discover a solution, not about giving you the answers. This principle, one of the key differences between coaching and mentoring, is stated well by one of the founders of the coaching movement, John Whitmore:

"Coaching is helping people learn instead of teaching them."

This is one key difference between coaching and mentoring. Here's another important coaching distinctive. Malcolm Knowles (known as "the father of adult education" in the U.S.) states, "One of the most significant findings from adult learning research...

Coaching vs. Mentoring

Coaching and mentoring are one-on-one relationships that use support and accountability to grow people toward a better future. Here's an example of the difference. A person has a job opportunity that would move his career forward but requires relocating and leaving friends and family behind.

The Mentoring Approach

"That sounds like a great opening! It must be rewarding to be recognized like this."

"Yeah, it sure is!"

"I had a few similar opportunities when I was a youth pastor. One was a great move; the other was sort of a disaster."

"What was the difference?"

"One position was in a college town with a lot of people in our age group. My wife thrived on the fellowship and loved the cultural events she could go to in the city.

"Then we moved to a country church in Nebraska. People were spread out all over. They'd offered me 40% more than what I'd been making, plus the senior pastor role, which was a big step up. But my wife never felt like she fit in; she had a hard time making friends, and it was tough on her and on our marriage. In retrospect, she didn't really want to go, but she was deferring to me. I didn't tune into what my wife was saying, and that was a mistake. What is your wife saying about this decision?"

The Coaching Approach

"That sounds like a great opening! It must be rewarding to be recognized like this."

"Yeah, it sure is!"

"How would this move change your life?"

"Well, probably the biggest difference is going to be the relationship with my parents. We'll miss going over for Sunday dinner and the free babysitting. Vacations and dates will be a lot tougher. Oh—mom and dad are going to really miss doing the grandparent thing. I better talk this through with them."

"Is that a step you want to take?"

"Yes. I'll do it this Sunday."

"How else will this affect your relational life?"

"We'll be able to make new friends eventually. It'll be harder for Patrice, because I'll be spending a lot of time at the church while she is stuck at home with the kids. Her mom's group is a big deal for her. We better talk that one over, too. I can check and see if the new church has a mom's support group or something like it..."

Coaching vs. Mentoring (Cont'd)

In the example on the previous page, the mentor is showing the younger pastor the ropes and giving wise counsel gained from life experience. A mentor is a more senior individual who *imparts* what God has given (wisdom, opportunities and counsel) to a more junior person. In the same situation, the coach is building the client's decision-making ability by asking him to think things through in a structured way. A coach *draws out* the abilities God has put in someone else.

When I'm mentoring, I'm teaching a person, letting him draw from me or learn from my experience. When I'm coaching, I'm pushing a person to draw from his or her own resources and experiences. Coaching is helping people learn instead of teaching them.

is that when adults learn something naturally instead of 'being taught,' they are highly self-directing [i.e. they feel ownership and act on it]... What adults learn on their own initiative they learn more keenly and permanently than what they learn by being 'taught.' (Malcolm Knowles, *Designs for Adult Learning*, page 10.) Put into a catch phrase, that nugget might sound something like this:

"Your own insight is much more powerful than my advice."

If you develop a solution for an issue you want to work on, you'll be much more likely to act on it than if I tell you what to do and how to do it. One of the many places Jesus uses this principle is in the story of the Good Samaritan. At the end of the parable, Jesus asks, "Which of these three do you think proved to be a neighbor...?" He lets His hearers figure out the lesson for themselves, so they own it, instead of telling them the moral of the story.

Adults learn best when they are *learning from life:* taking real challenges that they are motivated to address, developing their own solutions, immediately applying them and seeing the results. As leaders, they take responsibility for their own growth and their own problems. Part of what makes coaching so effective is that it is designed around the basic principles of how adult leaders learn.

Exercise 1.2: Support Structures

Let's do another exercise while we continue our dialogue with Doug. Coaching is a support structure for change. As you read the story, look for that structure: what is Doug's coach doing in this appointment to bolster him and keep him moving toward his goals? Underline the places where you see this structure and try to name or define what the coach is doing in each instance.

The Progress Report

"Hey, Doug, how are you doin' today?"

"Pretty good—and yourself?"

"Looking forward to the day. Tonight I'm going to the hockey game with Taylor. That'll be fun!"

"How old is he again?"

"Ten. His favorite part is when they shoot T-shirts into the crowd with an air cannon during half-time. So—what's the most interesting thing that's happened in your life in the past week?"

"The most interesting thing... Well, that's sort of what I wanted to talk about today. I was stuck in traffic last Thursday on the way home, running 45 minutes behind and already missing supper. I was bored, so I started thinking back to some of the stuff I used to do with my dad when I was a kid—going to basketball games, working on our old VW together out in the garage, that kind of thing. Suddenly it hit me: my boys aren't going to be boys for too much longer. I want to make sure I make the most of the years before they grow up."

"It sounds like you hit on something that's important to you. Before we go into that, can I ask you to give me a quick progress report on your action steps from last time?"

"Sure. Let me get my list in front of me. OK—I had two things I was going to delegate to get them off my plate. I asked Bob about leading pre-service prayer, and he seemed excited about it. He said he could do it three times a month, so that was easy."

"Quick question: Bob is going to do it three times a month; what do you want to do with the fourth Sunday?"

"Well, I guess I was just going to keep doing it. But now that

you ask, I could probably try to find someone for those off weeks... Or, here's an even better idea: I'll ask Bob to take initiative to find someone for the Sundays he is out of town. That way he is really taking on the leadership role and that responsibility is off my plate completely."

"Sounds like a great solution. So is that a step you are going to take?"

"Yeah, definitely," Doug replied, "I'll call Bob this week and ask him about taking care of that as well."

"Excellent. What other steps were you working on?"

"I talked to the Johnson's about leading the college-age group. It seemed like we were right on the same wave length, so I'm going to transition out of that role. I'll go another month or two to wrap things up, but I should be done by the end of the summer. That will free up one evening a week. I also talked to the elders about having a limit of no more than three counseling clients at a time. They agreed to hold me accountable to that."

"Sounds like you really made some progress. Anything else?"

"Well," Doug offered sheepishly, "I let go of working on the bulletin all together. My step was to give it to the secretary to format and then come back and check everything after she was done—you know how picky I am about how things look. But, after sitting there for 10 minutes going over everything with a fine-toothed comb, I just thought, 'You know, if she's ever going to get the confidence to do this, I can't keep looking over her shoulder.' So, I gritted my teeth, and told her I didn't need to look at it any more and that she could just run with it." Doug sighed, "It's hard for me to let go of stuff like that, but I guess it'll probably be a good thing in the long run."

"So, what do you think—will it be a good thing to let go of that or not?"

Doug thought for a moment, then laughed. "Yeah, it will. If I don't quit piddling away my time on trivia we'll stop growing and I'll burn myself out."

"Good insight. One last thing—I want to keep checking in on your exercise goal for a while even though you've been doing great. Did you get to the gym three times in the last week?"

"Yeah, no problem—except for the one time I got there and had forgotten my clothes!" Doug chuckled. "I just stop by on my way in on Tuesday, Thursday and Friday and then go straight from there to *work. That's going well."*

"It seems like overall you're making a lot of progress. You feeling good about that?"

"Absolutely!"

"OK. Then let's get back to your agenda for today. You mentioned that you wanted to make the most of your time with your boys..."

Supporting Change

What did you discover in this story about how coaching facilitates change? Doug came eager to talk about getting more family time, but instead his coach redirected the conversation to first get a progress report on the action steps they'd established at the last appointment. In fact, each time Doug settles on a step, his coach makes a note of it and then asks for a progress report on that step the next time they met.

It's amazing how much difference accountability makes. It's easy to put things off or let circumstances interfere with reaching our goals—until we know we are going to be asked about them! Whether you are dieting, developing a Bible study habit or trying to complete a task you've been avoiding at work, accountability makes it more likely that you'll succeed. It's a simple but powerful principle for supporting change.

Did you also notice the repeated affirmation that came from the coach? When Doug accomplished something it was recognized. Workplace studies have found that the top motivator for employees is not job security, promotion opportunities or even good pay—it's appreciation. When what we do is recognized, cheered and affirmed, we perform at a higher level. Support, encouragement and accountability form a support structure the coach deploys to help the client get things done.

Coaching is a support structure for change.

If you thought a little more broadly about this story, you may have noticed that coaching revolves around taking action to create a better future. Coaching is about focusing forward, not about fixing the past. At each appointment we follow up on previous action steps and generate new ones. This future-orientation is one of the key differences between coaching and counseling.

Coaching vs. Counseling

Coaching and counseling are both one-on-one relationships focused on growth. However, counseling tends to concentrate on helping people get well, whereas coaching works with healthy people who want to further improve their lives.

For example, this individual is having trouble dreaming about future possibilities because of past baggage. Here's what a counseling and coaching approach might look like.

The Counseling Approach

"So what I'm hearing is that dreaming wasn't accepted in your family."

"Yeah—my dad was always denigrating 'those dreamers who want to have it all without doing an honest day's work.'"

"What else does your dad denigrate?"

"Oh, he's got an opinion about everything. That was tough when I was at home; he didn't like the way I did my hair, didn't like my friends, and didn't like my ideas. He's always pontificating about something."

"How do you feel about that?"

"How did I feel? Well...I'm not sure. Sometimes I got mad; sometimes I'd just leave the house. I don't even remember a lot of it. It just sort of all blends together in my mind now."

"So your dad treated you this way pretty often?"

"Yeah, he did it to mom, too."

"So it sounds like there was a pattern of verbal abuse in your family..."

The Coaching Approach

"So what I'm hearing is that dreaming wasn't accepted in your family."

"Yeah—my dad was always denigrating 'those dreamers who want to have it all without doing an honest day's work.'"

"So what do you think: is dreaming incompatible with doing an honest day's work?"

"No! Why should it have anything to do with my work ethic?"

"I agree—I've always known you to have a great work ethic, and I think being able to dream can only make you more focused and productive. So what do you need to do to get beyond this obstacle?"

"Good question... I'm thinking. I guess I just need to push through this. My dad is wrong. I think he got that idea from his dad—maybe it's a depression-era thing. It feels uncomfortable, but I'm just going to do it. And, if I get stuck, I'll sit down with my husband and we'll pray through it."

Coaching vs. Counseling (Cont'd)

The counselor is diagnosing the client's emotional or psychological state and helping the client become whole. By contrast, the coach pushes the client to set goals and take action to solve the problem on her own. Coaching improves your quality of life by focusing on creating a better future, instead of by fixing problems from the past.

Note that the coaching approach is not "superior" to the counseling approach, or vice versa. Both are valid, useful and different. Which one you use depends on the person you are working with and what you're attempting to accomplish.

In a coaching relationship, we're not meeting just to talk; we have an agenda, clear expectations and concrete goals we're shooting for. Coaching is a growth-centered relationship. There is a definite, up-front expectation that if an action step is decided on, it is going to get done! Establishing and maintaining this standard is a big part of what makes coaching work. Here's the way I state that principle:

Don't set any goals you aren't going to meet.

That's a pretty obvious idea, right? But it's utterly divergent from how our lives usually work. I just had a physical, and my doctor suggested some changes in my diet to improve my health. What percentage of his patients do you think actually do what he recommends? (Maybe I'll ask him next time I'm in.) I'd be surprised if it was 20%. How many of us actually follow through on those annual New Year's resolutions? How many times have you set out to improve your devotional life, watch less TV, spend more time with your kids, or exercise regularly? If you've ever mentored or discipled someone who never followed through on your advice or suggestions, you know how frustrating that can be.

This highlights another important coaching practice: coaches give very little advice and make few suggestions. That fact runs counter to every instinct: I'm going to pay a professional *not* to give me advice? Why would I do that? The answer can revolutionize the way you work with people: *Being motivated to make a change is more important than knowing what change to make.* Anyone can tell me what I ought to do; but internal motivation can only come from within me.

Most of the time we have a pretty clear idea what God is asking of us. *God initiates change* in our lives—He has a personalized change agenda for us and is always speaking and arranging circumstances to bring it to our attention. This is what I believe John was thinking about when he said, "And as for you, the anointing which you received from Him abides in you, and you have no need for anyone to teach you; but as his anointing teaches you about all things...abide in Him" (I John 2:27). The Holy Spirit is pretty skilled at getting our attention. We know what we need to work on. What we lack is the energy and motivation to get started and then to follow through. In coaching, we say:

Change is more a function of motivation than information.

Prioritizing motivation over information makes an enormous difference in how we do one-on-one ministry. When we believe that in order to change, people need us to tell them what they need to do, we give advice. However, when we believe the most important factor in change is motivation, we ask questions and encourage people to come up with their own solutions, because we know that buy-in and motivation are highest for steps that we develop and choose on our own. That's why the coaching approach of listening and asking questions (the disciplines of believing in people) is more effective at fostering change than the advice-giving approach. Coaching prioritizes buy-in and motivation over giving people the right solution.

In the next chapter, we'll continue exploring the key principles that make coaching work.

Chapter 1: Exercise Answers

1.1 The client sets the agenda in a coaching relationship. That's what it means to be *client-centered.*

1.2 Examples of things the coach is doing in the dialogue to support change:

- *"Before we go into that, can I ask you to give me a quick progress report on your action steps from last time?"* The progress report supplies accountability for the client's prior set of action steps.
- *"What do you want to do with the fourth Sunday?"* The coach asks for a follow-up action step to complete the hand-off of this responsibility.
- *"So is that a step you are going to take?"* The coach makes sure the client is committed to the step and verbalizes that commitment.
- *"Sounds like you really made some progress. Anything else?"* The coach affirms progress and makes sure that accountability is provided for all the client's steps.
- *"I want to keep checking in on your exercise goal for a while even though you've been doing great. Did you get to the gym three times in the last week?"* The coach continues to follow-up until the new habit is fully established.
- *"It seems like overall you're making a lot of progress. You feeling good about that?"* The coach encourages the client by calling attention to overall progress.

What is Coaching? Part II

> *"[My coach's] genuine encouragement and accountability helped me to complete my first book, which is at the time of this writing receiving serious consideration by a major publisher! His coaching was a crucial catalyst to completing the book... For me, the paramount characteristic of my coach is his ability to focus on my future potential—not my past mistakes."* Para-church Leader

Exercise 2.1: Exploration

During the next section of the coaching appointment, Doug explores how to make the most of his boys' growing-up years with his coach. As you read, look for the words or phrases that make you wonder, "Why did Doug say that?" In each of Doug's responses, underline the most interesting thing he says. At the end, we'll use the phrases you've highlighted to demonstrate how a coach manages an exploratory conversation.

"Doug, you mentioned earlier that you wanted to make the most of your time with your boys. Tell me more about that."

"Well, I don't feel like I'm getting enough time with my kids and I don't like that. Family is a pretty high priority for me, but frankly, I'm not sure you'd know it just by looking at my life."

"I'd like to get a better picture of what you are perceiving. Take

a look at your life and tell me what you see."

"OK. I've got two boys: Johnny is nine and Silas is eleven—they're neat kids. We love to wrestle and roughhouse in the living room, and I like to read to them before bed. We fly kites or go to games on Saturdays. They like being with me and I like being with them. The problem is, we just don't get enough time together."

"How much time would feel like enough?"

"I don't know," Doug mused. "More than we get now. More like what I had when we were in the apartment."

"What was different when you were living in the apartment?"

"Well, two months ago we bought a new house about 45 minutes away from my work. The church is in an upscale city neighborhood, meaning we could barely afford the rent on the two-bedroom apartment we had. Its only virtue was being five minutes from the church. Buying farther out was the only way we could afford the kind of house we wanted. It's in a great neighborhood with good schools, and my wife loves it. What's different is the commute. That makes my day over an hour longer—two if I'm driving during rush hour."

"So spell it out—how does the commute affect your time with the kids?"

"It really shouldn't have altered it that much. I mean, since we started coaching I've cut at least as much time out of my week as it takes to drive to work. I guess the main difference is that I've had to jigger my schedule around to miss the traffic, so a lot of weeks I don't see them from Tuesday night 'til Friday night. I've started leaving early and doing a lot of breakfast meetings, so three or four days a week the boys are still asleep when I leave. And on Wednesdays and Thursdays I have evening meetings, so they're in bed by the time I get home."

"So what's bothering you the most: not getting enough time in general with the boys, or those long stretches where you don't see them for two or three days?"

Doug mulled it over a few moments. "It's the long stretches," he mused. "I hate the idea of them going through their lives for days at a time without seeing their dad, and I miss seeing them, too. If it weren't for that, I'd feel good about the amount of time we have together."

"OK. So what I'm hearing is that you want to focus on the long

stretches where you don't see the kids..."

The Coaching Conversation

The exercise for this story was to highlight the most important word or phrase in each of Doug's responses. Now let's do one more thing: look back and see how many times the exact words or phrases you underlined are repeated in the coach's next question.

If you made a lot of connections, you've got a good picture of how exploratory dialogue works in a coaching conversation. The coach homes in on the most interesting, unusual or significant thing the client shares (this is called intuitive listening), and asks the client to go deeper at that point. The coach is leveraging the *client's* discernment to identify and solve the problem, instead of trying to figure it out himself. This approach is based on a key coaching principle:

> **The Advice-Giving Paradigm**
>
> *The best way to help you change is to give you wise* ***counsel*** *about what to do with your life in a convincing way, so that you'll make a* ***decision*** *to change.*

People can solve their own problems.

In this conversation, the coach believes that Doug has the ability to steward the life God has given to him. Therefore, identifying and solving a problem is simply a matter of helping Doug think it through and walking with him while he carries out his solution. Doug can solve his own problems without being told what to do by a coach. This shift—from a diagnostic, advice-giving approach where the coach figures out what the issue is and solves it for you, to a curiosity-based, asking method where you solve your own problem—is the central paradigm shift in learning to

> **The Coaching Paradigm**
>
> *The best way to help you change is to create a structured, supportive* ***relationship*** *that helps you take* ***responsibility*** *for your life and make the changes you want to make.*

A Coach's Expertise

One benefit of the coaching approach is that it doesn't require the coach to be a subject matter expert, like a mentor or consultant. Instead, coaches are generalists: they're *change experts*. The client supplies the change agenda, the goal, the solution and the action steps. What the coach brings to the table is an understanding of how change happens (See chapter 16), and the ability to create an optimal environment for growth. Coaches need to know how to listen, ask powerful questions, keep the client responsible and provide follow-up. Those principles are transferable to almost any human endeavor.

For instance, I've coached a successful entrepreneur and business owner in the real estate field for several years. Although I have a lot of sales and general business experience, I've never worked in real estate. But I don't have to: my client is the real estate expert, and he's the expert on his own life. My job is to use my coaching skills to help him make changes and solve his own problems.

Theoretically, a coach can work with a client on any issue, whether or not the coach is familiar with that issue or profession. Practically, some experience is a big help—you have a much better idea of what to ask!

The fact that the client is the expert instead of the coach has far-reaching implications. For instance, coaching is often a better fit for cross-cultural ministry than mentoring, because the coach doesn't supply answers to the client—answers that may not work in a different culture. Instead, the clients use their understanding of their own culture to craft solutions that work in their context. I've trained a number of coaches from Southeast Asia. I'm no expert at translating Christian principles into Asian cultures—but they are. Coaching has had a huge impact on them, in ways that I never could have anticipated or communicated. Thank goodness it wasn't my job to tell them how to live their lives!

coach. The box on page 21 shows the basic assumptions of the advice-giving approach, juxtaposed against the corresponding postulates of the coaching paradigm. The advice-giving approach centers on delivering information to spur grow. The coaching approach focuses on relationship as the agent of change, and uses questions instead of suggestions to keep the client responsible and moving forward. In coaching, we remind ourselves of this by saying:

Ask, don't tell.

There is another key reason why coaching depends on the client to develop goals, solutions and action steps: *each person is unique.* We each have different gifts and personality types; we are at different stages in our personal and leadership development; and we have one-of-a-kind histories, callings and relationships. When we counsel others, our tendency is to recommend that they do what worked for us in the past. But human beings are so different from each other that there is a good chance that my solution won't work for you at all—and if it does work, you may have to go about it in a totally different way. A solution developed by the client is much more likely to fit the client's capabilities, needs and circumstances than one developed by the coach.

Problem Solving in Coaching

As Doug's coach listens and asks questions, he isn't angling to lead Doug to a certain solution. A coach believes that if you listen intently and intuitively to your clients, they will eventually tell you the answer. If you are caught up in what we call "the conversation in your head"—diagnosing and solving the client's problems—you might miss it. Exploration involves listening closely; picking out what makes you most curious; then asking the client to expand on that.

For instance, at one point in the conversation, the coach asked, "How much time would feel like enough?" Doug's reply was, "I don't know. More than we get now. More like what I had when we were in the apartment." That response is very intriguing! Doug begins by saying he doesn't know how much is enough, but only a sentence later says he *does* know: enough is like when he was living in the apartment. So the coach's follow-up question is, "What was different when you were living in the apartment?"

Exercise 2.2: Assumptions about Change

Here's a quiz to help you ascertain your assumptions about change. Identify the most recent occasion when someone came to you for help with a problem. You'll need a *specific, real, recent situation*—general impressions of how you respond to people won't do! Once you have a situation in mind, jot down an answer to each of the following questions:

- What did this person need from me?
- What of value did I provide to him/her?
- If a problem was solved in the conversation, who proposed that solution?
- What kind of follow-up support was provided for implementing the solution?

Now, look critically at what you actually did in light of the two paradigms listed below. Which best fits how you acted?

The "Telling" Paradigm

1. My own knowledge and experience lets me accurately discern what you need to change and how to change it.
2. You need right information to make right choices.
3. My value to you is in the knowledge, life stories, ideas, and wisdom I can deliver to you in a convincing way.
4. You can't solve this without my help.
5. Change is a choice—with the right answers, you'll succeed.

The Coaching Paradigm

1. It's not my job to figure out what you should do: you're responsible for your life.
2. Transformation is a function of experience and relationship (teachable moments), not information.
3. My value to you is in helping you draw from your own knowledge, life experience, ideas and wisdom.
4. You are able to steward the life God has given you.
5. Successful change is more a function of support and motivation than information.

Notice that the coach's question even uses the same phrase the client did: "...in the apartment." When you reference the client's own words, your questions don't feel like interruptions, but natural extensions of the person's internal thought process. Soon the client is on a roll, thinking more deeply and creatively than before, and the breakthroughs come naturally. As a coach, your job is to create an environment for free exploration. Let the client do the thinking, while you keep the conversation focused and push it toward action.

Let the client do the thinking.

Exercise 2.3: Action Steps

In the final section of our coaching conversation with Doug, we'll start developing solutions and convert them into action steps. (It should tell you something about coaching that we've taken this much time to listen before we've started problem-solving!) As you read, look for how the coach ensures a high level of buy-in for the agreed-on action steps. Can you identify at least three different techniques the coach uses to help the client own each step? Record your answers in the blanks at the end of the story.

"Doug, if I understand you right, the thing that's bothering you is not so much the amount of time you have with your boys as it is the long stretches where you don't see them. Is that accurate?"

"Yeah, you've got it."

"Good. So, let's brainstorm a little. What could you do to change your situation? Give me three or four options."

"OK. One, I could come home for lunch once or twice in that stretch. But that's 90 minutes of driving to see them for half an hour—I don't think that's a very efficient use of my time. Or I could switch my Wednesday or Thursday evening meetings to another night. Those are both team meetings so I'd have to check with everyone else to see if we could switch."

"What else could you do?"

"Well, I could go in later on those mornings—after the rush hour instead of before. I'm already working late those days, so I don't need the hours. The reason I haven't wanted to do that is that my assistant pastor has had a real problem with tardiness and his work ethic. So I feel like I need to be in the office when he gets there

in the morning to model good work habits and to provide some accountability."

"Can you think of any other options?"

"Maybe the church will get me a Star Trek transporter so I can just materialize at home without having to make the trip," Doug laughed.

"Maybe there is an idea there, though—is there a way you could make contact with your boys without being there in person?"

"I could call them on the days I don't get home. I already do that sometimes, but it feels sort of hollow. I think what I really want is to be there in the flesh."

"So you could come home for lunch, switch your evening meetings, or go in later some mornings. Which options stand out to you?"

"None. They all have a downside."

"Well, let's see if there's one where we can minimize the negatives. With the idea of going home for lunch—can you see any way around the 90-minute drive?

Doug deliberated for a moment. "I could meet them half-way, which would only take 45 minutes... No, they'd miss too much home-school time. And if they came all the way to see me it would be even worse."

"How about the idea of going in later? Tell me a little more about the situation with your assistant pastor."

"It's not real bad. It's just that he's supposed to be in at 8:30, and on days when I wasn't there I kept finding out he hadn't come in until 10:00 or 11:00. He has office hours three days a week, so those are the mornings I go in early."

"How could he get the accountability he needs without you always having to be there?"

"Well, he could fill out a time card. I'm not sure that would work—he's honest enough to write down when he actually comes in, but I don't think looking at a timecard once every two weeks would be enough to change the pattern. He seems to need someone right there to talk to him every day. Now, that's a thought," Doug brightened. "I could just call him on his cell every day at 8:30 and see if he's in. That could work."

The coach chuckled. "What have you learned about coaching from working with me that might make that step even easier?"

"Oh, right. I'll have him call me instead of me calling him. That

way it's his responsibility, not mine."

"Great! Would taking that step accomplish your objective?"

"Definitely."

"When will you start?"

"We have a meeting this afternoon—I'll talk to him about it then. He can start calling me this Wednesday."

"Good. Will that free you up to go in later?"

"It should. I'll have to pick a morning to stay home...let's say Thursday. That will cut the three-day stretch where I don't see the boys in half. If that works, maybe I'll do Fridays, too."

"When can you start taking Thursdays off?"

"Let me look. I've got a meeting this week," Doug reflected, pulling out his PDA. "That one I can't change on short notice. If I reschedule my breakfast meeting next Thursday I can start then."

"On a scale of one to ten, how likely is it that you'll go in late every Thursday morning, say for the next three months?"

"Maybe about a seven. I want to get this done."

"What would it take to make that seven into an eight or a nine?"

"Probably just sitting down and blocking out that morning on my calendar every week. Ouch! That hurts a little."

"What makes it hurt?"

"Oh, I guess I just enjoy being free to schedule meetings with people whenever I want to."

"So, when you put those two things up next to each other, what's most important for you—being at home with the boys or maintaining your freedom of action?"

"Well...." Then Doug continued more decisively. "Yeah, family is more important. I'll block those mornings out today."

"It sounds like you've got a plan that'll work. Are you excited about it?"

"Yeah, this is great! I feel better already. Thanks!"

Jot down three techniques the coach used to ensure buy-in:

#1: CLIENT BRAINSTORMING OUT LOUD

#2: REFLECTING BACK WHAT HE SAID

#3: CONSIDERING EMOTIONS 'ARE YOU EXCITED?'

Problem Solving

By the end of the conversation, Doug had a concrete plan to make his priority for family time a reality. What techniques did the coach use to ensure that Doug was committed to the plan he developed? Here are a few examples:

- The coach started by identifying the precise problem the client wanted to solve (in this case, the long stretches away and not the total amount of time).
- The coach helped Doug generate his own options instead of giving him suggestions.
- The client was asked to evaluate the options and choose which one he wanted to act on.
- The coach had Doug verbalize the steps he chose.
- The coach asked for an evaluation of how likely it was that a step would be taken, and then followed up by asking how that likelihood could be increased.
- When there was a conflict of priorities (family versus scheduling freedom), the coach asked for a clear choice between the two.

X Allowing the client to do the thinking, develop the options and make the choices maximized buy-in. The coach consistently kept Doug in the position of being responsible for his own life. This leads us to another guiding principle of coaching:

Coaching works through influence, not authority.

In healthy leadership and healthy relationships, authority and responsibility go together. The client is the one who bears the consequence for his choices (he's responsible and the coach isn't), so the client should also exercise the right to make those choices (he's the authority and the coach isn't). Since the authority to X decide rests with the client, a coach must function by influence, not by exercising authority.

There are two wonderful benefits to functioning solely through influence. Since you are not responsible for the client, you can relax. You don't have to make sure the client's life works: that's not your job. You are not responsible for the client's outcome. Letting go of this responsibility is what allows you to really believe in the client unconditionally.

Second, since the client chooses the goals and the steps, it's not your fault if they don't work. (Those of you who are pastors probably see the benefit of this immediately!) There is no room for blameshifting in a coaching relationship. If what the client decided to do isn't working, the client takes responsibility for it and together you just fix it.

You are not responsible for the client's outcome.

There is one more area we can highlight from this story. Coaching is a relationship, and coaching at its best is relationally transparent, authentic, deep, safe and fun. In my job as a coach trainer I review a lot of evaluations clients do of their coaches, and one of the most prevalent comments I see concerns the impact of the relationship itself on the client. Many people feel that just being with and knowing a coach has been transformational. It is a powerful thing to be heard, to be believed in, to be accepted and to be loved.

Coaching is a relationship.

I believe the biggest reason Christians in general experience so little transformation in their lives is that they ignore the Bible's relational mandate for how to affect change. We were never meant to live the Christian life alone. Christianity is an interdependent, community-oriented faith. And yet, when we set out to improve our prayer life, or deal with our anger problem, or increase our income, or become a better father; most of the time we work on it completely alone. Coaching puts change back into the context of a *learning community*, where God always intended for it to be. You cannot live the life you were born to live without relationships.

Fulfilling your destiny is only possible in community.

Characteristics of Coaching

It might be helpful to sum up in one place some of the

characteristics of coaching that we've touched on in this chapter. Coaching is:

- Believing in people
- Client-driven
- Action oriented
- Growth-centered
- Aligned toward the future
- Conversational
- A relational partnership
- Influence, not authority
- Listening and asking instead of telling
- Based on internal motivation
- A support system for change

A complete list of over 50 coaching principles can be found in Appendix A.

Chapter 2 Exercise Answers

2.1 The significant phrase in each of Doug's responses is listed below:

- Paragraph 2: *"...I'm not sure you'd know it just by looking at my life."*
- Paragraph 4: *"...we just don't get enough time together."*
- Paragraph 6: *"More like what I had when we were in the apartment."*
- Paragraph 8: *"What's different is the commute."*
- Paragraph 10: *"...a lot of weeks I don't see them from Tuesday night 'til Friday night."*
- Paragraph 12: *"I hate the idea of them going through their lives for days at a time without seeing their dad..."*

The Power of Coaching

"I discovered the need to always be coached. That was a watershed for me...I don't want to ever stop being coached." Assistant Pastor

Randy is an apostolic leader who does counseling, writing and travels internationally to speak and to develop leaders. He'd recently been through a difficult transitional time in his life: he and his wife had both switched jobs; his mother-in-law had endured a long illness and recently died; and family difficulties had exacerbated the situation. Randy was feeling unmotivated, tired and overwhelmed; so we were using a life purpose tool to identify his values and rethink what he wanted in different areas of life. The conversation was rolling along smoothly until we started talking about hobbies and recreation. Randy is an enthusiastic, verbal person who is usually not at a lack for words, but he was struggling to come up with anything that fit in that area of his life.

"Well, what do you like to do for fun?" I inquired, trying to help him get unstuck. Randy wasn't sure how to answer. Fun wasn't really an important part of his life. He rarely took time out from working to just play. The conversation soon turned to rest and recreation, and there wasn't much to say in that area either.

Ministry pretty much consumed his schedule and his life.

At that moment it occurred to me that the discipline God has given us to keep our work and rest in balance in our lives is the Sabbath. It seemed like a perfect teachable moment, so I followed my intuition and asked a challenging question: "When was the last time you took a Sabbath?"

After a lengthy silence, Randy quietly responded, "Probably 1998". It had been five years since he'd taken a day off simply to rest. I asked another question or two on the subject, but by then our appointment was nearly over. The Sabbath idea seemed to strike a chord in Randy, so to wrap up I requested that as an action step he look up Exodus 31:13 and meditate a little on it. Randy wholeheartedly agreed to that suggestion.

That evening, Randy looked up the verse, "...You shall surely observe my Sabbaths...that you may know that I am the Lord who sanctifies you."

"I couldn't sleep that night," Randy recalls. "I was up until three in the morning studying what the Bible said about Sabbath rest. The idea that rest was connected with God's way of sanctifying me was a completely new idea. My wife had been trying to convince me for years that I needed to take time off, but I never did. Before I went to bed I e-mailed my coach and told him what a 'Eureka!' moment that was."

As he reflects back now, Randy declares, "The idea of rest keeps coming up everywhere in my life now—I was just preparing to preach on the Sabbath the other day. Since then I've noticed a phenomenal difference in my productivity, clarity and creativity. I had been struggling to finish my book for months, and after I started taking a day a week to do nothing, I was able to finish it in about a week and a half."

Randy went on to describe the power of coaching to bring about change. "You think you are going to get under conviction in some meeting where there is preaching and teaching going on, and here we were just having a conversation. There has only been one other time in my whole life where I've been under that level of conviction—I would have thought it would have come through someone getting on my case and saying, 'You need to change! You ought to get some rest!' But instead it happened in a natural, casual, everyday conversation."

Coaching is Transformational

The reason I coach is because it's the most effective way I've found to transform the lives of leaders like Randy. What makes that kind of transformation happen?

> **Top 5 Reasons to Coach and Be Coached:**
>
> 1. **Experience More Transformation**
> Make radical changes in your own life and see more lasting change in others.
> 2. **Grow Faster/Get More Done**
> Accelerate change and accomplish more without overload.
> 3. **Unleash People**
> Stop creating dependence and free up your time by empowering others to take action.
> 4. **Develop Leaders**
> Invest more effectively and efficiently in leaders around you to multiply your impact.
> 5. **Improve Interpersonal Skills**
> Learn great tools for building deep relationships and having extraordinary conversations.

Over the years I've regularly asked groups of leaders to name the things that most transformed their lives. Every group comes up with the same answer: transformation doesn't primarily come from classes, seminars, books or large-group ministry events (which are all informational), but through *significant relationships* that influence us and *pivotal life experiences*. The power of coaching is that it leverages both these key ingredients of transformation, engaging the unique life circumstances of the client within the context of a transparent, growth-oriented relationship. Transformation is experiential and relational. Rearranging how I lead and minister around that transformation principle has led me to coaching, and that change has born tremendous fruit.

If that's not enough to get you excited about coaching, there's much more. The box on page 33 outlines five key reasons to coach other leaders and be coached yourself. Let's look at each of those reasons more closely.

1. Experience More Transformation

Transformation is deep, lasting, significant change. Paul Jeong, the head of Natural Church Development in Korea, trains thousands of Christian leaders each year. He embraced coach training for himself and the key leaders in his organization, because he wanted to see more genuine and consistent transformation in the lives of those he works with. In the process, he's become a vigorous advocate of the coaching movement in Southeast Asia. Here's his comment on how coaching transforms lives:

> *"Honey, what's happened to you? You've really changed!"*
>
> To a husband who'd just begun coach training

> *"...I believe coaching produces more transformation than teaching and consulting. Here's my reality. I've taught more than 40,000 pastors and leaders in the last five years. I believe that less than 10% of them experienced change. One year later, maybe 1 to 3% had experienced ongoing transformation. But through TLC coaching, more than 90% of those I work with are transformed.*
>
> *"Before [I learned about coaching], I personally hated one-to-one stuff, but I loved a big SHOW (big conferences and seminars). Now I am becoming much wiser after many pains, life lessons and teachable moments. My wife now also spends more time in coaching than any other hobby, job, or responsibility, because she has experienced its power to transform her clients. It is very hard for me to stop her now—and myself too!*
>
> *"...The TLC coaching process has totally revolutionized our ministry."*

Coaching transforms people because it zeros in at the place God is at work in the individual's life: the transformational experience. It is in these teachable moments, when circumstances put us under pressure, that we are most receptive to radical change. And, when you combine a teachable moment with a transparent, growth-oriented coaching relationship, the potential for transformation is enormous. The parable of the sower gives a good picture of this transformational process:

> *"Hear then the parable of the sower. When any one hears the word of the kingdom and does not understand it, the evil one comes and snatches away what is sown in his heart; this is what was sown along the path. As for what was sown on rocky ground, this is he who hears the word and immediately receives it with joy; yet he has no root in himself, but endures for a while, and when tribulation or persecution arises on account of the word, immediately he falls away. As for what was sown among thorns, this is he who hears the word, but the cares of the world and the delight in riches choke the word, and it proves unfruitful. As for what was sown on good soil, this is he who hears the word and understands it; he indeed bears fruit, and yields, in one case a hundredfold, in another sixty, and in another thirty."* Matthew 13:18-23

We tend to think of the different kinds of soil as different kinds of people, but they can also represent *different moments in our lives.* In certain circumstances and with certain people, we are much more receptive to God's voice than we are elsewhere. Have you ever learned a hard lesson your parents warned you about earlier in life, but as a teenager you didn't listen? Have you ever blown off a negative comment from someone you didn't know, and then been willing to listen to the same critique from a friend?

> *"Sometimes I wonder if I'm making progress; but then I look back to where I was at five months ago and think, man! I've grown more in the last five months than in the previous five years."*
>
> Christian Businessman

In the story at the beginning of this chapter, Randy's demanding life circumstances combined with a close relationship with his coach and the right question at the right moment made him open to a change he'd resisted for years. Coaching is extremely effective at transforming people, because you are always working at the point where your clients are most teachable: the place where *they* want to change.

When I was a kid, I remember my dad going out to seed our lawn with a hand-cranked seeder that hung from his neck. It threw seed around, all right—on the lawn, on the sidewalk, in the flower beds, in your shoes. There was no way to keep it all on the yard. But grass seed was cheap, so you could afford to waste some.

Advice-giving is like that old seeder. When you are telling people what to do, you are broadcasting your seed in all directions—who knows whether the individual is really ready to receive it? Your advice may fall on the path, where the person doesn't understand where you are coming from; or on the rocky soil, where they say, "Yes!" at first but don't have the ownership in your solution to press through when things get tough. Or your advice could fall in the weeds, when what you're focusing on isn't what the client wants to change, and other priorities choke it out.

But when you are coaching, your seed is always falling on fertile ground, because your clients lead you to the exact point where they want to change and where God is at work in their lives.

2. Grow Faster/Get More Done

A second key reason to coach and be coached is that coaching is an outstanding way to accelerate growth and accomplish more, both at home and at work. Here's a note I got the other day from Rebecca, a client of Sharon Graham, who specializes in nutritional coaching:

"The three months of coaching I've had with Sharon have been life changing. What I expected was to clean up some messes in my life, get rid of piles of paper, clean out my trunk, organize cluttered drawers, make a budget and a savings plan, etc, etc. All of that has happened, and is still happening, and as a result I have new disciplines that keep my life orderly. I feel peaceful when I come home. I don't feel guilty about spending time doing something fun; because I spent the time I needed keeping my life orderly.

"But I also gained some things I didn't expect. To tackle some of the messes I had made required facing fears and learning some new skills...mostly just experiencing that I can solve problems and make decisions in areas where my self-assurance was low. My confidence has rebounded and it's spilling over into areas that I couldn't have imagined.

"For example, I've toyed with the idea of taking the first in a series of certification exams at work for a couple of years now, but I always had a feeling that this technology stuff was just too hard for me. Now I am seeing myself differently. I call what I've found a "can do" attitude. I started studying for the exam two days ago, have finished eight of ten chapters and passed most of the practice tests after only one read of the book. I'm confident that in a few more weeks I'm going to pass this first exam of four toward a certification.

"With my life so pleasantly organized, I don't have nagging fears like wondering if I'm spending too much money, or if I have paid all my bills (because one might be hiding in a pile of paper somewhere). Instead of closing my eyes to problems and procrastinating, I just dig in and make decisions and they are dealt with.

> *"Accelerated growth describes this exactly ...I didn't think there would be this much going on in my head and applying to my life this fast."*
>
> Professional Counselor

"I appreciate my coach so much for being an instrument of transformation in my life. I believe God has used her to coach me into a more disciplined and organized life, and to clear the way for new responsibilities God wants to give me, like writing a grant proposal for a new women's ministry. Doing that work is a delight now because the clutter is not taking over my life. I can run without chains on my legs."

It's the support system that coaching provides that makes the difference for someone like Rebecca. The confidence and energy she gained through working with a coach (her "can do" attitude) is infusing every area of life and she's tackling things she never thought she could. Having someone to encourage and support her supplied the extra energy to overcome internal obstacles that had always stopped her in the past. We learn and grow much faster with relational support than we do alone.

> *"I have grown more in the last year and a half, than in my previous 14 years combined."*
>
> Para-church Leader

Research in the business world bears this out. One large study found that out of the billions of dollars spent on corporate training programs (seminars, e-learning, classes, etc.), only about 10% of those who attend show *any* measurable, lasting change in their actual work behavior. Trainees were taught new skills or ideas, but usually given no support or follow-up to help them implement what they learned. Consequently, 90% of them promptly went back to their old way of doing things.

By contrast, two studies (Oliver et. al. 1997, and Strayer and Rossett, 1994) found that following up training events with a coaching relationship had dramatic results. The first showed that training for executives followed by coaching increased performance four-and-a-half times as much as training alone. The second study, at a well-known realty organization, looked at the difference coaching made for new realtors fresh from their training. The coaching program cut the time new associates needed to get their first listing to one-third of the industry average, and their first month's commissions were nearly 300% greater than those who went through the same training but had no coaching follow-up.

We need support, encouragement and accountability (S.E.A.) to function at our full capacity. That's why leaders with a coach get more done.

3. Unleash People

One feeling I think every beginning coach struggles with is that coaching is inefficient. "I know what the answer is," the coach urges impatiently. "Wouldn't it be easier to just tell them?" In the short term, advice-giving saves you time by keeping your conversations short. It always takes longer to help someone discover an answer than it does to dispense solutions.

The downside is that advice-giving inevitably creates *more* work in the long run. If you give people answers, what happens the next time they have a problem? They aren't any more equipped to solve it on their own than they were the last time, so they come back to you again...and again and again and **again**!

Paul faced this problem with the churches he oversaw. In Hebrews he discussed how he expected the believers to face it:

> *"For though by this time you ought to be teachers, you need some one to teach you again the first principles of God's word. You need milk, not solid food; for every one who lives on milk is unskilled in the word of righteousness, for he is a child. But solid food is for the mature, for those who have their faculties trained by practice to distinguish good from evil."* Hebrews 5:12-13

The group he was addressing had been taught the basic principles of the Christian faith. Paul's expectation was that they would not continue to remain dependent on being taught, but would mature and become teachers themselves. Those who are children in the faith are dependent on others to show them how to live the Christian life. Maturity is achieved by applying basic biblical principles to your own decisions, and learning by practice to distinguish right from wrong. An infant is someone who primarily receives. A mature believer is someone who gives.

> *"The greatest thing I'm learning from [coach training] is how to work at change while keeping others responsible... After 22 years of pastoral experience giving people advice and providing answers, this is a whole different way of working with people... I've gotten a taste now of what it can do."*
>
> Apostolic Leader

Paul was all about unleashing people and making them into fully developed leaders. He didn't want to create churches filled with bottle-fed baby Christians, stunted by over-dependence on leaders who keep telling them what to do long after they should be making decisions on their own. Paul's objective was to raise up robust, mature believers who knew how to chew the meat of responsibility.

Coaching mirrors that approach: it is more interested in building capable, responsible adults than in feeding people solutions to immediate problems. Coaching is about teaching people to fish instead of just giving them a meal.

For instance, when someone comes to me for coaching on a major decision, we almost always end up talking about how that person makes decisions. Do you have confidence in your ability to hear God? Do you know who you are and how this opportunity fits with your life purpose?

I'm much more interested in helping people become great decision-makers than in helping them make a right decision. If they make a good choice, I've influenced that one situation. But if I help them grow in their ability to make great choices, *I've affected every decision they make for the rest of their life.* If you are a leader, taking this approach produces a healthy long-term payoff for you. The more you help those you lead take responsibility for their own lives, the less work it is for you! Coaching cuts the cord of dependence and unleashes people.

Janice is a good illustration of this principle. She and her husband are bringing the gospel to a remote area of South America, using a boat to bring medical care and ministry to needy children. An experience Janice had while being coached was instrumental to pursuing her call to missions.

One of the issues Janice chose to work on with her coach was "speaking the truth in love". After several appointments, her coach began to sense that things were not going well in one of Janice's peer mentoring relationships, so she asked about it.

"When Sharon asked me how it was going with my peer, I didn't really want to say anything because I grew up protecting people who were judged by my mother and grandmother. I never allowed myself to say anything negative about anyone because I grew up protecting my dad—I never held him accountable for anything." Janice's father was an alcoholic who died when she was 13, and his problems were never discussed openly in the family. "I choose to shut off my desires and emotions to take care of my family and their needs. I had developed a pattern of watching my words and protecting others by not saying things that were difficult."

As her coach probed, the real state of her peer relationship began to trickle out. "Because she was my coach, I felt like that was OK," Janice declared. "But, even so, I was very careful about what I shared." Eventually, it became clear that her peer was taking advantage of her in a number of ways. "Most of the time we met at my house, and because we were getting ready to move she would say things like, 'I want that.' I didn't know what to say, so I'd reply, 'Let me ask my husband,' because I didn't have the freedom to say, 'Why are you trying to claim all my stuff?'"

> *"When I started this coaching, I thought of it as routine, just another thing to do for my job... but now that I've seen the power of it...if I had a coach like you when I was 20 or 30, my life would be so different! I want to be a coach and do this for other people."*
>
> Korean Pastor

With a chuckle, her coach recalls the pivotal moment in the conversation. "I asked her, 'What are you going to do about it?' And her mouth dropped open—I think it suddenly hit her that I wasn't going to fix things for her and she needed to address the situation herself."

"That opened a door about what I needed to do," Janice remembers. "I had to tell my friend the truth in love—tell her the things that concerned me in this relationship. I e-mailed her, apologized for not telling the truth and then shared my concerns about our relationship."

It was a breakthrough moment for Janice to stand up for herself and confront someone. It was also a moment that changed her life. "I am able to tell the whole truth now and not just the good parts," Janice affirms. "I had wanted to be in full-time missions for 20 years. God closed the doors years ago due to my deep need for healing... This was a major, final piece of my healing that allows me to go. In order to work with the people we are joining, I'm going to have to be able to do this [challenge people] or it won't work."

"Now...my husband and I will be able to do what we've always dreamed of."

When Janice's coach asked her to solve her own problem instead of doing it for her, not only did it unleash her to confront—it freed her to pursue her dreams and make a much larger impact in the world. The coaching approach is an extremely efficient use of a leader's time in the long run. It takes more time up front, but the long-term payoff is enormous!

4. Develop Leaders and Multiply Yourself

Setting goals, taking action, taking responsibility, making choices, problem solving—these are all important parts of being a leader. Because coaching exercises people's abilities in these areas, it naturally increases their ability and capacity as leaders. Here's a story that shows how coaching can improve performance while developing the leader at the same time.

Sparked by a presentation on leadership coaching given by Wyatt Fisher, Anthony asked about the possibility of being coached on further developing his leadership skills. As a manager at his computer services firm, Anthony supervised over 40 staff involved in product development. His company provided funds for professional development that he was able to tap into to launch the coaching relationship.

"He responded to the presentation and was pretty motivated to be coached," Wyatt recalls. "He wasn't sure what to focus on first, so we decided to set growth goals based on the outcome of a 360 feedback process." Anthony was a hard-charging, detail-oriented individual with a high capacity for work. However, the feedback he received from his co-workers in the 360 process indicated he tended to micromanage and needed to delegate more.

At the time, Anthony was shouldering a very heavy workload and was experiencing stress-related health problems. The growth objective that emerged from the feedback process was to work on delegation. Wyatt and Anthony spent several sessions hammering out a plan for what could be delegated and how. Even so, it was difficult at first for Anthony to let go.

"I think a breakthrough moment came when we started working with the IDEAL model." (IDEAL stands for: Identify a problem, Define the problem, Examine Alternatives, Act on one of the options, and Look to see how it worked.) *"He would give his team a problem, have them work through the IDEAL model to develop a plan and bring it back to him. It was liberating for him that he could gradually let go."*

After only eight weekly coaching sessions, Anthony was successfully farming out 20 hours per week of tasks, that he had been doing himself, to his team. In a wrap-up evaluation, staff members noticed (without being told what he was working on) that Anthony was more relaxed, was going home earlier at night and had made good progress in delegating more work to others. Anthony himself estimated that learning to delegate more effectively (so he could concentrate on more important issues) would save the company $30,000 a year.

Anthony is a more effective leader because of his coaching relationship. A boss could have mandated these kinds of changes from above and that may have gotten short-term results. But because Anthony's coach pushed him to take responsibility for his situation, he was able to see that trying to do it all by himself wasn't working. He owned the problem, and he owned the solution.

Here's why that's crucial. If someone else uses power or position to get us to change, we'll change—for as long as we are forced to do so. We'll grumble about what the boss is making us do, and then as soon as the pressure is off we'll revert back to the old way of running things. Our outward behavior changes, but that's all.

> *"The hour I spend with this guy [I'm coaching] is the best hour of my week—this is the best investment I'm making."*
>
> Senior Pastor

On the other hand, if I am the one who identifies and solves a problem, I have to believe in the solution I came up with in order to act on it. I'm freely choosing it, so I really embrace it. The change starts on the inside, then percolates out to alter my behavior. In other words, *who I am changes, not just what I do.* My choices alter my fundamental understanding of myself, of the situation and maybe even my values and beliefs. Because I am much more invested in this solution, embracing it changes me more deeply and more permanently. Coaching keeps responsibility with the client, because taking responsibility for your own situation is one of the surest ways to foster lasting behavioral change and increased leadership ability.

This idea is clearly reflected in Jesus' leadership development practices. He preached the Kingdom message to thousands far and wide, but He walked with His disciples instead of only talking to them. He sent them out to preach and to heal, gave them responsibilities (like finding a place for the Passover meal or keeping the purse), asked them to speak for themselves ("But who do you say that I am?") and pushed them to make hard choices. After Jesus' ascension, which group supplied the leaders for His movement?

The first leaders of the early church came from the group of those who bore responsibility with Him, not the crowds who heard Him speak from a distance. You can develop leaders in the same way Jesus did: give them responsibility and then walk with them as they carry it out. Coaching provides the tools and the structure you need to do a great job of raising up leaders.

5. Improve Interpersonal Skills

Below are three interesting questions about relational skills. See if you can put a number to each one:

- What percentage of your ministry, work or leadership time is spent in conversations? 60-70 %
- On a scale of one to ten, to what degree does your success as a leader depend on maintaining healthy relationships with the people around you? 10
- What percentage of the time you've spent in higher education was focused on practicing conversational or relational skills? 10 %

What really matters in organizational leadership is not what you know but whether you can relate. Research by the Center for Creative Leadership found that two of the top three primary causes of derailment in executives are "not being able to work in a team" and "poor interpersonal relations". Most ministry leaders would agree that relational skills are constantly used and very important to their success.

However, there is a disconnect between the training leaders receive and the skills they actually need in real life. A large seminary recently did a survey of divinity graduates, asking them what they felt they had most missed in a seminary education. Four of the top five answers involved relational skills (they were: conflict resolution, developing leaders, team building and interpersonal communication). Rounding out the top five, the number one answer was "being mentored/coached by an experienced leader". Obviously, these leaders felt that relational skills were much needed but not well addressed in their formal education.

Coach training is all about upgrading your conversational and relational skills. Will Meier talks about the impact of formal coach training on his own leadership:

"My experience of becoming a coach and being coached has radically changed the way I relate to people. As a manager in a Fortune 50 company, the primary leadership style in our corporate culture is the "command and pace setting" style. This method was reinforced by my personality type and corporate culture. I found that this technique worked fine for me in time of crisis, but when used consistently over time, it only created relational tension and breakdowns. I was not effective as a leader and could not sustain positive relationships over the long term. People were only loyal to me as it related to my position and the power I possessed.

"Over time, I observed that my leadership style was ineffective, but I didn't have the ability or energy to change my ways. But, after going through coach training and coaching others for 125 hours, I'm a changed person! I am now confident that I can manage people effectively over the long term. My capabilities as a manager have been enhanced significantly.

> *"Have you noticed that people around here in the office are different? They really listen to you now!"*
>
> After coach training for staff

"Part of that transformation resulted from developing a personal listening growth plan. I measured my listening events and behaviors, and through that process I became aware of the ways I was not listening to people effectively. I began eliminating my poor listening behaviors. Today, people really feel heard when they speak to me. I never dreamed that I could develop such a powerful ability.

"My coaching experience has provided another significant breakthrough: allowing people to come up with their own solutions. I am a person who loves to speak, and I have always prided myself on the counsel, discernment, and insights I have given people. Over the years, though, I found that many of my words were ineffective because people didn't own them. Coaching has given me a tool to help others take a greater ownership of the solution, guaranteeing a greater impact. I am still free to 'tell,' but I have found that I am more influential and effective by listening."

Because coaching uses relational influence instead of command and control to get things done, it is uniquely suited to our times. As a leader, your ability to compel others to follow you simply because you are the leader isn't what it used to be. People expect to be listened to. They want to have a say, to understand the vision and have the chance to buy into it—much more than they did a generation or two ago. As Will discovered, positional authority works in times of crisis, but when used as a matter of course it erodes your ability to lead over the long haul. In this generation, *if you can't lead by influence, you can't lead.*

I think this is a good thing. The great move of God inside the church in our times has been the explosive, worldwide unleashing of the laity to do ministry. The move toward empowerment in the business world parallels and complements what God is doing in the church. I believe coaching is a primary strategy God is raising up to meet the leadership needs of this generation.

If what God is doing in these days is empowering and unleashing people, we need leaders with potent new tools to raise others up and the radical belief in them to unleash them to pursue their destinies. That's the power of coaching.

Chapter 4

The Heart of a Coach

"Coaching has taught me that my life isn't about me."
Denominational Executive

Upgrading your listening skills won't make you into a coach. Neither will learning how to ask incisive questions, or how to hold someone accountable, or any of the other coaching skills. To truly tap into the power of coaching, you have to go beyond skills alone to grasp what makes those techniques important and why you are employing them. Great coaching starts with heart.

Here's an example. A wealth of techniques can be employed to give others a sense that they are being listened to. You can make eye contact, demonstrate open body language, nod or make those little "agreeing noises" as they speak. Or you might face toward the person, avoid looking around the room or at your watch and make sure they get the majority of the airtime.

> *Technique without Heart is Manipulation*

However, it's possible to employ all of these techniques and still barely hear a word a person is saying. *Great listening technique doesn't equal great listening.* Inside your head you could be daydreaming about your team's run to the Final Four, or be totally distracted by the fight you had last night with your spouse. The outward impression given by practicing a skill can be completely different than the internal reality.

True listening comes from caring about what another person says. It's tuning your own thoughts out because you believe it's imperative to tune in to another person's heart. Great listening technique can let you appear to care when you don't, or it can be a window that lets a genuine heart for others shine through. The point is this: skills channel character. What you give to others comes from your heart. Skills simply provide a conduit to give what you have more effectively.

The bedrock of great coaching is what's in your heart for the person you are coaching. If you truly believe in a person, great questions and excellent listening technique will make that empowering belief shine through in your conversations. But, coaching without heart is simply an elegant way to try to coerce people to change. Technique without heart is manipulation.

Imitating Jesus

How do you cultivate a coach's heart for people? The place in our own experience that most exemplifies the heart of a coach is our relationship with God. Powerful coaching comes from studying, internalizing and imitating the Father's heart toward us.

Let's step back for a moment and look at the way God works with us on the change issues in our lives. Even before you ever became a Christian, God had already chosen you and decided he wanted to work with you. In fact, Paul states in Ephesians,

> *"And you he made alive, when you were dead through the trespasses and sins in which you once walked, following the course of this world, following the prince of the power of the air, the spirit that is now at work in the sons of disobedience. Among these we all once lived in the passions of our flesh, following the desires of body and mind, and so were by nature children of wrath like the rest of mankind."* — *Ephesians 2:1-3*

A pretty ugly picture, isn't it? We were God's enemies, thumbing our nose at Him and freely aligning ourselves with the prince of darkness. We chose to take over the life God had given us and to live it in direct opposition to His intentions. We were dead—walking corpses in God's eyes—wallowing in the empty pursuit of our lowest animal desires. Everything about us screamed out for God to give us what we deserved and blot us off of the face of the earth. But, amazingly, God saw something different:

> *"But God, who is rich in mercy, out of the great love with which he loved us, even when we were dead through our trespasses, made us alive together with Christ (by grace you have been saved), and raised us up with him, and made us sit with him in the heavenly places in Christ Jesus, that in the coming ages he might show the immeasurable riches of his grace in kindness toward us in Christ Jesus."* *Ephesians 2:4-7*

God's response to us was totally out of keeping with what we looked like on the surface. Think about it: what did God see in *you* when he made that incomprehensible choice? What motive made Him willing to send His own son to be inhumanly tortured and to die for you, when you preferred to be His enemy? What in all the problems and failures and lost promise of your life led Christ to put off His divine nature and be betrayed by His best friends just to reach out to you? Paul cites two reasons for this amazing gift: grace and destiny:

> *"For by grace you have been saved through faith, and this is not your own doing, it is the gift of God—not because of works, lest any man should boast. For we are his workmanship, created in Christ Jesus for good works, which God prepared beforehand, that we should walk in them."* *Ephesians 2:8-10*

God gave you something you didn't deserve (life in place of death) simply as an expression of His own character. He is grace and he is mercy, and therefore he chose to act toward you out of His own heart instead of out of what you had coming. But, there's a second reason: God made you *for* something. Even when your life was a mess, God never lost sight of your destiny—the good works He had created you for. God's perception wasn't limited to your obvious problems. He looked at what you were made to be, and seeing that, He loved you—enough to choose you to become part of the bride for His only son.

The Power of Destiny

God works with all of us in terms of our destiny. Before we'd even started the process of being transformed into His likeness; when we hadn't done any changing and were still an infinite distance from what we needed to be in order to marry into God's family, God saw our destiny and believed in what we could become. But, God didn't stop with just seeing our potential: He did something concrete to bring it to fruition. It was obvious that in our hopelessly messed-up state we couldn't affect the changes we needed to make us fit into God's family on our own. (The whole Old Testament is a demonstration that human efforts can never meet God's standards.) God solved this problem in an incredible way: through Jesus' sacrifice He set up a relationship with us, and through that relationship we received the power to change in ways we never could on our own.

> **Value**
>
> God initiates change, using every life circumstance to develop our character and prepare us for our destiny.

In effect, God said, "You don't have to change before you can be part of the family. If you choose Jesus, I'll accept you into the family right now, and you'll end up changing because you *are* part of the family." God can accept us because Jesus is sitting right next to Him vouching for us: "Father, this is the bride I want to marry. I see her in terms of her destiny—who you made her to be and who she really is—and I know that through me that's what she will become."

> *The Relationship Comes First, then the Change.*

Jesus sees us with an unconditional love as well as an unconditional belief in our destiny. The freedom we gain from that unconditional relationship empowers us to change from the inside out, because we want to, instead of trying to adjust how we look on the outside so that we'll be accepted. The relationship comes first, then the change.

There are plenty of religions that say, "Clean up your act and then you'll be acceptable to God." Christianity acknowledges the impossibility of that proposition. We can know what is right, we can even set our wills on acting right, but we simply can't do it. The gift of unconditional, sacrificial, believing relationship is what makes our transformation possible.

Believing in People

The gift of relationship is the linchpin of God's strategy for transforming people. Therefore, if we're working at change, it would make a lot of sense for us to imitate God's approach. Coaching does exactly that. The key to the heart of coaching is learning to see people as God sees them. As coaches, we consciously choose to interact with our clients in terms of their destiny, not their problems. We get to know them at a deep level: their dreams,

The Power of Believing in People

"Coaching was ideal for Abigail. She reveled in having someone listen as she talked about her inner life. She has said many times since beginning coaching that the thing that has been most transformational is having someone actually believe in her. As a result, she accepted the challenge to begin to think of herself as God does. She created action steps that included journaling, meditating on Scripture and practicing assertiveness in groups. The progress came quickly as she changed what she believed about herself.

"Just as impressive were the changes Abigail made in her eating and health habits. She got a personal trainer and began keeping a food journal to track what she ate, and the pounds fell off.

"Abigail now believes that she can solve her own problems in partnership with Christ, and her confidence is soaring—so much so that she began coach training so she can help others find the freedom and confidence that she's found."

hopes, fears, strengths and weaknesses. We rejoice with them when they get a victory and grieve with them when things don't work out. We see them in their best moments and at their worst—and then believe in them.

Believing in people doesn't work at a superficial level. You can't do this by giving an encouraging word to an acquaintance as you pass each other in the hall. *People do not truly feel believed in until they are truly known.* The power of belief only flows fully through the channel of open, authentic, personal relationships.

God knows us fully as unique individuals. He doesn't relate to us as part of the mass of humanity, but takes the time to work with us as valuable, individual sons and daughters. It's not merely that He loves us in a generic sense: He loves *me* and knows *me* and believes in *me*! When we imitate God by taking the time to really know our clients as unique individuals, giving them unconditional belief and support, the transforming power of God flows in like a tidal wave. Relationships animated by the heart of a coach empower our clients to change in ways they never could on their own.

If there is a New Testament mandate for coaches, it's given in this verse:

> *"From now on, therefore, we regard no one from a human point of view; even though we once regarded Christ from a human point of view, we regard him thus no longer. Therefore, if any one is in Christ, he is a new creation; the old has passed away, behold, the new has come."*
>
> *II Corinthians 5:16-17*

Our assignment as coaches is to look at people from God's point of view, in terms of their destined place in the Bride of Christ. We want to instinctively tune into their God-given capacity, their untapped potential, the fleeting glimpses we see in them of the image of God—and consistently relate to them in those terms. By seeing them this way, we change how they see themselves. That opens the door to incredible transformation.

Here's what this means in practical terms. If my clients are doing things I don't understand, my default setting as a coach is to reserve judgment and believe they have a good reason for what they do. When my clients have a problem or growth issue, I choose to believe that they are capable of stewarding their own lives and solving the problem. If I think a client is making a mistake, I still act out my belief in that person's capacity to manage their life by not stepping in and making the decision for them. In every situation, my default posture is to believe in the person, in order to be the same kind of advocate Jesus is. I do this because I know that the gift of belief unleashes the potential for transformation. The relationship comes first, then the change.

The Two Mindsets

The Coaching Mindset

If I'm coaching, I ***believe*** that God is already active the lives of others and that they can take responsibility and solve their own problems much better than I can. They most need me to believe in them and to provide support, encouragement and accountability as they act on what they know.

The Advice-Giving Mindset

If I'm giving advice, I ***believe*** that God wants to do something in the lives of others, but they don't have the ability to figure things out and need answers. They most need me to solve their problems, and once they have the right ideas, they ought to be able to walk them out on their own.

Coaching and Faith

"Now faith is the assurance of things hoped for; the conviction of things not seen" (Heb. 11:1). Coaching is a faith discipline. I often compare it to healing. If I have the faith to pray for healing, I believe that I can lay my hands on a person and God will step in and do something incredible. Faith operates in coaching in a virtually identical way (with one interesting twist): if I have the faith to coach a person, I believe that *I can take my hands off* that individual's life and God will step in and do something incredible.

When I pray for healing, I don't have any confidence that I myself can heal the person: I believe God will step into the situation through my simple act of faith and do the impossible. Likewise, when I coach, I don't have any confidence that I can "fix" anybody. But, I do believe that through my simple act of faith—choosing to see people as God sees them—that God will enter into the situation and do something beyond my abilities.

When I first got to know Joseph Umidi, he was a well-known leader and seminary professor and I was a nobody. We met at a mentoring conclave I helped sponsor, where he shared his dream of founding an international coaching movement and invited others to join him. So, I mustered up my courage and e-mailed him after the conference with an offer to help out. I was thinking I'd do a few things for him on the side—maybe some writing or some web site work. I was very surprised when he replied that he didn't want me to help out, he wanted me to partner with him in launching his dream.

He believed in me more than I did in myself. And I found that given the opportunity, I could do more than I ever dreamed I could. In the next four years, I accomplished a ministry goal that I thought would take a lifetime to fulfill.

Believing in people has tremendous power. So how do we learn to believe in others in a whole new way? You can't just manufacture faith. It doesn't work very well to say, "I'm now a coach, so starting today I'm going to believe unconditionally in all my clients all the time." Beliefs don't tend to change by force of will. Have you ever tried to grit your teeth and "believe" that you'd get well? It's sort of like saying, "I won't get angry!" or "I won't have any more impure thoughts!" Sometimes the more you try to believe in something, the harder it is to do it!

The Disciplines of Believing in People

However, there is a simple, effective way to strengthen our belief in our clients: it's what I call *the disciplines of believing in people*. Here's how it works.

A spiritual discipline is something we practice to build an internal habit. For example, take our relationship with God. Instead of trying to manufacture communion with God out of thin air, God has provided a set of disciplines (fasting, silence, meditation, Bible study etc.) that we practice to develop our ability to commune with God. The discipline itself isn't the communion—for instance, abstaining from food doesn't equate to being close to God (otherwise, starvation would equal glorification)! Instead, the discipline is a channel that communion flows through.

As we exercise these outward disciplines, our hearts are changed from within. Gradually, imperceptibly, we take on the mind of Christ. His thoughts become our thoughts, our desires are aligned with His and we start to naturally see things the way He sees them. When we start acting as if God is "the friend who sticks closer than a brother," we discover that He really is. Practicing the spiritual disciplines make us into people who are attuned to the Spirit, and who reflect more and more of God's heart and character.

Coaching training is learning and practicing the disciplines of believing in people. We aren't just developing a new set of skills: we're learning a disciplined way of treating others that focuses on their destiny and not their problems. We practice these skills over and over because they breed in us the heart of a coach. When we start to consistently act on our belief in people, we find out what they are really capable of, and our belief grows deeper and more profound each day. When that discipline has fully molded us, it becomes a powerful channel where the heart of a coach can reach out to touch and transform everyone we work with.

The Disciplines

The three most crucial disciplines of believing in people are:

- Listening
- Asking questions
- Keeping the client responsible

The three most important disciplines of believing in people are listening, asking questions, and keeping responsibility with the client. Take listening: one of my personal commitments as a coach is to be "all there" in my appointments. I don't want any interference that sets my mind wandering when I'm listening to my clients; so I've systematically removed distractions from my environment; and I make sure to take time before each call to center in so I don't drag my own agenda into the appointment. Genuine, I'm-100%-here-right-now listening sends a message to the client: "You are so very important, and what you are saying is so valuable, that I am going to put aside all my own thoughts and everything that is going on in my life just to focus on **you**". To really listen is to say in unmistakable language, "I believe in you". Listening *is* believing in people.

No question, listening like that is a discipline—I've worked on it for years. The interesting thing is, the more I listen, the more I believe in people and the more I *want* to listen. I've been in so many coaching appointments when I've thought the problem was simple and I had the solution. But because I was disciplined enough to bite my tongue and listen, I saw the client create an elegant, effective solution I wouldn't have thought of in a million years.

I remember one thorny, emotional situation where I was ready to put a full-court press on the client to make a change—and then he solved the whole problem by putting a post-it note on his steering wheel. That never would have worked for me! I've had clients who've shouldered what I saw as a crushing workload and flourished, or (I thought) didn't have what it took to start a business and went out and succeeded anyway. If I would have stopped listening and told these people what to do, I never would have witnessed what they were capable of doing. The more I listen to people, the more reason I have to stop talking and listen to what they have to say.

The Discipline of Asking

Asking questions is another key discipline for a coach. Posing questions instead of dispensing answers is a tangible way of honoring a person's capacity to run their own life. It's saying, "God gave you the gift of your life and I believe you can steward it well." Coaches ask because they expect you to be able to arrive at a great answer—probably a better answer than the coach could give. Asking questions is an unmistakable way of saying, "I believe in your capacity and ability!"

> *"You need someone older and wiser, telling you what to do... I am 17 going on 18; I'll take care of you!"*
>
> The Sound of Music

By contrast, when I "tell" instead of ask, the message I am sending is, "You aren't an adult. You aren't capable of living your life without my help." As it goes in the classic song, "You need someone older and wiser telling you what to do." Often in our eagerness to help we end up actually sapping people's confidence by sending the message that they aren't capable of doing the job. When we treat people as less than what God made them to be, they tend to live down to our low expectations.

The more I ask, the more convinced I am of the power of asking. When I discipline myself to ask, I embolden my clients and honor their abilities. As their confidence grows, their ability and their performance grows with it. At a recent speaking engagement, one of the leaders in the congregation I was addressing shared his own coaching experience with his church. After he recounted the phenomenal growth he'd experienced, I asked what had been most transformational for him. He felt that it was reflecting on the powerful questions his coach had asked him.

I've never gotten those kinds of results by giving advice! The more I ask, the more I see the potential and the destiny I've believed in become reality—and the more I grow in my capacity to believe in people.

Skills to Disciplines to Heart

Practicing the coaching skills as disciplines is the way you develop the heart of a coach. Study the disciplines outlined in this book, then practice them diligently over time. As with any discipline, you'll start out doing it by rote. But, as consistent choices solidify into a practiced habit, your hard work will change who you are. The more you believe in people, the more reason you'll see to believe in them. One day you'll wake up, realize you've been transformed and you'll never look at people the same way again.

The requirement to practice coaching as a discipline is why coach training must be spread out over a significant period of time to be truly effective. You can learn a skill in a day, but to practice a discipline takes months.

A few years ago a large organization brought me in to do a day of coach training. I had worked hard to convince them to spread the training out over time, but with their existing structures a one-day workshop was the only option. So, I did a one-day coach-training event without any follow-up. The experience was summed up by a life-long pastor who attended that event. "This is *hard!*" he exclaimed. "You can't learn to be a coach in a day!" I totally agree. Coaching is a habit.

Imitating the Way God Deals with Us

Coaching is imitating how God works at change with us. Below are seven practical examples:

1. A Coach Listens

When you pray, who is doing most of the talking? Is God giving you a constant stream of advice and telling you what to do, or is he mostly listening? God is a great listener. Likewise, in coaching, the client gets 80% of the airtime, while the coach listens.

2. A Coach Asks

The Bible is filled with questions. From "Adam, where are you?" to "But who do *you* say that I am?", questions are used constantly to push us to reflect, take a stand and shoulder responsibility. You can learn a lot about coaching questions from Jesus, the master conversationalist. Read through the gospels and highlight all of Jesus' questions—you'll be surprised at what you find!

3. A Coach Sees More than He/She Says

Stop for a moment and evaluate yourself. How many things are wrong in your life right now? Could you be a better parent, a more loving spouse, make better use of your time? Of course! The gap between God's holiness and your performance is infinite. Yet, God has the patience to work with you on only one or two growth issues at a time. Likewise, a coach may see many areas for improvement in a client's life, but chooses to let go of them and focus in on the client's change agenda. If God can overlook my faults, I can do the same with my clients!

4. A Coach Gives Responsibility

God gives us responsibility to grow us up into maturity. We are Christ's representatives on earth. Jesus even handed the

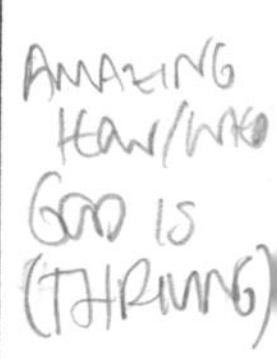

Imitating the Way God Deals with Us

church the keys to the Kingdom, and said, "Whatever you bind on earth is bound in heaven." Responsibility is the tool God uses to grow leaders. In the same way, a coach keeps the client responsible to grow his or her leadership capacity.

5. A Coach Works through Internal Motivation

We all believe in destiny: that God created us for something. But destiny has powerful implications: it means that God's best for our lives is implanted inside us. Our destiny is not something we ought to do; it's something we yearn for, that is more fulfilling for us than any other task. God is into buy-in—He specifically made us to want what he created us for. In the same way, coaches let clients set their own agenda for change. We major in internal motivation, because that's how God works with us.

6. A Coach Respects Free Will

God works with whatever we give him—he doesn't push his way into our lives against our will or force us to do anything (even though he could). God gave us free will, and he respects it. The line a coach doesn't cross is to never do anything that takes away a client's freedom of choice.

7. A Coach Honors Human Uniqueness

Have you ever wondered why the New Testament doesn't prescribe exactly how and when to pray? While other religions specify the times and even provide all the words for you, God lets you choose. He allows flexibility in how you carry out his commands because you are a unique individual. Similarly, a coach doesn't dispense one-size-fits-all solutions, because each person is different and the coach's solution may not work for you. Coaching honors human uniqueness.

A Coach's Eye View of Life

> *"I don't say this much, so I take it seriously when I do: Thank you for changing my life. My family (wife and kids), school-work, perspective and even my goals are the better for having gone through this process. Thank you!"*
>
> Divinity Student

A few years ago, a retired military officer who wanted to be coached on his career path approached me. After leaving the service, Brett had turned down an offer to stay in a similar role as a civilian contractor, sold his beautiful home in Hawaii and returned to the states to start a second career as a lawyer. He was now in his final semester of law school prior to graduation.

Brett was having second thoughts about his choice of careers. The farther he went in school, the more he felt he was just going through the motions. A real go-getter who didn't stop often to really reflect, Brett had managed to ignore his growing sense of uneasiness for some time. But, with only two months of classes to go, he finally had to admit to himself that his heart was not in being a lawyer. He was also concerned about his marriage. The stress of relocating and not having an income had taken a toll, and he and his wife had begun seeing a counselor.

As he talked through what was going on inside, Brett finally stated, "You know, all the biggest mistakes in my life I've made in the last three years. I shouldn't have left the Navy—I really enjoyed what I was doing there. I shouldn't have turned down the chance to stay on as a civilian, either. I got several offers when I retired, but I was so sure I wanted to go to law school that I didn't explore them.

I wish we hadn't sold our house! I loved Honolulu more than anywhere we ever lived—the beautiful weather, the skies, the scent of the flowers wafting through our windows at night—but housing prices have gone up so much that we could never afford to go back. I've spent all this money and three years of my life training to be a lawyer, and now I wish I'd just stayed where I was. I feel like I've totally missed God's will for my life."

Who Are You Becoming?

How you respond to a situation like this illustrates what you believe about how God works with people. On the surface, it appeared that Brett had made some mistakes (he admitted he'd simply gone with what made rational sense to him instead of praying about it) and was reaping the consequences. We could have moved straight ahead into some career planning. But as Brett's coach, I saw some larger dynamics at work.

"Brett," I offered, "Can I give you another perspective on that?"

"Sure, go ahead," he replied.

"You mentioned that you feel like you've missed God's will for your life. Here's what I see. For the first time in twenty-some years, you're asking fundamental questions about your destiny. You've told me you want to learn how to pray so you can hear what God has for you instead of just following what seems logical. You mentioned that you and your wife had been struggling for years, but for the first time you've gotten help and you're working with a counselor. And now you've hired me as a coach to help you really dig in and discover what you should be doing with the rest of your life. God seems to be much more a part of your thinking and your actions than he was three years ago. From where I sit, you are more in the center of God's will for your life than you've ever been."

What does it mean to be "in God's will" for your life? Here's one way to readjust your perspective. Think back for a moment to when you were dating your spouse-to-be. When you were with the man of your dreams, was your attraction based on who he was, or on what he had done in the past? As a man, would you ask a woman to marry you because of her track record—because she always made the right choices—or because you saw her as the kind of person you wanted to marry?

Mistakes

Even if you've made a mistake, God can still accomplish His purpose for your life; because His purpose is for you to become more like Christ.

The answer is obvious: you don't marry a person's past. You don't keep a scorecard and rank your dates based on how many mistakes they made before you met: you fall in love with who someone is. You love their identity, their "being," not their track record.

Our relationship with Jesus is the same way. He's not marrying us because we've done everything right in the past—He's coming back for a bride who is the right kind of person. This leads to a powerful insight on how God develops leaders:

God is more interested in who you are becoming than in what you are doing.

Take Brett's situation. Brett made some mistakes in his decision-making, his marriage and in his priorities. If you look at his situation in terms of what he is *doing*, he is out of God's will. In other words, if God's will for Brett is to make certain decisions, be at the right place at the right time and do the right thing, he's missed it. However, if you look at Brett's destiny in terms of what he is *becoming* (like his coach did), a different picture emerges. Through this painful experience, Brett started to seek God in a new way, to invest in his relationship with his wife, to make changes to his character—he is becoming a whole new man. Which is the more important outcome?

When what a person is becoming is the priority, you see things in a new light. It would have been possible for Brett to make the "right" decision about his career without growing as a person or getting any closer to God. But something much more profound happened. In spite of making some wrong choices, he was transformed by his experiences and became more like Christ—and that is a big part of God's ultimate purpose for Brett's life. Accomplishing our destiny is less a measure of being in the right spot at the right time than it is to draw near to God, to grow up into the measure of the stature of the fullness of Christ.

God's Purpose for His Bride

Jesus Christ is coming back some day for His bride. Scripture says that we are being prepared to reign and rule with Him. We will sit on Christ's throne with Him (Rev. 3:21) as bride, as brothers (Rom. 8:29) and as joint heirs with Christ (Rom. 8:17). As part of our reign with Christ, Paul says that we will judge the world and the angels (I Cor. 6:2-3). John says that we will share His glory (John 17:22). The bride is to be Christ's partner in marriage, in glory, in inheritance and in rule.

God's purpose in history is that we are first restored to relationship with Him, then become regenerated and remade in His image and finally become joined with Him as part of His own ruling family. The point of all this is that our destiny far exceeds what we'll do in this life. We are made for something beyond our time on earth. Life is a training school, preparing us for what we will be in heaven.

Heaven is not a place where we will just sit passively by while God takes care of our every need. The fact that leisure alone does not produce lasting fulfillment here on earth should be a clue that it isn't what we are made for in heaven. Instead, we co-labor with God in this life, not because He needs our help, but because He is training us to bear a greater weight of responsibility in the future when we will labor with Him in heaven. We minister here because we will minister to Him there. We bear responsibility here because we will rule and judge with Christ there. We grow in character and purity here because we are preparing ourselves to be wed there. We practice wielding Christ's authority in prayer here (Matt.

> **Eternal Life**
>
> We won't be couch potatoes in heaven. Taking responsibility here is preparing us for greater things in eternity.

16:19) because we will also wield it in glory with Christ.

Life is not a punitive obstacle course to be endured, so we can fold up our tents and become couch potatoes in heaven. It's not about doing the right things and being a good boy so you won't get in trouble with God. Life is preparation. Life has purpose. The heart of that purpose is becoming a fitting bride for the Son of God. God made our lives purposeful here, and even better, He's designed things so that fulfilling our destiny in this life also prepares us for an incredible destiny that our human mind can't conceive; an eternal weight of glory beyond all comparison, in the next one.

Build People, Don't Solve Problems

As coaches, we can choose to focus on becoming or on doing: on preparing people's character for eternity or on making sure things are done right today. In practical terms, we can build people or we can solve problems. Transformational coaching is about building people. This approach is a far more powerful method of producing leaders, and yields long-term results (in this life alone) that are orders of magnitude greater than merely solving problems. Here's an example.

Not long ago I coached a woman who was trying to decide whether to buy an investment home. The more we talked, the more it seemed that she'd done a fair amount of planning—she knew what she could afford and what kind of property she wanted. She had talked to a number of friends and advisors and had gotten their opinions. When I asked how she was going to make the decision, she replied that she planned to ask a brother she respected who was a realtor and whatever he advised she'd go with.

That last statement made me curious! She'd mentioned several times that she had sought counsel, but she had never shared her own opinion about what to do. So I inquired, "What would it take for you to feel confident enough to make this decision without asking anyone else's opinion?"

After pondering a while, she answered, "I'd need to know that God had spoken to me."

"So how would that look?" I challenged. "How do you know when God has spoken to you?"

That question opened up a deeper discussion: hearing God's voice. She admitted she didn't have very much confidence in her ability to hear God, but she was hungry to learn.

So let's look at this situation in terms of doing or becoming. Which would be the most life-changing outcome: for this woman to make the right decision about an investment property, or for her to learn to confidently hear God's voice? If she makes the right decision, I've helped her today. But if she develops confidence in her ability to hear God, I've impacted every decision she will make for the rest of her life.

If you want to help your clients in the short-term, focus on solving problems. If you want to see them radically transformed for life, concentrate on building people. Transformational coaching produces far-reaching change because it prioritizes who you are becoming over what you are doing. The question isn't, "Are you succeeding?" or "Did you do the right thing?" but "What are you learning?" and "How is this changing you?" In most situations, who you become is a much more significant outcome than what you do.

Taking the Long View

Transformational coaching is taking the long view in working with people. Companies that are managed to generate short-term profits ignore research, product development and employee training because they don't contribute to the immediate bottom line. The downside of this approach is that it mortgages the company's long-term growth.

Coaching offers similar choices. We can coach for short-term outcomes like getting today's problem fixed or making the right decision. However, the more we focus on the short-term, the more likely we are to tell and give advice. If our belief system says that the point of the Christian life is to do things right, we have a very hard time letting go and letting others make choices because they might fail. We become risk-adverse in terms of personal growth and try to take responsibility for others in order to make sure things turn out right. This approach is like a business that prioritizes the short-term bottom line at the expense of the company's future. Telling is not only an unfortunate habit: it springs out of a works-righteousness worldview that says that Christianity is about doing things right.

The other option is to take the long view. In coaching, that means the important thing is growing the company—learning, taking risks, and investing in the future. Short-term profits can often (though not always) be sacrificed for future potential. In other words, if our ultimate objective is leadership and character development, we can allow our clients to make choices and risk failure because risk and responsibility are what produce long-term growth.

Believing that our most important task as coaches is helping people grow to maturity allows us to let go of responsibility for their lives. It becomes OK for people to fail, because failure is a catalyst for growth. We can take the risk of letting clients try things we aren't sure will work, because it is more important for them to grow in their ability to take initiative than it is for them to make no mistakes. When we believe that who people are becoming is more important than what they are doing, we stop telling and start coaching naturally.

> **Value**
>
> Ministry flows out of being. Who you are is what you have to give.

The catch phrase we use to express this value is, *ministry flows out of being*. What it means is, our contribution to the Kingdom comes from our being, not our doing. Who you are is what you have to give. If you want to change what people do, change who they are.

Building Leadership Capacity

The idea of focusing on becoming and taking the long view works out practically in the coaching technique of keeping responsibility with the client. Giving responsibility to others instead of taking responsibility for them is a key to developing leaders. Here's why. Our capacity for leadership is directly tied to our capacity for responsibility. The more responsibility we can effectively handle, the greater the sphere of influence we are ready for. For example, a bank branch manager needs to have the leadership capacity to watch over five or ten people, schedule their work and manage a single location, all while following a well-defined set of procedures. A bank president may need to supervise hundreds of employees, multiple facilities in multiple locations and a budget of many millions of dollars. A leader would never move directly from managing a single branch to running a whole bank—it's too big of a leap in responsibility.

In order to grow as a leader, a person must gradually increase in ability to take initiative and bear responsibility. Our coaching catch phrase for this value is "leaders take responsibility" for their own growth. Keeping clients responsible is an intentional strategy for fostering growth.

So, when I take responsibility for other adults and tell them what to do, I'm not doing the person any favors. In fact, I may be making things worse by stepping in to fix a situation that God has specifically designed for that person's development as a leader. Leadership coaches keep their clients responsible because taking responsibility is how you grow in leadership capacity.

> **Out on His Own**
>
> *"I realized that my 14 year-old son didn't know how to do anything, because I had always done it for him. If I don't take more of a coaching approach, he'll never learn how to live on his own."*

Here's another example. When your daughter is an infant, you do a lot of things for her: you feed her, change her and burp her. As she gets a little older, you still do the cooking and the driving, you help her get dressed for church and you make rules for where she can and can't go. You do a lot of "telling" ("Jana—clean your room!"), and you pay for everything. Most of the responsibility in a child's life still rests with the parent.

As she moves into the teen years, things start to change. You're still driving and setting boundaries, but (hopefully) she is doing chores around the house, learning to clean up after herself and making more of a contribution. At 17, the contrast is even greater. Now she can drive herself to school, go out on her own (with a curfew), set her own bedtime and pick out her own clothes. She may have a job that is providing for some of her own expenses, even though you're still paying most of the tab. But, as a teenager, she is more independent and less receptive to being told what to do.

Now imagine that same individual at 22. What would happen if her parents treated her in the same way as if she were a 10-year-old? We instinctively realize that something's wrong with that picture. We'd say either that the daughter never grew up, or that her parents are terribly controlling. In child rearing, the objective is to gradually transfer responsibility so that when our children come of age they are ready to function as responsible adults. We start in a discipling mode, but in the teen and adult years parents must move to a coaching approach (where we stop giving advice and taking responsibility and start giving responsibility) for our kids to mature.

Leadership development operates in a similar way. Since our objective is to increase the person's leadership capacity (ability to take responsibility), we must allow them to make choices and take risks, instead of doing everything for them. The coaching approach is a perfect fit.

Getting Results

Another way to look at the difference between building people and solving problems is to examine the results. Let's say a leader in your sphere of influence comes to you for help with a question: "How do I build a sense of community in my small group?" You give him a number of good suggestions, hand him a book, and even offer to come to the group and do a relationship-building workshop. A month later the group is doing much better—problem solved, right?

However, the next month that leader has another problem: "How do I teach my group to pray for each other more effectively?" How do you think he'll solve his problem? He'll do what you (inadvertently) taught him to do: come back and ask you for help. Because someone else solved his problem for him the first time around, he isn't any more equipped to overcome leadership challenges than he was a month ago.

Giving Responsibility

Here are seven simple ways to keep responsibility with your clients:

1. The client makes the phone calls.
2. The client sets the agenda.
3. The client chooses the goals.
4. The client develops the action steps.
5. The client is accountable to report on each action step the following week.
6. A client who misses an appointment pays for it anyway.
7. The coach doesn't tell the client what to do.

Solving people's problems for them creates dependence, not empowerment.

Many pastors and ministry leaders fall into this trap. They are overwhelmed by their workload, and wish that more people would get involved and carry more of the load. But, often what's delegated is the chore, not the choice. People are given tasks to do, but the leader still keeps one hand on the reins to make sure that things are done right. When there is a problem, the leader quickly steps in to offer solutions, not realizing that handling things this way is training people to be dependent.

The way to get beyond this roadblock is not to provide more teaching or instruction for your leaders; but to walk with them as they shoulder real responsibility, the authority to make significant choices and the opportunity to conquer their own challenges. They need to be coached!

The Destiny Perspective

Coaching focuses on helping people become what they were born to be. Christianity has a unique perspective on destiny that is both personal and corporate, sacrificial and fulfilling. Concentrating on personal happiness and ignoring sacrificial commitment, or focusing exclusively on our individual destiny without understanding its connection to the body of Christ are both ways we sell ourselves short.

Below are seven fundamental assumptions a Christian coach makes about destiny:

1) You have a God-given destiny.

Life has meaning because God made you *for* something. The purpose of life is to reach for that unique calling (Eph. 2:10).

2) You were specially designed for your destiny.

It isn't an arbitrary task given to you by God—it springs out of your personality, gifts, experiences and make-up. When you are walking in your destiny, it fits you like a glove. The desires of your heart reflect God's purpose for your life (Ps. 37:4).

The Destiny Perspective (Cont'd)

3) Destiny is something you are, not something you do.

It is not a predetermined, static endpoint you can miss; but a dynamic, evolving interplay between what we were born to be and what you've done with your life thus far. The more you become who you were made to be, the more you'll do what you were born to do (Eph. 1:4-5).

4) Your whole life prepares you for your destiny.

Every event and circumstance has meaning, because God leverages each experience to help you accomplish His purpose for your life. This refining transforms you into the image of Christ and prepares you to be part of His bride (Rom. 8:28).

5) Your destiny is bigger than you.

Our ultimate fulfillment comes not from pursuing happiness for ourselves, but from bringing life to others for the sake of the Kingdom. If your dream doesn't involve serving others in a way that stretches you to your limits and beyond, it isn't big enough. It really is more blessed to give than to receive (Acts 20:35).

6) You must die to fulfill your destiny.

While God's desire is that we live an abundant life, a direct pursuit of happiness can never reach it. True joy only comes through a sacrificial death to self and a fundamental realignment of our wills with God's purposes. Only those who lose their life will truly find it (John 12:24-25).

7) Living your destiny brings productivity and fulfillment.

When you do what you were born to do, you function with maximum effectiveness and exceptional joy in the doing. Having fun without serving productively does not satisfy. Producing fruit without joy in the process is soul deadening. Productivity with fulfillment is the symptom of a life aligned with its destiny (III John 1:4).

Chapter 6

A Coaching Value Set

"[Coach Training] is changing me, whereas my other classes aren't changing me: they are teaching me but not changing me." Professional Counselor

Values are our core beliefs. They are the rationale for our decisions, the passions we live for and the explanation for why we make the choices we do. While a goal is something you set out to accomplish, a value describes who you already are. Values are part of our being.

In the first section of this book we've been talking about the "being" issues of coaching: the heart and perspective of a coach. Since becoming a coach involves a change of heart, or being, a values change is going to be part of the equation. And values change is powerful: when you embrace the coaching values, the way you work with others will automatically change. Values change is another way to work at developing the heart of a coach.

Below is a list of the ten fundamental biblical coaching values we've touched on in the preceding chapters:

1. *Believing in People*
2. *God Initiates Change*

3. *Leaders Take Responsibility*
4. *Transformation Happens Experientially*
5. *Learning from Life*
6. *Ministry Flows out of Being*
7. *Learning Community*
8. *Authentic Relationships*
9. *Own-Life Stewardship*
10. *Each Person is Unique*

Each value in the list has been expressed as a short catch phrase to make it memorable. These catch phrases are employed throughout the book to explicitly tie exercises and examples into the underlying values, so that it is immediately apparent how coaching skills flow out of the coaching values. If you "get" the values and truly adopt them as your own, you'll automatically begin to function like a coach.

Below are these same ten values examined in more detail.

1. Believing in People

Like Jesus' belief in us, the unconditional belief of a coach unleashes the power of God for change in the client's life. Therefore, coaching uses listening, asking questions and keeping the client responsible instead of advice-giving; because these disciplines are practical ways to show belief in another person.

> *"From now on, therefore, we regard no one from a human point of view... Therefore, if any one is in Christ, he is a new creation; the old has passed away, behold, the new has come."* II Corinthians 5:16-17

2. God Initiates Change

God is the sovereign initiator of our growth, setting the agenda and motivating us to move forward through the real events in our lives. Change starts with God's action. Therefore, a coach waits to see what God is doing in the client's life before engaging it, instead of trying to push a change agenda on the client.

> *"...The Son can do nothing by himself. He does only what*

he sees the Father doing, and in the same way."

John 5:19; TLB

3. Leaders Take Responsibility

Coaches develop leaders by keeping them responsible and allowing them to solve their own problems. Taking responsibility for others stunts their growth. Therefore, a coach diligently allows the client to choose agendas, goals, solutions and action steps instead of spoon-feeding them to the client.

> *"But solid food is for the mature, for those who have their faculties trained by practice to distinguish good from evil."*
>
> Hebrews 5:14

4. Transformation Happens Experientially

The things that most deeply shape us happen through experiences and relationships, not by accumulating information. Therefore, transformational coaching focuses on engaging the teachable moments of life in the context of a transparent coaching relationship to produce lasting change.

> *"I have heard of Thee by the hearing of the ear, but now my eye sees Thee...and I repent in dust and ashes."*
>
> Job 42:5-6

5. Learning from Life

Life is an ongoing development process custom designed by God for our growth. Coaching works because it takes seriously what life brings as God's agenda for change. Therefore, coaches listen intently and intuitively, because each incident in the client's life is meaningful and important.

> *"All things work together for good for those that love the Lord and are called according to His purposes."*
>
> Romans 8:28

6. Ministry Flows Out of Being

Ultimately, behavior comes out of character. What we do is a function of who we are. Identity, character and destiny issues hold great potential for transformation. Therefore, transformational coaching concentrates on changing what you do by changing who you are.

> *"The good man out of the good treasure of his heart produces good, and the evil man out of his evil treasure produces evil; for out of the abundance of the heart his mouth speaks."* Luke 6:45

7. Learning Community

Maximized growth and destiny fulfillment are only possible within an interdependent learning community. Coaching provides the relational context we need to go farthest and reach highest. Therefore, coaches intentionally invest in relationship as a vital part of the change process.

> *"Iron sharpens iron, and one man sharpens another."*
> Proverbs 27:17

8. Authentic Relationships

Transparent relationships free us from secret sins and hidden fears that tie us down, and give God access to our lives in a deeper way. Therefore, coaches intentionally foster an authentic atmosphere because of its intrinsic power to open us to God's work in our lives.

> *"Our mouth is open to you, Corinthians; our heart is wide. You are not restricted by us, but you are restricted in your own affections. In return—I speak as to children—widen your hearts also."* II Corinthians 6:11-13

9. Own-Life Stewardship

God has entrusted to each person the stewardship of his or her own life. We are individually responsible for our choices and for fulfilling our God-given destiny. Coaches never take freedom of choice away by telling a client what to do, because free will is a gift from God.

> *"So each of us shall give account of himself to God."*
> Romans 14:12

"For the gifts and the call of God are irrevocable."
Romans 11:29

10. Each Person is Unique

Each person is a uniquely valuable individual with a distinctive gifting, history and call. Coaching is an individualized process because people are individuals. Therefore, coaching follows the client's discernment and uses the client's solutions, because what worked for one individual may not work for another.

"If the whole body were an eye, where would be the hearing? If the whole body were an ear, where would be the sense of smell?...As it is, there are many parts, yet one body." I Corinthians 12:17-20

The Coaching Process

The Seven Elements of the Coaching Model

Up to this point, we've been looking at the coaching paradigm: what coaching is, how it looks in action, and the underlying values and philosophy that drive it. Coaching also has a unique set of tools and disciplines for fostering change—the coaching process. Up to this point you've been immersed in the heart and values of coaching. This section will take you through the practical nuts and bolts of how to coach. We'll begin by presenting a model that explains the seven key elements of the coaching process, and then focus in on each of these fundamental skills that coaches use to transform lives and maximize potential.

The Coaching Context

The coaching process is a *conversation* that happens in a unique *context*. A big part of that milieu is the relationship formed between client and coach. At its heart, coaching is *relationship-based.* The power of coaching to change lives comes from the belief, trust and support that flow through the transparent bond between coach and client. The relationship comes first, then the change. Take away the relationship and you eliminate much of coaching's potential for change.

Second, coaching is *client-centered.* Here's what that means.

If the relationship were coach-centered, the coach would define what needed to be talked about, solve the problems, and impart insight and advice to the client. The relationship would be centered on what the coach has to give. Instead, the client is the center of attention in the coaching relationship. The client generates all the agenda, goals, solutions and action steps. In the coaching methodology, the client does the heavy lifting, not the coach.

Third, coaching relationships are *goal-driven*. This is a relationship that is going somewhere. We aren't here merely to chat—we formed this relationship for the express purpose of accomplishing a growth goal and we've covenanted together to diligently work toward it. Coaching relationships are high-commitment, professional, growth-oriented relationships with clear, written goals and expectations.

These three elements—relationship-based, client-centered and goal-driven—form the context within which the coaching conversation takes place (See diagram).

The Coaching Conversation

Within that context lies the centerpiece of the coaching process: *the coaching conversation*. This is where the work of the coaching relationship gets done. (Some coaches say, "Coaching **is** the conversation.") However, this is not an ordinary, everyday dialogue. For instance, in a normal friendship we'd expect that each person would speak about half the time and listen for the other half. But, since a coaching conversation is client-centered, the client gets the lion's share of the airtime. We don't discuss the coach's needs or agenda, because the client is in the spotlight.

In the same way, since a coaching conversation is goal-driven, it is always focused around a specific change objective. We don't ramble on about what is going on in the sports world that week.

Instead, we intentionally stick to the agenda we've set and work together to reach a goal.

The coaching conversation has four key elements: *listening, asking, acting* and *supporting*. Listening and asking are the primary ways the coach moves the conversation forward. These disciplines allow the coach to move clients forward without telling: the client is allowed to discover the answers and make choices, instead of being told what to do. Intuitive listening and powerful questions push clients to explore more deeply, discover new insights and commit decisively to action, all while retaining responsibility for the outcome.

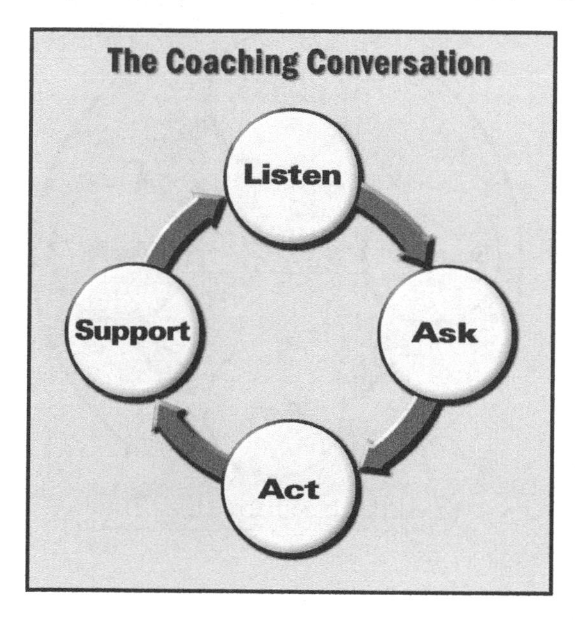

The coaching conversation also revolves around *action*. Once a goal has been set and strategies discussed, the coach's job is to help the client translate that goal into concrete action steps that get done. Coaching has a special set of tools for problem solving that help clients generate options, choose the best solution and develop strategies to implement it. The endpoint of a coaching conversation is always an action step. The client sets the agenda in a coaching conversation: the coach's job is to focus the conversation and push it to action.

It's easy to say we will do something, but much harder to actually get it done. Once the client has committed to a course of action, a coach provides the on-going *support* needed to give the client the best possible chance to succeed. Coaches provide consistent accountability for action steps, celebrate progress, affirm their clients' abilities, and help them get up off the ground and try again when things don't work. Effective support is a vital part of what makes coaching so successful at engendering change.

The coaching context is *relationship-based, client-centered* and *goal-driven*. Within that context, the coaching process is comprised of *listening, asking, acting* and *supporting*. Taken together, these seven elements make up the unique coaching methodology (See diagram). Each characteristic flows directly out of the coaching values listed in the previous chapter. The coaching values coupled with this methodology are an interlocking, consistent process for producing change.

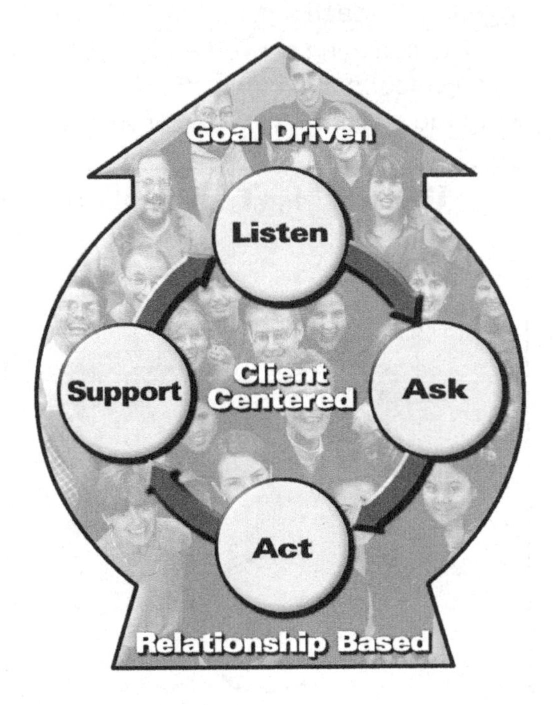

Formal and Informal Coaching

This section of the book walks you through how those seven elements would play out in a formal coaching relationship—one where you have regular coaching appointments, a coaching covenant and accountability for action steps. However, the same techniques can be used to great effect in informal situations. I'm constantly using the coaching process when I talk to people after church, at work, with my kids and my spouse (intuitive listening can do a lot for your marriage!). I also use coaching skills constantly in situations where I know I'll only talk to the person about the issue at hand once. If you spend a significant amount of your time managing employees, developing leaders, working with volunteers, or leading a team, coaching skills are tremendously beneficial, even if you never employ them in a formal coaching relationship.

Learning to Coach

I'm a coach trainer at heart, so my objective in these chapters is for you to learn what you need to begin actually coaching. To that end, instead of *telling* you about the coaching process, I'm going to *show* you how it works and how to coach. Each chapter discusses one of the seven elements of the coaching process. Interspersed between these chapters are "Master Class" sections to help you develop specific skills and practice them in real-life situations. Most chapters offer exercises, case studies or self-evaluations designed to provide real-world practice. Appendix D also includes additional coaching resources for certain chapters.

Case studies are great, but listening to actual coaching sessions will take you to another level in your understanding of how coaching works. If you are hungry for more than a book alone can provide, the "Leadership Coaching Live" CD set that goes with this book includes demos, live coaching appointments (with commentary from experienced trainers) and more that will show you how to coach.

One last thought before you begin. It's easy to just absorb the information in this section and skip over the hands-on exercises that require you to set the book down and actually *do* something. However, *information does not produce transformation.* Simply reading about coaching will not make you a coach. As a graduate professor in communications once told me, "At first glance, this looks easy—until you try to do it." To truly understand the coaching process, you have to apply it in real life. Practice really does make perfect.

Chapter 7

The Coaching Relationship

> *"I look back on my life as never before. Every past moment and difficulty God has used to teach me humility, patience and understanding of others. Now I feel like I understand God's mind. My coach sponsored me, loved me, and helped me...Before, I could not dream, but now coaching has made me a new person, [and given me a] new life."*
>
> Pastor's Wife

Years ago I used to run a helps ministry at our church called the "Maintenance Team". I had some experience working on a professional painting crew, so when we did a painting project I always asked volunteers if they knew how to paint. Invariably, the answer was, "Sure!" Painting looks easy, right?

I remember one epic situation where I came around a corner and witnessed a young man—who had, of course, assured me he knew what he was doing—using one of my expensive brushes with roughly the same motion you'd employ with an ice pick. Stab! Stab! Stab! (That's the recommended technique for ruining a brush in the shortest possible time.) I managed to restrain myself from snatching it out of his hand and instead gave an impromptu demonstration on the correct way to hold a paintbrush.

Shortly thereafter, we cleaned up and broke for lunch. While the volunteers took off for Pizza Hut, I grabbed a sandwich from the car and took a walk around the house to check our progress. Rounding the last corner, I was dumbstruck to find my brush, bristles bent and loaded with paint clear up to the heel, now totally ruined. Clearly, my instructions had fallen on deaf ears. To add insult to injury, instead of cleaning out the brush, my faithful volunteer had attempted to save time by wrapping it in a paper towel and leaving it out in the sun. The brush was already permanently bonded to the paper by the rapidly hardening enamel. After that day, I bought cheap disposable brushes for volunteers and kept the good ones for myself.

Evaluating Our Relationships

Relationships are like house painting. We all have relationships. We all have friends. So when leaders are first introduced to coaching, they look at the relational element and think, "Hey, I already know how to do that—no big deal!" Unfortunately, the statistics belie that view. Sixty percent of U.S. pastors don't feel they have *anyone* in their life that they can talk to honestly about their job. Another study found that seventy percent do not have a close friend, confidant or mentor. Three quarters of all pastors spend less than one evening a month engaging in purely social interaction with other couples (i.e. not "ministering" to them). Ninety percent said the hardest thing about ministry is dealing with uncooperative people. We're not as good at relationships as we think we are. For a more objective measure of your relational abilities, try the relational check-up on the opposite page.

Coaching relationships are extraordinary, influential, life changing partnerships. Think of an influential person in your life: someone who really believed in you in an extraordinary way and made a big difference in your development. Maybe it was a teacher who took a special interest in you, a business leader who sponsored you, or a ministry leader who reached out and mentored you.

I'm thinking of an art teacher I had in second grade. She used to take several of us kids out on painting expeditions on Saturday mornings. I can still remember one of the paintings I did looking off the balcony of her 12th floor apartment. One of the reasons I'm good at art (I spent 15 years in the design profession) is that she believed in me. Do you have someone in mind that did that for you? That's a good image of the impact of a coach.

Exercise 7.1: Relational Check-Up

Here's a quick check-up to evaluate your relational health. Circle "yes" or "no" for each of the following questions, then add up your total.

Yes	No	I am content with the state of my relationships right now.
Yes	No	If I got hurt or upset, I can think of at least three friends I could pick up the phone and talk to about it right now.
Yes	No	I have at least one really close friend, a "soul mate" that I can share anything with (in addition to my spouse).
Yes	No	I have a wonderful, formal relationship with a coach, mentor or peer mentor in my life that helps me grow.
Yes	No	I have someone I talk to regularly to hold me accountable for basic personal holiness issues.
Yes	No	My home is a peaceful, healthy, respectful environment. We don't fight, tear each other down or snipe at each other.
Yes	No	I have a good relationship with my parents.
Yes	No	I can't think of anywhere I am carrying anger or a grudge inside me toward another person.
Yes	No	I do things with people from work outside the office. We have more than just professional relationships.
Yes	No	In the last two weeks I had a conversation with someone where they opened up and became very transparent with me.
Yes	No	I have a healthy social life, with people I can hang out, relax and recharge with.

There is no "right" score for this evaluation. But here's a challenge: will you commit to taking one proactive step that would change just one "No" to a "Yes"? Write down your step!

A coaching relationship is an extra-ordinary relationship. It's an investment in another person that allows them to honestly say, "It made so much difference having someone who believed in me." It's more than being able to relate: it's relating in a way that empowers, energizes and challenges everyone you meet. Learning to consistently develop these great relationships is the first step toward becoming a coach.

Authentic Relationships

The first element of the coaching methodology is that it is relationship-based. Two words that describe a great coaching relationship are *authentic* and *unconditional. Authentic relationships* are ones in which we are real: we don't have to maintain different public and private faces. Who we are inside is who we are outside.

When we're afraid of being judged or rejected, we hide who we really are and throw up a façade (a false front) so no one can see that we aren't as good as we appear. The problem with façades in a coaching relationship is that they prevent the coaching conversation from dealing with the real person or the genuine issue. Developing solutions for surface problems won't transform the client's life. The power of authenticity in coaching is that when the relationship is genuinely transparent and safe, you can begin working with reality and not just appearances.

Authenticity doesn't just happen. The coach must cultivate the ability to take relational risks and the discipline of going first at being real. One of the things I customarily do to build an authentic relationship with my clients is to share life stories. During our first session, I take 15 to 20 minutes to share my own story, making it a point to include failures, reverses and wilderness times in my life. I go first because I'm setting the tone: I'm giving the client an example of the depth of sharing we'll do together. Once I've been honest about my life, my clients find it easy to be equally open when sharing their stories with me.

A while back I had a relationship with a client that seemed *different*. After about the fifth session I figured it out—she was still trying to impress me and look good for her coach. I was mystified, because I'd never had a coaching relationship where that pattern had persisted beyond the first meeting or two. Then I realized a crucial difference: because of time constraints in our first appointment, we'd never shared life stories with each other. Because I hadn't taken the initiative to go first in being real, the client hadn't gone there either.

Not all coaches use life stories, but whatever you do, find a way to be vulnerable with your client and jump-start an authentic atmosphere early in your coaching relationships. A good measure of your ability to catalyze authenticity is to look at your present relationships: how

Exercise 7.2: Authentic Stories

If you had only three to five minutes to take a relationship to deeper level, what story would you tell? Here are some guidelines for what to pick:

- ***Self-Revealing***
  Share something about yourself that you wouldn't tell to just anyone.
- ***Significant***
  Tell a story about something you care about deeply—your dreams, hopes, fears, relationships, or a life changing experience.
- ***Specific***
  Share concrete details instead of generalizing. Get beyond "I had a problem and now it is all better" and talk about what really happened.
- ***Human***
  Don't share something that makes you look like you have it all together. Laugh at yourself. Struggle with basic human needs. Treat failure as a gift. Be real.

Once you have a story in mind, choose a person you'd like to be closer to, share your story and watch what happens.

many really transparent relationships do you have in your life now? Who are the people in your life that you could tell anything to?

Unconditional Relationships

Coaching is also an *unconditional relationship.* This means that as a coach you offer full acceptance and unqualified belief to your client, independent of performance. This agape' concept comes straight from the gospels:

> *"But love your enemies, and do good, and lend, expecting nothing in return...and you will be sons of the Most High; for he is kind to the ungrateful and the selfish. Be merciful, even as your Father is merciful. Judge not and you will not be judged; condemn not, and you will not be condemned; forgive and you will be forgiven; give and it will be given to you..."* Luke 6:35-38

Because God loved us when we were unlovable, because God believed in us while we were messed up: we can do the same for those we coach. To love unconditionally is to imitate God. We discussed this concept in-depth in chapter four—now let's develop the skills to apply it.

Years ago, I was coaching a leader from my church through a training course. Midway through the program, she began missing our coaching appointments. She always e-mailed me afterward and apologized profusely, but when we rescheduled she'd miss again.

It was a challenging situation for me as a coach. Because she spent three quarters of her time at her company's overseas site, all of our appointments were in the early morning or the middle of the evening. It was frustrating and inconvenient for me to keep sitting by the phone at odd hours waiting for calls that never came. After five missed appointments in a row, I discovered that she was so embarrassed at standing me up that she had decided to drop the course without even telling me or her peer partner (and I was director of the coaching school)!

One of my personal commitments to my clients is that when we have a coaching appointment it's going to be about you, not me. That means I'm going to leave my own agenda at the door, so when I'm coaching we're talking about your growth and not about my frustrations with you. It took a fair amount of prayer to get to the point where I could coach this situation with a clean slate!

We finally managed to set up a meeting to bring some closure to the training experience. To prepare, I carefully planned the question I wanted to ask to initiate our discussion. I wanted a gentle, neutral, non-judgmental opening that gave her a chance to explain herself.

On the surface, it seemed like she had really blown it. But I believe that *people have a good reason for what they do.* If things break down or the client does something that seems irrational to me, there is a good reason (at least from their own perspective) for why it happened. I decided to try to understand (and help the client understand) the beliefs that were driving her actions.

> **Principle:**
> *People have a good reason for what they do.*

After chatting for a few moments, I asked my opening question: "I know we missed a number of appointments over the last while. Could you talk a little about what was happening there?" She slowly started to open up, and in a few minutes began to share about her experience with an alcoholic father. Whenever she did anything that wasn't perfect—shut a door too loudly, didn't do her chores on time, got a "B" in a class at school—her father would hit her or abuse her verbally. The only way to stay safe was to hide from her father until he forgot about the problem. For the first time, she realized that even as an adult she was still running away and hiding whenever she made a mistake.

But this time things were different. We faced the breakdown together, we talked things through, she apologized and I forgave her. She actually rejoined the training program and from there on she didn't miss a call. We didn't go through any special healing process—I don't remember if I even prayed with her during that appointment. But she was so transformed that I began to get e-mails from others in her organization: "What happened to Stephanie? She's a totally different person now!" That appointment changed her life, *because this time no one beat her when she failed.*

The Power of Agape

There is power in simple, unconditional love to transform people's lives. The simple act of listening and withholding judgment is a compelling way to love people. Coaching relationships have special boundaries that free the coach to offer this kind of unconditional belief and support. The first of those boundaries is illustrated in the story above: the coaching relationship focuses solely on the issues of the client, not those of the coach. We say it like this: *It's about the client, not about you.*

During the coaching appointment, the client and the client's growth is the sole focus. Everything I do and say as a coach is directed toward that end. In the story above, I didn't choose to share my own frustrations about the missed appointments, because our coaching relationship is *client-centered.* It isn't about me. Instead, I dealt with my personal agenda outside the coaching relationship, so that when we met I could function in the way that best facilitated the client's growth. This approach is a practical way to express agape love—the love that gives, expecting nothing in return—to the client. The coaching relationship gives clients a very personal picture of the way that God loves them.

> **Principle:**
> Coaching is client-centered: It's about the client, not about you.

Being client-centered doesn't mean the coach is a doormat. The coaching relationship with this client couldn't continue until we'd talked about the missed appointments and come up with a workable solution. I certainly wasn't willing to continue that pattern!

Sometimes the best course in a breakdown is to confront the client directly about not meeting agreed-on expectations, while in other circumstances an indirect approach is most effective. But the guiding principle for both is that coaches get their own issues taken care of outside the coaching relationship, so what happens in your appointments is about the client, not the coach.

The Challenge of Giving

A year or so ago I realized that my conversations with my wife were becoming uncomfortably one-sided. Two-thirds of the time we were talking about me, and only a third of the time about her. Then it hit me: I was spending five or six hours on the phone talking exclusively about others, offering them something and expecting nothing in return, and I needed a little balance! It spurred me to invest in spending more time with friends to make sure my needs were better met.

This highlights one of the deepest personal challenges of being a coach: you are constantly giving the gift of relationship, the gift of listening and the gift of acceptance. You can't maintain that degree of outflow unless you are a whole person and your own needs are met.

Ministry flows out of being: who you are is what you have to give. It's tough to focus intently on other people when you have an aching wound inside begging for attention. It is difficult to be there for someone else when no one is there for you. If no one believes in you, how will you believe in anyone else? If you have few friends you can share authentically with, how will you know how to be a true friend to others? Jesus once stated that the key of knowledge was to enter into something yourself—then you would be equipped to pass it on to others.

A coach's first responsibility is to steward his or her own life. That means having healthy relationships with God and others, living a balanced life, enjoying your work, keeping priorities in order and making a sacrificial contribution to your church and society. I call this "living the lifestyle of a coach." Part of being a coach is living the kind of life you want for your clients. If you are stressed out, unhappy at work, aggravated at home, or insecure in your relationships, you won't make an effective coach. Who you are is what you have to give. Needy people don't make good coaches.

Exercise 7.3: Living the Lifestyle of a Coach

Jesus said, "That which is born of the flesh is flesh, and that which is born of the Spirit is spirit" (John 3:6). Start by asking yourself: what's the one area of personal stewardship that most stands in the way of your being a great coach? Where are you most needy? Which area of your life would you ***least*** like to replicate into another Christian leader?

Here's a challenge: If you believe that who you are is what you have to give, set up a coaching or peer mentoring relationship and go to work to make yourself more whole, so you are better able to foster wholeness in others.

Influence, Authority and Responsibility

A second key principle that allows coaching relationships to be unconditional is that they are purely *influence-based.* As a coach, you don't hold a position of authority in your client's life like a boss, pastor, mentor or counselor would. There is absolutely no expectation that your clients have to listen to you just because you are "the coach". It is not your job to tell your clients what to do or to hold them to your own standards. The clients set the goals and make the choices. Your relationship gives you influence with your clients, but all the authority to make the decisions rests with them.

> **Influence**
>
> *Coaching is a pure influence relationship. The coach does not hold an authority position in the life of the client.*

Here's the payoff. In effective leadership (and healthy organizations) authority and responsibility go together. The person who is responsible for something should be able to make decisions in that area. Likewise, whoever makes the decisions should also be responsible for the consequences of them. In coaching, the clients keep all the *authority* to make choices about their lives, so they carry all the *responsibility* for those choices as well. Stated as a coaching principle, it goes like this:

You are not responsible for the client's outcome.

You won't realize just how freeing that is until you start coaching! If your clients make wrong choices, they are responsible for them: it isn't your fault. If your clients do something great, you can celebrate with them, but they get all the credit. Because you are not responsible for the client's outcome, *you can let go of having to make sure your clients do things right*. You are free to relax and believe in them.

Here's an example to help flesh this out. Say that you're a manager and you hire an individual into your department. Because you hired and you oversee that employee, her performance reflects on you. For instance, if she skips work half the time and quits after three weeks, you made a bad hire. It's your department and you are responsible.

Bearing responsibility for the outcome changes how you work with that person. Say that one day this gal comes in all excited about a new product idea, but you think it might lose the company a bunch of money. Because you are responsible, you'll have to be convinced that this will work before you OK it. Your ability to unconditionally believe in her is limited by your responsibility for the outcome of her choices.

If I'm a coach retained by this same individual, my response is different. I'm not there to be an expert on this business, and it's not my job to determine whether this is a good idea or not. I'm there to partner with her and help give her the best chance to succeed at what she believes she should do. Because I'm not responsible, I'm free to be genuinely excited about her idea. We'll brainstorm together, think things through and maybe come up with a plan to present the idea to the boss. But when the appointment is over, I won't waste a moment worrying if it is the right idea or not: that's her responsibility to carry.

Here's another way to look at it. As a Christian, do your sinful acts reflect negatively on God? Is His character sullied because you did something wrong? Does it mean He made a bad call when he invited you into the Kingdom? Thankfully, it doesn't. The reason why is because God has given us the gift of free will. We have our lives as a gift from Him, and we are solely responsible for how we steward them. God could use His authority to force us to do what's right, but he has temporarily laid down His potter's right, and instead given the authority and responsibility for our earthly choices to us. The gift of free will is what enables us to be sons and daughters instead of slaves. The choice of how to live our life is ours, so the outcome of that choice is also ours to bear.

At the last judgment, no one will be able to claim that God made them sin, or that it was God's fault that they turned out the way they did. On that day, when God reasserts His full authority over all His creation, those who freely gave their lives to Him as Lord will be able to live under His total authority and still maintain their freedom as sons. Those who freely rejected His rule will receive the outcome that they chose and that God's holiness will then demand: to be separated from Him forever. God is not responsible for our choices—we are.

Coaching honors the free will of the client because God honors free will. A coach keeps people responsible for their own lives because God does the same. Coaching is imitating how God relates to us.

But Shouldn't I Say Something?

Helping people change by believing in them unconditionally is a counter intuitive concept. At first hearing, people always raise a million practical objections. The discussion usually boils down to a question like this: "If I see my client doing something wrong, don't I have an obligation to say something about it?"

Here's how I respond. Pause for a moment to really ponder the following question, and answer it with a number:

> *How many things does God see right now that are wrong with your life or that don't meet His standards?* ______

As the expression goes, there's a hole with no bottom. The gulf between God's holiness and yours is larger than the universe. If we saw a true picture of God's holiness alongside our own depravity, it would literally kill us (See Exodus 33:18-23). Yet of all our infinite number of shortcomings, how many is God explicitly prompting you to work on right now? My experience is that I can count that number on the fingers of one hand. Of all that God sees in me that needs to change, He only chooses to reveal a few things at once. Applied to coaching, I call this the See/Say principle: *Just because I see something doesn't mean I'm supposed to say it.*

Seeing a problem in a client's life does not make me responsible to address it. At any moment, God sees many things wrong, but asks for change on only a few. Therefore, I need to figure out what things God is speaking to the client about and limit my agenda to match His. I'm only responsible to say the things that God prompts me to say. Even Jesus accepted this limitation when He stated, "...The Son can do nothing of his own accord, but only what he sees the Father doing"

> **See/Say Principle**
>
> *Just because I see something doesn't mean I'm supposed to say it.*

(John 5:19). You are not responsible to speak to everything you see in others. Your mandate is only to address what God specifically prompts you to address. Accepting this principle frees you to let go, love your clients and believe in them unconditionally. That letting go of responsibility for others is a big part of the greatness of the coaching relationship.

Master Class: Setting Up a Coaching Relationship

> *"I had lots of good friends, but none who were helping me in the areas I needed to grow...I could fool a lot of people because I'm authentic up to a point. [Through coaching] I found that I wasn't as transparent as I thought... and that God wants me to have those kinds of relationships in my life."*
>
> Coaching Client

Because coaching has its own unique set of ground rules and expectations, time spent at the beginning talking through what to expect and setting up the relationship will yield big dividends down the road. There are four key steps you need to take by the end of your first appointment to get off and running:

1. ***Lay the Groundwork:*** Keeping records and introducing coaching.
2. ***Build Relationship:*** Telling life stories.
3. ***Clarify Expectations:*** Reviewing and signing a covenant.
4. ***Set a S.M.A.R.T. Goal:*** Defining the agenda.

One caveat: we're going to look at the process of setting up unpaid (pro-bono) coaching relationships. If you plan to coach for an income, formal training through a professional coaching certification program will greatly enhance your skills and your chances of success. These programs will show you what you need to do to establish paid coaching relationships.

Let's look at these four key steps in turn.

1. Lay the Groundwork

The single most important success factor in a coaching relationship is the motivation of the client. So before you begin, stop and do a motivation check-up. Clients who are paying out of their own pockets to be coached usually have a high degree of buy-in. Those who approach you out of the blue and ask for your services are also usually well motivated. But that isn't always the way unpaid coaching relationships get started. You may have approached an emerging leader and offered your coaching services. Or you may be coaching one of your direct reports at work, a team member at church, or even someone assigned to you as a client.

> **Checking Motivation**
>
> - "What got you interested in coaching?"
> - "What do you expect to get out of this coaching relationship?"
> - "What goal would you like to work on?"
> - "On a scale of one to ten, how motivated are you to reach that objective?"
> - "How many hours a week are you willing to devote to working on that goal?"

When a person says, "Yes," to being coached, that response can mean many different things. If we've been asked by a leader to find a coach, "Yes," might mean, "OK, I'll do it if you want me to". If we are offered free coaching, our yes might mean, "OK, I'll do it as a favor to you". We can also say, "Yes," and mean, "OK, I'll give it try and see if it's worth doing". None of these answers is a good enough motivation on which to build a coaching relationship. (Now, from what you know of coaching principles and values, can you express exactly *why* this isn't good enough?)

Or we might answer, "Yes," and mean, "I don't know how say 'No,' so I'll agree to this and then never show up for the meetings".

Obviously, that kind of approach isn't going to work either. What you want is an enthusiastic, well-considered, informed "Yes!"

The box on the previous page offers several powerful questions used to check a potential client's motivation. You're looking for internal inspiration as opposed to outward pressure. To be coached, clients have to find a powerful reason to *want* to change from within, and they have to believe the coaching process can help them do it.

You can sometimes convert a weak "Yes" into a strong one by helping the person develop a compelling reason to change. I call this approach *connecting with your motivation.* The idea is to help people paint a graphic picture of the better future coaching could launch them toward. This technique also works great for times when a client has lost energy for a change goal or is ready to give up. The box at left lists five questions that I use to help people catch a vision for change. If there is a spark of internal motivation in the client, these queries will help you find it and fan it into a flame.

Connecting with Your Motivation

- "How would your life be different if you achieved this goal? Paint me a picture!"
- "What would it be worth to you to get this accomplished?"
- "What would it be like if two years from now you weren't any further toward this goal than you are now?"
- Have you been successful in the past in making this kind of change on your own? What do you need that you don't have to make this change?
- "What has God been saying to you over the last three months about this area of your life?"

Here's another tip on motivation. I've often used a request for an action step before the first appointment as a test of motivation for non-paying clients. I'll ask the person if they would read a few chapters of a book on coaching and then call me when they're finished to set up the first appointment. The ones who are really motivated to work call me shortly thereafter. Those who aren't motivated never call at all—and I've saved both of us the hassle and awkwardness of starting something we won't finish.

There are two practical steps to take before your first appointment that will get things going smoothly. First, keeping records of your coaching appointments is imperative. You won't be able to provide effective accountability for your clients unless you know what their goals and action steps are—and the two weeks between appointments is plenty long enough to forget! Some coaches create a binder with a section for each client, some create file folders for each individual, while others create a folder on their computer and take electronic notes. (If you choose to type in your notes, make sure you inform the client! The sound of the keyboard will carry over the phone, and there is nothing that turns a client off quicker than thinking you are doing your e-mail instead of listening!)

Whatever you do, have a foolproof system. I once got my notes for two clients confused, and for weeks I had one person's life history in mind when I was listening to someone else. I finally had to confess what happened and ask for their help to straighten things out. That was quite embarrassing!

Second, make sure your client has an accurate understanding

Exercise 8.1: Coaching in 60 Seconds

You have one minute to tell a prospective client what coaching is. What would you say? Sit down and jot out a brief outline of coaching so you are ready when opportunity knocks. Here are some ideas of what to include:

- A definition of coaching (See chapter 1).
- A testimonial or story of a victory from someone you've coached.
- A reason why coaching works (See chapter three).
- A coaching statistic.
- How you personally have benefited from coaching.
- Why you're sold on coaching.

Now, to get good at this you need to do one more thing. Practice giving your description several times in front of the mirror, or to friends or family members, and ask for feedback!

of what coaching is all about. Most of us learn a new concept by association: we compare it to similar things we already know. So be aware that when you're talking about coaching, the images in a person's mind may actually be counseling or mentoring. Or they could be thinking of the NFL coach they watched screaming at the refs last week on Monday Night Football.

A person can't make an informed decision about whether to be coached without understanding what coaching is all about. Since it's tough to describe coaching without demonstrating it, most professional coaches offer short complimentary sessions where they actually coach the prospective client for 20 to 30 minutes. The demonstration is what defines what coaching is. Then the prospective client can decide if coaching is the right way to go based on actual experience.

Another way to educate potential clients might be to ask them to read the first three chapters of this book as an action step before your first appointment. I've intentionally included a lot of coaching dialog and first person stories to make coaching easier to grasp. However you choose to do it, give a good introduction to coaching so the client knows what to expect.

2. Build Relationship

Since coaching is first and foremost a relationship, investing in creating a safe, transparent friendship pays off big in the long run. Here's an easy way to take your relationship deep right from the start (which is vital if you want to do transformational coaching.) For your initial appointment, get together for twice as long as usual. In other words, if you plan to do 45-minute appointments, make the first one a double session 90 minutes long. (If possible, I also like to have the first session face-to-face.) Now, take the first half of that appointment and tell each other your life stories.

A life story can include your salvation story, family background, work history, spouse and children, and whatever else seems significant. I always tell my own story to the client first, for several important reasons:

- I'm demonstrating how to tell a life story and giving the person an idea what I'd like to hear from them (i.e. the same kinds of things I am sharing about).

- I'm catalyzing authenticity by taking the risk of opening up first. I make sure and include several difficult experiences or places I made wrong choices in my story, to send the message that it is OK to talk about real life with me.
- I'm managing time by modeling how much to share and how long it should take.

When we both tell life stories, I'm also sending a message: this will not be a relationship where I am an authority figure; dwelling in unapproachable light, revealing nothing of myself but expecting you to be vulnerable; admitting no faults of my own but telling you how to deal with yours.

The main objective of sharing life stories is to get comfortable with each other. When you feel like you really know the person you are talking to, it becomes much easier to share freely and honestly about what is going on in your own life. You want your clients to feel *known*. Then you can value them for who they really are. The more deeply you know them, the more powerful the impact of your acceptance. It's important to get the details, like the names of the person's spouse and children, the company they work for, etc. Knowing the details allows you to coach people in the context of their life histories. What they share will often mean much more to you if you understand

> **By Phone or In Person?**
>
> Here are the top three reasons why I love to coach by phone:
>
> 1. ***Save Travel Time.*** If you have to drive 20 minutes to a restaurant to meet, your appointment just got twice as long.
> 2. ***Don't Get Stood Up.*** There's nothing as frustrating as driving that 20 minutes and then having a no-show. Save yourself the aggravation by coaching from home.
> 3. ***Maintain Boundaries.*** It is much easier to do an hour appointment in an hour when meeting by phone. Just saying "Hello" and "Goodbye" in person can take 15 extra minutes.

where they've come from.

3. Clarify Expectations

The third crucial step in launching a coaching relationship is to clarify expectations. Back when I was in my twenties I bought an investment property with a close friend. After owning it and living in it together for several years, I got married and wanted to get my money out of the house. The circumstances I left under weren't what we had anticipated, and the only thing that kept the situation from souring our relationship was that we'd written out a plan years before for how we were going to divvy up the profits.

Clear, written expectations make for productive, long-term coaching relationships. Here are three great reasons to have a written agreement with every client, whether they are paying you or not:

1. It can save your friendship if things don't turn out the way you expect.
2. It can uncover unrealistic expectations before they cause trouble.
3. The client will take the relationship more seriously if there is a written agreement.

That third reason is particularly important. I spoke recently with a denominational executive who was a reluctant convert to this principle. He was a highly relational person who had coached pastors for several years with no written agreements. It felt uncomfortable to him to sign contracts with co-workers whom he considered friends. However, he found that when he started requiring his clients to sign on the dotted line, they became more consistent about making appointments, took the coaching relationship more seriously and got more done. Now he's a true believer in coaching covenants.

I've often heard aspiring coaches say something to this effect: "I don't like the idea of having a coaching agreement. It doesn't make it feel like I trust the person or value their friendship if we have to sign a contract in order to work together."

Here's how I answer that objection: "I value our relationship so much that I want to make sure that nothing happens that could damage it. Signing a coaching agreement will ensure that we both know what we're getting into, and that we both want the same thing." It seems counter intuitive for some gift types (those who are highly relational—NF's on the MBTI, I's on the DiSC™, or Exhorter motivation gifts) to sign a contract. But serious coaches almost universally say: *don't coach anyone without a written coaching agreement.* (A sample is provided in Appendix B.)

The box at right is a checklist for clarifying expectations. Most of these items are normally included in a coaching agreement. (Professional coaches will want a more in-depth contract that covers things like remuneration and termination.) Most coaches meet with their clients by phone two to four times per month. Meeting lengths are commonly between 30 and 60 minutes. When you're doing performance coaching in the workplace, or the client's goal is to change a daily habit (like diet or exercise), shorter, more frequent meetings are the norm. For transformational coaching it helps to have longer sessions (I often do an hour) so the client has more time to reflect on and process what is being learned.

Expectations Checklist

- ❑ How often will we meet?
- ❑ How long will appointments be?
- ❑ How long will we work together? When will we reevaluate?
- ❑ Will we meet by phone or in person?
- ❑ If by phone, who will make the calls?
- ❑ Do we have each other's contact information?
- ❑ Have we signed an agreement?

Discuss the Following

- ❑ Timeliness and rescheduling boundaries.
- ❑ Taking initiative versus waiting for me to do things for you.
- ❑ Phone etiquette.
- ❑ Taking action between appointments.
- ❑ Being honest and authentic.
- ❑ Handling what is shared with discretion.
- ❑ Having fun and accomplishing great things together!

Most paid coaching relationships are open-ended—in other words, the client pays month-to-month and there is no set end-point for the relationship. Periodically the relationship is refocused when the client finishes up a major project or switches from one goal to another. In between, a quick check-up every six or eight weeks will keep you on track. Here's what to ask:

> **Exercise 8.2: How Often to Meet**
>
> Why do you think you wouldn't want to meet only once a month with a client? (check your answer at the end of the chapter.)

- Are we focusing on the goal you most want to work on?
- Are you happy with the progress you are making?
- Is there anything about our coaching relationship you want to change?

For unpaid relationships, it's better to commit for a certain time period and then re-evaluate. If you're coaching for an income, usually it's the client that ends the relationship. Nobody minds getting paid! On the other hand, if you are giving your coaching services away, often you will be the one to end the relationship. It's amazing how much frustration and entitlement can surface when a free service is withdrawn. Young leaders are prone to unconsciously expect a gift of coaching time to turn into a long-term investment in them. Pre-established times to stop and reevaluate give you a graceful way out if you feel it is time to move on.

> **Exercise 8.3: Phone Calls**
>
> In a coaching conversation, who do you think should make the calls: coach or client? Apply the coaching principles you've learned so far to come up with an answer (and check yourself at the end of this chapter).

4. Set a Goal

Your last task for the initial appointment is to help the client select a growth goal and develop their first set of action steps.

When clients leave their first meeting with a clear, compelling goal and some practical steps, you'll have a satisfied, enthusiastic client. The process of setting a S.M.A.R.T. growth goal is covered in depth in chapter 10. Here are a few tips for getting it done in your first meeting.

The key is for the client to come prepared. I send my clients a welcome packet (See box below) with several important action steps to take *before* the first appointment. Doing some groundwork before you meet will get you a lot farther in that first meeting. While some clients will have settled on what they want to work on, others will have three or four potential issues rolling around in their minds. It can take a fair amount of time to sort that out—and by then you may have run out of time to develop a set of action steps. If the client has done the wheel of life or written out a goal statement before the meeting, you've got a great head start.

Exercise 8.4: Make a Welcome Packet

A great way to add professionalism to your coaching is to start new clients off with a welcome packet. Send the packet to the client before your first appointment; it gets your relationship off to a fast start. Your welcome packet should include:

- A welcome letter (A sample you can modify is included in Appendix B).
- A copy of the coaching agreement for the client to review before the appointment (A sample is included in Appendix B).
- The Wheel of Life (Appendix B) or other instructions to help the client select a growth goal to work on.
- Any reading you want clients to do to familiarize them with coaching.

And here's a bonus: if you are certified to administer a gift or personality assessment, add that to your packet as well. Knowing the client's gift type will enable you to provide better coaching, and is an added win for the client as well.

Here's another quick tip for your first session. It's easy to make assumptions about what the client can and can't do in terms of action steps. I've had clients who have an hour or two a week to devote to their steps, and I've had some who want to dedicate eight or even twelve hours a week to their goal (that'll make you work hard as a coach just to keep up)! So I make a habit of asking up front: "How many hours a week can you devote to this goal?" Once you have a number, you can help your clients manage the number of action steps they take on so they don't get overloaded.

Chapter 8 Exercise Answers

8.2 *When your meetings get to be three or four weeks apart, there is not enough contact with the coach to keep things on track and provide effective accountability. You lose continuity and the client tends to lose energy for the action steps. The effectiveness of the relationship rapidly decreases when appointments get more than two weeks apart.*

8.3 *While different coaches treat this differently, having the client make the calls sends a message: "You are the initiator in this relationship and the responsibility is yours." When the client is responsible to make the call, I believe they are more likely to remember the appointments as well. I believe it is more consistent with coaching values to have the client call the coach.*

The Client's Agenda

"The thing [in coach training] that has changed my life the most is just working with a person's internal motivation and drawing out of them what is in their heart...that for me was absolutely life changing. I approach people now totally differently than I did before." Senior Pastor

Several years ago I was demonstrating coaching to our small group and a young man volunteered to do a coaching role-play with me. Peter was a fairly new Christian, but one who bubbled over with excitement about his new life and eagerly got involved in the church. That evening he seemed more subdued than usual, so I was curious to see what would happen in the role-play.

I began by simply asking, "Peter, what would you like to talk about tonight?" After hemming and hawing around for a bit, he finally offered that he hadn't been reading his Bible for the past few weeks. With the kids, work and everything else that was going on, he was having a hard time getting motivated to get up early and spend time in the Word.

It takes courage to be vulnerable like that in front of a group, so I took a moment to affirm him for his openness. Then, to get a little more information on the table, I inquired about what he normally did during his devotional times. Looking at the floor, Peter admitted,

"To be perfectly honest, I really haven't had devotions at all for several weeks. God feels pretty distant right now and I don't feel very good about trying to talk to Him."

Exercise 9.1: Discerning the Agenda

Before we go on with Peter's story, I want to give you a discernment challenge. Grab a pencil and jot down an answer to these two questions before you turn the page:

- What do you think is the root issue that needs to be addressed here? ______________________________
____
- What do you think the solution is to this young man's problem? ______________________________
____

Now, let's get back to the coaching conversation. Peter's last statement caught my attention; so I asked him to reflect on what might have changed in the last few weeks to disrupt his devotional habit. At first, he thought it was his own fault and that he had just gotten lazy. However, as I probed further, the conversation took an unexpected turn. Peter began to recount an incident that had happened a month before with his sister. He was attempting to share how he talked with God in his devotions, and she blurted out, "If what it means to be a Christian is to be like you, I don't want any part of it!" Peter was deeply hurt and confused. Six months before he'd made a vow to his mother on her deathbed that he'd take care of his sister. Now in trying to help her he felt like he was driving her further away from God. Somehow things got turned around in Peter's unconscious mind to the point where he believed that his devotions were turning his sister off to God, so to keep his vow he had to stop doing them.

We talked through how to respond to his sister's comment, and whether his vow to his mother was appropriate. The chance to talk things through and get perspective slowly untangled Peter's feelings. After 20 minutes or so he was ready to get back on track with his relationship with God.

That role-play was a turning point for our small group as well.

Peter's honesty set a new standard of authenticity in the group. From that point on we were much more transparent with each other. It turned out to be a great demonstration of coaching

Now, let's go back and finish up exercise 9.1. Look back at the problem and the solution that you identified. Did you correctly identify Peter's root problem and how to solve it?

Don't feel bad—I didn't have any idea our coaching session would go in that direction either. In fact, I've done this exercise often in groups, and I've yet to have a single observer correctly identify both the key issue and the solution the client chooses.

The Arrogance of Diagnosis

One of the sobering things I've learned in my years of coaching is that I'm not nearly as good as I thought I was at identifying God's agenda in a person's life. I discovered how poor I was at this when I began to really listen to people. Oh, I had listened for a few minutes when someone came to me for help. But I was never very far into the conversation before I began to formulate an idea of what the problem was and what needed to be done about it. While the other person was talking, I'd be engineering strategies in my head to fix the problem. Once I had a solution, my listening became progressively less about hearing the person's heart and more about looking for confirmation of my pre-existing conclusions—and for an opening to direct the conversation toward my answers.

> *"If one gives answer before he hears, it is his folly and shame."*
>
> Proverbs 18:13

In ministry we've gotten the idea that our discernment allows us to rapidly pinpoint another person's difficulties and prescribe an ideal solution. In this way of thinking, the more mature or "spiritual" we are, the more quickly and accurately we can intervene. If people would only follow our godly counsel and focus on the important issues we've confronted them with, they'd be able to live victoriously. While we certainly should aspire to grow in wisdom and discernment, is this the way we should employ it?

I've struggled with a sleep disorder ever since my teenage daughter was born. I can never seem to get a really good night's sleep. I've tried stress reduction, diet, exercise, doctors, herbal remedies, earplugs, prayer, quoting Scripture, medication, a chiropractor, buying a $1000 mattress—the works. After years of asking God to heal me, it began to dawn on me that much of the power of my ministry came out of my struggle with always being tired. I understand what it is like to try to change when all you have the energy to do is collapse on the couch and watch TV. Ironically, being unable to sleep has turned out to be one of God's greatest gifts to me. I've wondered if Paul had a similar experience with his thorn in the flesh. When he came to see his weakness as a gift, he began to understand that when he was most inadequate the power of God was most fully revealed in him.

I often share about my sleep problem in public settings to catalyze authenticity. I'm not asking for help by sharing the story—I'm simply opening up myself to invite others to be real about life with me. But inevitably someone will come up to me and tell me that if I would only take this vitamin or pray this special prayer or count sheep (Yes! I've actually been advised to do that!)—in other words, *if I'd just do the thing that worked for them*, my problems would be a thing of the past. I wish the solution was that easy!

There is arrogance in diagnosing a problem a person has lived with for 10 years in two minutes. Are we saying that the person is too passive and apathetic to have even tried to come up with a solution? Or is it that we are so much more spiritually mature that we can see in an instant what they've missed for years? This form of spiritual one-upmanship is endemic in ministry.

One of the things I love about coaching is that it is *client-centered.* It's a way to work with others that honors their ability to hear God for themselves. Coaching is totally different than most of what we do in ministry, in that it is directed by the discernment of the client. It looks to the client to set the agenda and solve the problems, not the coach.

Exercise 9.2: Why the Client Knows Best

There's a compelling reason why a coach allows a client to set the agenda. Say a leader comes to you asking for coaching on a personal growth issue. Given that situation, circle the correct answers to the following questions:

- "Who will God speak to 'the firstest and the mostest' about the situation?" — ***Coach*** or ***Client?***
- "Who has the most information about the issue, decision or situation?" — ***Coach*** or ***Client?***
- "Who is most affected by the outcome of this situation?" — ***Coach*** or ***Client?***
- "Who has likely invested more time praying and thinking over the situation?" — ***Coach*** or ***Client?***
- "Who has the most responsibility to take action in this situation?" — ***Coach*** or ***Client?***

The person with the most information, authority, responsibility, and investment, the person who God speaks to first, is *not the coach!* The coaching client has more information about and more investment in his or her own life than the coach. Therefore, it's a natural to let the client set the agenda. Coaches don't direct their clients. Instead, they help clients succeed at directing themselves.

Letting the Client Lead

This client-centered approach is a predictable outgrowth of the coaching values. Coaching is based on *internal motivation*. The biggest obstacle to growth and change is motivation, not information. You can come up with a great idea for how to make a client's life better, but if that person isn't looking to change in that area, proposing it is a complete waste of time. People are the most motivated to act on their own plans and

> **Client-Centered**
>
> *In a coaching conversation, the client's discernment leads, not the coach's.*

ideas. Therefore, if you want to maximize growth, you'll allow people to set their own agenda, because that's where the motivation is highest.

Letting the client lead is also an expression of faith in God's work in the person's life. *God initiates change.* That means God was at work in this person's life before a coach ever came on the scene, and He is actively leveraging every circumstance in the person's life to bring him or her to maturity. It's the Holy Spirit's job to convict people, speak to them about what they need to be doing and use life circumstances to motivate them to change. He's pretty good at getting people's attention—He's worked with a few billion more people than you have. When you believe that God is already at work in a person's life, it follows that the one who has the best handle on God's change agenda is that person. Therefore, the most dependable way to get in line with what God is doing is to let the client set the agenda.

Here's what that looks like practically. When I am in a coaching conversation, I'm not spending any time attempting to discern what problem we should work on. Setting the agenda is the client's job. I'm not hunting for blind spots or wrong behaviors in other areas of the client's life so that I can turn on the light—that's the Holy Spirit's job. I believe that God is able to spur the client to want to work at the area He intends for them to work on. And I believe that if the client isn't seeing the light, God will divinely order circumstances to bring the pertinent issue to the surface. This doesn't mean that I'm passive or I never challenge the client—it simply indicates that I let God and the client lead the process.

Who's in charge has a tremendous impact on how a coaching conversation develops. Here are several practical examples of how this works:

Example 1: Deciding What to Talk About

The coaching appointment is just starting. If the client is in charge, the coach might begin like this: "What is the most important thing we could talk about today in order to move you toward your goal?" If the coach is in charge, he or she might begin by saying, "I've been praying about your progress this week and there were a couple things I wanted to share with you today."

Example 2: Developing Action Steps

The client is contemplating the effect of a staff change on morale. If the client's discernment is leading, a coach might say, "What action could you take that would strengthen your relationship with your staff?" If the coach is in charge, he might counsel, "I think you should talk it over with your boss first and then announce the change."

Example 3: Problem Solving

The client is frustrated with an ongoing conflict with a co-worker. If the client's discernment is directing the process, a coach might ask, "What could you do to make things better?" If the coach is leading, it might come out like this: "I think your anger got the better of you and you overreacted. You better go back and ask forgiveness and make things right."

What Does a Coach Do?

You might be wondering, "If a coach doesn't set the agenda, discern the problem, generate options or solve problems, what exactly *does* a coach do?" Here's an interesting example. A few years ago I was doing a workshop with a newly-minted coach. I'd tapped Linda to do a role-play for the group about coaching decisions without telling. Once they got settled, the volunteer client started sharing with Linda about the decision she needed to make and how stuck she felt. Five or six minutes into the role-play, the client suddenly exclaimed, "I know what I need to do!" She proceeded to lay out her solution, thanked the coach profusely for being so helpful, and went back to her table and sat down. Perplexed, the coach looked up at me and shrugged apologetically. Her job was to demonstrate coaching for the group, but she had only asked three questions, and one of them was, "What do you want to talk about today?"

> **The Coach's Role**
>
> The coach's job is to focus the conversation and push it toward action, not to set the agenda.

I thought it was a fantastic demonstration. This client had been completely stuck, but after only a few minutes with a coach, she knew exactly what to do. It clearly wasn't anything the coach said that made the difference. There was no amazing question that broke open the situation. The fundamental gift that Linda gave her client was not advice, or even great questions, but a listening environment that unlocked her own creativity.

The second great paradigm shift in coaching is that you are not giving your clients a product (information, expertise or answers), but a service: an environment that helps them think more clearly; an acceptance that frees them to explore without shame; and an unconditional belief that leaves them energized and motivated to change. Coaching is like putting a plant in a greenhouse: with the right amount of sun, heat, fertilizer and water, the plant will grow much larger than it will out in the cold.

Certain things are hard for human beings to do by themselves. One of those things is getting perspective on our own lives. We just aren't that rational when we are looking in the mirror. Our emotions trip us up and make it hard to think clearly. Since we only see ourselves from the inside we miss things that are obvious to others. We experience internal resistance and don't understand why. We are easily distracted and lose focus even on what's most important to us. We talk about accomplishing something, but fail to nail ourselves down and really commit to a certain course of action. Sometimes, our lack of confidence keeps us from even trying things, which we could easily master if we could muster up the courage to get started.

Being human means having limitations. Coaching provides the missing ingredient that helps us accomplish some of those things in life that are difficult to do alone. The simple act of listening intently to someone without saying a word (like in the role-play above) can make a huge difference. When you combine listening with unconditional acceptance, powerful questions and a support structure for change, you have a real hothouse for growth.

The Coach's Job Description

The fact that coaches don't direct the conversation doesn't mean they are passive. Once the client sets the agenda, the coach takes responsibility to focus the conversation and push it toward

Seven Ways to Keep the Client in Charge

Keeping the client in charge of the coaching relationship is a challenge. The gravitational pull of the old advice-giving habit tends to suck us back toward taking over. A great way to reinforce the client-centered principle is to build structures into your coaching relationships that reinforce this ideal. Here are seven ways to do it (can you think of an eighth?):

1. Ask the client to set the main agenda during each appointment. I often ask, "What could we talk about today that is most important to move you toward your goal?"
2. Have the client keep the list of action steps. When you do a progress report, work from the client's list, not yours.
3. When asked for suggestions, offer multiple options (instead of just one) and ask the client to choose which to pursue.
4. When there are multiple directions the coaching conversation could go, present the alternatives to the client and let him or her make the call.
5. Use the words "action steps," not "homework" or "assignments". An assignment is something a coach gives out; the client develops action steps. Let your language reflect your values!
6. Ask the client to develop options and action steps first before you offer any ideas.
7. Make sure the final wording for a goal or action step comes out of the client's mouth, not yours. A statement made by the client is the client's statement.
8. ______________________________

   ____

   ____

action. The coach's job is to help you think more clearly, to push you to go deeper and reach higher, to provide the structure you need to stay focused on the agenda you've chosen. A coach has three main logistical responsibilities during an appointment:

1. Ask for a progress report to provide accountability.
2. Manage the coaching conversation so it moves the client forward toward the goal.
3. Make sure the client arrives at a set of concrete, committed action steps.

The coach manages the time and the flow of the conversation in an appointment to make sure these three steps take place. The coach also tracks progress over multiple appointments. For instance, by keeping records of the client's goals and steps, a coach can ensure that the relationship stays focused around the long-term agenda. Within the boundaries of these responsibilities, the coach uses listening, powerful questions and other techniques to move clients forward toward their goals.

Master Class: Tools for Setting the Agenda

Much of the time new clients come into a coaching relationship with a well thought-out idea of what they want to work on. In that case, you can move directly into setting a growth goal and starting the coaching process (See chapter 10). You'll also work with clients who are considering several possible objectives and need help deciding where to start. Occasionally, an individual will approach you who doesn't have a clear idea what to work on—just a sense that life is not what it could be and a desire to make it better. Here are three tools you can use to help a client choose the agenda they are most motivated to work on.

1. The Wheel of Life

It's easy to live day to day and never stop to reflect on whether we even like what we are doing. When we've not reflected, we may have a sense that our life isn't going the way we want it to, but we can't put our finger on where things have gone awry. The Wheel of Life is a simple self-evaluation used to help clients reflect on how satisfied they are with 12 different areas of life. Ranking satisfaction in each area and then discussing the client's answers will often provide significant insight into what's working and what needs to be changed.

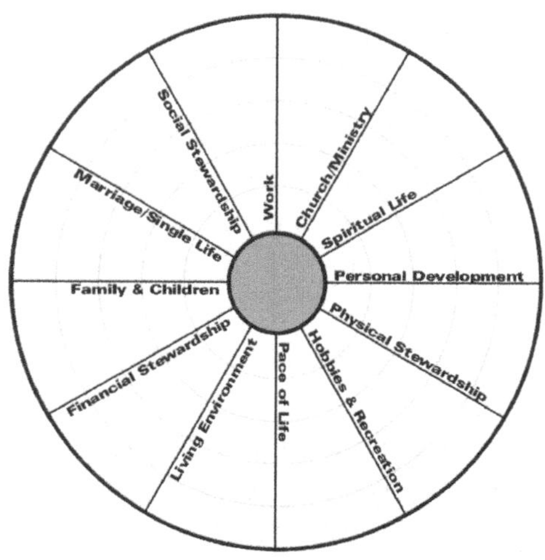

The wheel is shown at right (a full page version is shown in Appendix B). Ask the client this question: "On a scale of one to ten, how satisfied are you with each area of your life?" Then have the client color in the wheel from the center outward to represent their answer in each quadrant.

The first step in evaluating the Wheel of Life is to ask clients to reflect on what their answers mean. The areas in which the client scored the lowest usually indicate where there is the most motivation to change. Defining what the person wants in those areas versus what life is really like will often result in a clear goal with high buy-in.

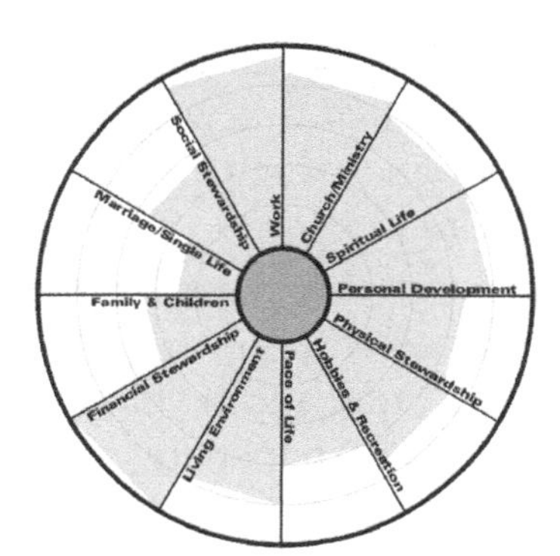

A "Flat Wheel"
Relationship Needed

Much more sophisticated evaluation of the wheel is possible. For instance, like categories are arranged together around the wheel, so a "flat tire" with low scores on several adjacent categories could mean that a whole segment of life (such as the client's inner world, relational life or service to others) is underdeveloped. Here are a few ideas for taking the wheel of life one step further:

- Ask the client to go back around their completed wheel and mark where they'd realistically like to be in a year.
- Go for a quick win instead of tackling a giant. For clients with low energy or confidence, identify the area where the client could see the biggest gain with the least effort, as opposed to tackling the highest mountain right off the bat.
- Ask the client to go around the wheel again, and rank where God has been speaking to them the most about making changes over the past six months.

2. Identifying Pressure Points

Where there is pressure, there is motivation to change. If clients can consciously identify the pressure points in their lives, they can be proactive about making changes instead of merely letting life happen to them. When a client doesn't know what to work on, pressure points can be a good place to start.

Here's a simple reflection exercise. Ask the client to reflect on and answer any one or all of the following questions:

Pressure Points

Proverbs states "A man's gift makes room for him, and will bring him before Kings." The converse is also true: "A man's flesh makes room for him, and will drag him through the mud."

1. "What are the pressure points in your life? Where is life difficult right now?"
2. "What do you want more of in your life? What do you want less of?"
3. "What is your biggest energy drain? Your second biggest?"
4. "Name five minor annoyances that sap your energy and drag you down."

Be aware that people tend to gravitate toward changing external circumstances in order to relieve the pressure instead of looking within. It's much easier to blame circumstances or the people around us than it is to take a hard look at ourselves. However, conflict, stress or difficulty is often the natural outcome of the quality of our character.

For instance, a person comes to you needing coaching on a job search. The reason he's out of work is that he was unable to get along with his co-workers—and this is the third time he's lost a job for that reason. The fact that things aren't going well in this area is not an external problem—he's reaping what he sowed. His employment picture won't change long term until his character changes.

If the client is focusing on externals, try an ownership question:

- "What could change about *you* that would make this situation different?"
- "If you were going to make some fundamental changes so this never happened again, what would you have to do?"
- "What do you think God is saying to you through this situation?"

3. Finding God's Agenda

One of our coaching values is that God initiates change. If that's true, then at any moment God has a personalized change agenda for each individual, and He has already begun implementing it through that person's life circumstances. These reflection questions can help clients tune into God's change agenda for their lives:

1. "If you were to list what you think the top three items are on God's agenda for you, what would they be?"
2. "If your current circumstances were part of God's plan to develop you as a person, what would you say He is up to?"
3. "What area of your life has God been speaking to you the most about in the last six weeks?"
4. "What would need to change to take your personal life, work or ministry to a whole new level?"
5. "What in your life are you most motivated to change?"

Exercise 9.3: Choosing the Agenda

Try out one of the three tools above on yourself. What is the change agenda you want to be working on at this point in your life?

Chapter 10

Goals: Defining the Outcome

> *"My productivity has gone up to a level it hasn't been at for 20 years...because I've focused on the goals I need to be working on."* Apostolic Leader

Bob is a pastoral leader who didn't pay a whole lot of attention to his financial future until recently. The sudden realization that retirement was not far off galvanized him to begin saving and investing for tomorrow. And that got him thinking about his sons' future as well. Bob had a strong desire to help them get off to a good start in life and avoid getting encumbered with debt. So, even though he didn't have the money at the time, he made it a personal goal to help his sons through college and provide each of them with a first car.

Not long after setting that goal, a solution arrived out of the blue. An elderly relative was purchasing a new car, and instead of trading in her current model, she decided to give it to Bob's eldest son. "I didn't have any money for a car, but my son got one anyway," Bob remembers. "Amazing things happen when you set a goal."

Over the years, I've heard story after story about the power of goal setting, and I've accumulated a few stories myself. Recently I was transitioning out of a staff role that no longer fit me in order to have more time to write. At first, I thought I'd make up the salary I was losing by doing more coaching and training. But as time went on, I began to see that God had called me to write and wanted to provide for me through that call. So one day I started praying differently. "OK, God, I'll focus on writing this year. Give me the opportunities I need to replace my salary through that." I started to think, act and talk like I was going to spend the bulk of my time developing new training programs. Within a week, I had five new opportunities to make the income I needed by writing.

Attaining Your Life Goals

A few years ago during a move, I dug out a list of life goals I'd written 13 years before, when I was 29. Back then, I was trying to envision what I'd want to accomplish in my whole life. But scanning over the 15 things on my list, I was surprised to see that there was only one item that I had not either already finished or come close to achieving. I had written a book, taken a three-month sabbatical retreat, built a telescope with an 18" mirror, created a leadership school and much more. It was fun to reset the bar higher knowing I had accomplished more than I thought I could!

Stop and think of a time something like that happened to you—where once you made a decisive choice and declared a goal, it seemed like the whole universe got behind you and an obstacle that seemed to be an unclimbable mountain became easy. Why does that kind of thing happen?

Exercising Our Faith

Goal setting is an act of faith. In some ways it functions like believing prayer. As a Christian, setting a goal is making a decisive choice to step out into the thing you feel God is asking you to do. When you commit yourself to a certain path, not only are your own internal resources focused and brought to bear, but the faith step of setting the goal releases the power of God on your behalf. God waits for you to choose because He really has given you the stewardship of your own life and he wants to work with you. He delights to see you set goals with Him, because He loves stewards who are willing to take risks and use the gifts and the abilities He has invested in them (See the Parable of the Talents in Matthew 25).

God has designed the world to work on the basis of faith. You can't know God without faith, because you can't see Him or touch Him. Without faith it is impossible to please God (Heb. 11:6). Faith is the engine that powers our prayers, that causes us to align our lives toward an unseen eternity instead of the here-and-now that is all around us. God has created a universe that responds to faith steps such as goal-setting (even for non-Christians); because those steps build the same muscles we use to get to know Him.

The story of the centurion in Matthew 8 is a great example of this principle. He was a leader used to functioning in an environment where once he made a decision his subordinates would carry it out—no questions asked. The centurion had so much practice in seeing what was declared come to

Staying Focused

"The group coaching session we had moved [our district leadership team] to talking about what was important to our district: working with churches in transition. I still have the goal sheets we developed up on my office wall. It clarified our most important task: we all realized that was where we really wanted to put our energy, and we saw the value of it above everything else.

"Having this goal in mind has dramatically changed the way we do business. We are much more focused on transitions, clear that that is the priority, and we're letting other things go. For instance, the other day a pastor called wanting help acquiring a van for one of his church programs. In the past, we would have gotten involved with that need, because we'd never defined our focus. Now we say, 'Work it out in your own congregation.' [Having a clear goal] just helps us stay focused."

District Executive

pass that he readily believed that Jesus could speak a word and his servant would be healed—without Jesus even being there in person! Jesus was astounded. He had never seen such faith, even among the Israelites, the people of God. The centurion's constant practice in the use of faith principles prepared him to meet Jesus and see his prayer answered.

Setting a goal to make a change or pursue a dream is a faith step. Coaching leverages this power of goal-setting to get things done. Part of the privilege of being a Christian coach is helping clients understand how the power they find in goal-setting points toward their creator.

Goals and Coaching

A goal is the end toward which your efforts are directed, the finishing line of a race, a picture of where you are headed. *Setting a goal is making a decisive choice to reach a certain end.* It's starting with the final objective in mind. Coaching is a goal-driven process, because at every point you are explicitly working toward specific objectives.

It's the client's job to choose the goal (set the agenda) for the coaching relationship. That decisive choice focuses the client's efforts and sets things in motion. Your job as a coach is to focus the coaching conversation around that goal so that the client develops and carries out the kinds of action steps that bring the person to the goal. In essence, the goal provides both a mandate and a set of boundaries for the coach. It is a mandate because it represents the client's clear, specific request to be coached on that agenda. It's a boundary because that stated objective is where you need to focus your coaching.

Here's why that's important. Let's say you and a client have talked about several different issues but not decided where to put the primary focus. She wants to get organized so she can improve her productivity, spend more time with the kids, start taking care of herself by going to the gym regularly and realign her priorities with what God wants for her life. So state your opinion: which of these four issues is the most important one to focus on?

The problem is that when there is no definite goal, it's easy for the coach to choose it for the client by default. My personal calling is to build leadership character, so if I was coaching this gal I'd naturally be attracted to the fourth option. It would be a challenge for me not to skew the conversation in that direction. But that's not my job. Of those four issues, the one that is most important is the one that the *client* thinks is most important. Having the client decisively choose a goal keeps the coach from inadvertently changing the agenda.

Here are five key reasons why being goal-driven is vital to coaching effectively:

1. ***Clarity.*** A goal represents a decisive choice by the client to pursue a particular end.
2. ***Power.*** Declaring a goal unleashes God's power on the client's behalf.
3. ***Motivation.*** Visualizing the end result motivates the client to pursue a better future.
4. ***A Mandate.*** A goal gives you a clear picture of the client's priorities, a mandate for how to focus your coaching conversations and boundaries to stay within.
5. ***Action.*** Clear goals make it easy to develop effective action steps. It's hard to plan if you don't know where you're going!

The Coaching Funnel

Start your coaching relationships by defining a growth goal in your first appointment. Any time the client reaches a major objective, or the relationship begins to feel less focused or fruitful, it is the coach's job to help the client either refocus around the existing goal, change it to fit with the changed circumstances, or set a new goal.

Throughout the remainder of the book we'll be referring to a simple model of how a coaching conversation develops called the *coaching funnel*. It's a graphical representation of how a coach moves from a goal to action steps. The process can take place in as little as 10 or 15 minutes with simple practical issues, or extend over a number of coaching appointments when you're working on a major challenge or decision.

In this model, the coaching conversation starts with a narrow, concrete focus: a specific, measurable goal. The more clearly defined the goal is, the better. "I want to be more content," is a poor change goal—it is so vague that it provides little direction for the coaching conversation. "I want to identify the top three areas of stress in my life, and develop a plan to reduce stress in each of those areas by 50%," is much better.

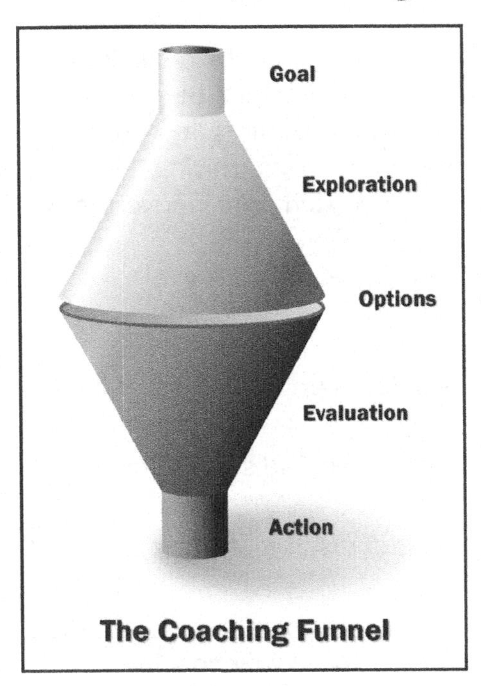

The Coaching Funnel

Once the goal is defined, the coach broadens out the conversation using open questions and exploration techniques to help the client discover new insights and think creatively. Many possible sources of stress are examined. Once the top three are identified, the coach pushes the client to develop multiple options for reducing the strain.

Up to this point, the conversation has been wide-ranging and exploratory—we've reached the widest part of the funnel. However, everything that has been discussed pertains to the original objective. Starting with a goal keeps us from going off on bunny trails or side issues that aren't really top priority for the client.

Next, the coach helps the client narrow the conversation back down to specific action steps. Here again, the original goal forms a mandate the coach uses to ensure that the proposed action steps move the client toward the objective. Any solutions or actions that don't clearly move the client toward the desired outcome are rejected. The boundaries of the funnel, the coaching conversation, are defined by the original goal.

If we hadn't set a goal at the beginning, our conversation could end up anywhere—maybe the client would vent, or we'd swap stories or joke around. The goal is what makes the coaching conversation strategic—we are going somewhere, and the place we've decided to go is important enough that we're willing to work to get there.

Practical Goal-Setting Tips for Coaches

Below are five top goal-setting tips for coaches:

1. Focus on the Destination

It's easy to make setting a growth goal too complicated. *Just establish where you are going and don't worry yet about how you are going to get there.* Here's an analogy: a client is in Chicago and wants to take her family on vacation. When you are making the goal statement, all you have to establish is the deadline and the destination: whether she is going to New York or Los Angeles, and when she'll get there. You don't need to know whether she is driving or flying, how much the trip will cost, or how many pieces of luggage they need. Leave the action plan for later.

For instance, if a client's goal is to increase his income, you don't need to ask yet about how he'll do it. All you need to determine is how much of an increase he wants and when he wants it by. The goal says *where* you are going; the action plan states *how* you'll get there.

2. Start with One Goal

Sometimes a new client will be all fired up about working on three or four things at once. Unless the person has an unusual amount of time and energy available, I request that we start with a single growth goal. Setting your expectations a little low and then increasing them is much better than placing the bar too high and starting off with a failure.

The pattern you want to establish with your clients is that *every time we set a goal we meet it.* Success breeds success. When clients meet their goals or make great progress, they get excited, begin to believe in themselves, and suddenly can do things they never thought possible. Not long ago I had a client whose initial goal was to clean up his office. He got so excited about the changes he was making ("I'm on fire! This is really helping me, and I can't thank you enough!") that his next goal was to retrain himself to launch a new career.

Many goals take a lot of work at the start and then gradually consume less energy as the new habit takes hold. By staggering the start times of the goals you can even out the amount of energy the client is expending and increase the overall chances of success.

3. Major in Motivation.

The best goal is the one the client is most motivated to work on. If the client is unsure what to focus on, an assessment tool like the *Wheel of Life* (see chapter 9) can help unearth where the greatest felt need for change is. The area where there is the largest gap between the client's aspirations and reality is usually where there is the most motivation to change.

Another thing to look for is a recent teachable moment. For instance, a person might ignore her health for years, but when a close friend the same age dies from a heart attack, suddenly the motivation to exercise skyrockets. A client with a great reason to change is a client who is ready to make some great changes.

Signs of a Motivated Client

1. Motivated clients take initiative and approach you about being coached.
2. Motivated clients know what they want to work on.
3. A recent circumstance has made them more aware of their growth issue and inspired them to deal with it now.
4. They are visibly excited about getting started.
5. They are willing to work.

4. Be Concise

Most of us ramble, especially when we are talking about things we haven't fully thought through before. The problem is, the best goal statements are concise and to the point—preferably a single sentence. Often the first time you ask a client to state his goal, you'll get something like this:

> *"Well, the thing that has been bothering me is that I just don't have that many years of work left. I'm 54, and until now I haven't really focused on getting ready for retirement. The clock is ticking and the sound is starting to echo around inside my head. We've got some money saved up, and we've got the house, but we've starting getting the bills from two kids who are in college. We've promised to help them, but I don't know where the money is going to come from. So all of the sudden I'm thinking a lot more about our financial future..."*

We all talk like this sometimes. But the seeds of a goal are there: retirement, college bills and his financial future. Your job as a coach is to help this person turn his jumbled thoughts into a clearly expressed goal. As the client talks, I jot down the main points he's focusing on. Then I summarize the key ideas for him, like this: "So, you are thinking about your financial plans for retirement and how to put your kids through college—is that correct?" Making a summary statement will usually draw even more out of the client.

Once he's gotten everything out on the table, I'll list the key ideas and then ask

Visualization

A goal represents a new or better future you are shooting for. One way to help clients flesh out a goal is to have them describe that future in visual language:

- "Draw me a picture: what will your life be like when you achieve this goal?"
- "What will be different? Describe the change in how you will look, feel, think, act, etc. when we've reached this objective."
- "What will your average day look like once you've reached this goal?"

him to state the goal in one sentence: "You mentioned that this year you want to work on developing a budget to account for college expenses, creating a long-term financial plan and saving for retirement. Can you roll those three things into a one-sentence goal statement?" I'm careful to let the client state the growth goal whenever possible. This ensures that it is truly his goal and that he fully owns it.

5. Change Horses in Midstream

In my experience, it is very common in the third, fourth or fifth appointment for a new client to want to change the original growth goal to something completely different. This pattern is deeply disturbing to beginning coaches. The knee-jerk reaction is to treat it as a betrayal: "But we agreed we were going to work on your prayer life! Let's go back to our original coaching covenant and review what you decided to focus on..." It's perfectly understandable: the coach has invested a lot of time and energy in getting the coaching relationship going, and now the client doesn't like things the way they are and wants to work on something else. It shakes the coach's confidence.

However, in most cases this shouldn't be a blow: it's actually a confirmation that the coaching process is working. Probably one of two things is happening. It may be that your client was not quite ready to open up to you at first. But now that you've gotten to know each other, the client feels safe enough to work on something much more important than what was first mentioned. That's a good sign!

The second common scenario is that a God-initiated set of circumstances has gotten a client's attention, and now the person wants to use the coaching relationship as a primary place to respond to God's initiative. That's a positive development as well.

Remember, coaching is about believing in people. If your clients want to change growth goals, the default setting for a coach is to believe that those individuals know what they are doing and that this is a great choice. When changes like this upset us, it may indicate that our default setting is to suspect the motives of others and believe that they don't know how to follow through with their commitments. As Jesus said, "Out of the abundance of the heart the mouth speaks." Our instinctive responses reveal what we really believe about people!

Master Class: S.M.A.R.T. Goal Statements

Congratulations—this month you've signed up two new clients! By coincidence, each wants to work on roughly the same thing. At your first coaching appointment, each individual hands you a goal statement he's developed for the coaching relationship. They're listed below:

1. *"I want to be a better husband."*
2. *"My goal over the next three months is to take practical steps to increase the quantity of my communication with my wife by 50%, and to increase the quality of our communication by planning ahead for regular talks when we don't have the kids."*

Exercise 10.1: What Makes a Workable Goal?

Which of these two goal statements do you think would be most conducive to a successful coaching relationship? Why exactly would one goal be harder to coach than the other? (Answers are at the end of this chapter.) To help think it through, take each goal statement above and try to envision yourself doing the following:

- Holding this person accountable.
- Helping this client develop clear, concrete action steps.
- Encouraging this client by pointing out tangible progress toward his goal.
- Celebrating the achievement of the goal together.

The S.M.A.R.T. Format

Because vague, ill-defined goals are much harder to coach, the first step in coaching a certain issue is to develop a clear, concrete goal. The S.M.A.R.T. format is an excellent tool for refining a goal. SMART goals are *Specific, Measurable, Attainable, Relevant* and *Time-Specific.*

Here's what each of those five characteristics means. A *specific* goal is one where you know exactly what you are shooting for. "I want to be a better husband" fails the SMART test because it is not specific—what exactly does it mean to be "better"? The second sample goal in exercise 10.1 is more focused: it calls for implementing practical steps to increase communication and starts with a clear example: date nights.

S.M.A.R.T. Goals

- **S**pecific
- **M**easurable
- **A**ttainable
- **R**elevant
- **T**ime-Specific

A *measurable* goal is one where you know when you've reached it. If your goal is to scale Mount McKinley, you know you've accomplished that objective when you're perched on the summit. You can even take a picture of it to prove you were there. The problem with setting out to be "better" at something is you can never celebrate that you've arrived. To make a goal measurable, find an objective way to quantify or measure progress—cutting stress by half, or increasing your sales by 10%, or having devotions six days a week.

Attainable goals are ones where the outcome is possible and you are in control of whether that outcome is reached. The usual reason client goals aren't attainable is that other people's wills are

Unattainable vs. Attainable

Here are three potentially unattainable goals, with each goal adjusted to become definitely attainable:

Unattainable: I want to reconcile with my father.
Attainable: I want to find five practical ways to show my father I love him.

Unattainable: I want to lead my brother to the Lord.
Attainable: I want to give my brother a chance to hear the gospel.

Unattainable: I want to be the top salesman in the company.
Attainable: I want to beat our company's current sales record.

involved. For instance, if the goal is to get promoted, the outcome depends on the boss as well as your performance! Rework the goal so it doesn't depend on anyone's actions but the client's. I like to say, *"Set a goal that you control."*

The other reason goals are unattainable is that they don't take into account real, intrinsic limitations. For instance, if you are 45 years old, stand 5'7" and haven't played ball since high school: we could say with pretty complete confidence that NBA stardom is not in your future!

Goals that are *relevant* are ones that are important to you—ones you care enough about to work hard to achieve. Usually, coming up with a relevant goal is simply a matter of asking your clients what they want to work on. However, be aware that new clients may choose a less important goal if they aren't sure they want to open up to you yet.

If you don't have a deadline, you haven't set a goal. Without time limits, procrastination can continue forever. Pinning yourself down to a *time-specific* deadline is what makes accountability possible. So take your best guess for when the goal will be completed—you can always revise the estimate later if you have to.

Example: Making a Goal SMART

When a client comes to you with a vague goal, your first task as a coach is to help make it SMART. The left column below is an example of that process. The right column offers a window into the mind of the coach, letting you see the coaching techniques that make the process work. This dialogue shows how to work through each step of the SMART format, which makes it longer than it would usually take in real life to define a goal.

"Ed, what would you like to work on in our coaching relationship?"	*The client sets the agenda.*
"Well, mainly some things on the home front. I want to be a better husband for my wife."	*The client's first goal statement is vague and unmeasurable.*
"OK, that sounds great! Let's see if we can make your goal a little more specific. What does it mean to you to be a better husband?"	*The coach begins to help make it more specific.*

"I guess I want to get more things done around the house—the honey-do stuff she wants me to take care of that always seems to end up on the back burner."

"Give me an example: what are some of those things you want to start getting done?"

Asking for examples helps the client become clearer about the goal.

"You know, working on the lawn, raking the leaves in the fall, planting in the spring, that sort of thing."

"OK. So is getting these practical things done what you want to focus on in our coaching relationship?

The coach asks for a commitment to a specific direction.

"Yeah. Because once Jan and I get this stuff out of the way we can focus on the more important things."

Surprise: the client discovers a deeper, more relevant agenda. The coach picks up on it and the conversation goes to a deeper level.

"Say more about that. What are the more important things?"

"Communication. That's something I really want to work on. And being a good father—that's an important part of being a better husband for me, too."

"Alright. You've put three things out on the table that would help you be a better husband: practical chores like lawn care, communication and being a good father. Does one of those three stand out to you?"

The coach asks again for the client to choose an agenda.

"Um... I think communication. Yeah, that's what's most important to me."

"Sounds great. So now draw me a picture: how will the communication in your marriage look different once you have achieved this goal?

The goal is where you are going. It is what your life will look like when you've arrived. So the coach asks the client to visualize that end point.

"Well, we'd definitely spend more time communicating. We don't have much time or structure in life right now for that. And I want to have better quality communication. To do that I think we need to plan times to talk when we're fresh and not just at 10:00 pm. I want to set aside time when we have a babysitter so we can focus and enjoy talking."

"Let's quantify that. How much more communication do you want than you have now?"

"Fifty percent more."

"And how will you be able to tell that your conversations are higher quality?"

"I want to have at least one time a week when we have an evening without the kids to talk and to enjoy being together."

"Good! Now we've got a specific, measurable target to shoot at. How long will it take to develop this pattern? In other words, how long do you expect us to be working on this?"

"Probably about three months."

"Last question. You and your wife will need to do this together. Is this something she'll get on board with?"

Ed laughed. "That's a pretty sure bet."

"OK—let me see if I've heard you correctly. You want to focus on communication; increase the time you spend communicating 50%; plan quality times to talk when you have a babysitter, and you think that will take about three months to implement. Is that right?"

"Yeah, sounds good."

"Put that in a goal statement for me—can you say what you want in one sentence?

"Sure. My goal over the next three months is to take practical steps to increase the quantity of my communication with my wife by 50%, and to increase the quality of our communication by planning ahead for regular talks when we don't have the kids."

"Great—that's an excellent goal statement! Let's both write that down, because that goal is going to guide what we do over the next three months."

The coach helps the client make the goal measurable by asking for a number.

The coach asks for a time-specific deadline for when the goal will be reached.

Is the goal attainable?

The coach summarizes what's been decided so far from his notes.

The coach asks the client to express the final goal statement in his own words. This maintains ownership and makes sure the nuances of the goal are right for the client.

Both coach and client write down any goal statements that are made!

S.M.A.R.T. Goal Questions

Powerful coaching questions used to refine a client's goal:

Specific

- "Can you define more clearly what you want to accomplish?"
- "How could you sum that up in one sentence?"
- "Sharpen that: what's the heart of what you want to do?"

Measurable

- "How will you know when you've reached this goal?"
- "Can you quantify that outcome?"
- "What will be different about your life when you attain this goal?"

Attainable

- "Does meeting this goal depend on someone else?"
- "Can you restate that goal so it doesn't depend on anyone's actions but yours?"
- "Are there any 'givens' in your life that would keep you from reaching this goal?"

Relevant

- "What would you like to work on?"
- "Of the things you've mentioned, which would you most like to change?"
- "Is there anything else that is more important to focus on right now?"

Time-Specific

- "Give me a time limit: by when will you reach this goal?"
- "What's your best guess for when this will be done?"
- "How long would it take to develop a long-term, sustainable habit instead of merely making a surface change in this area?"

Exercise 10.2: SMART Practice

For each goal listed below, answer the following questions: Is this a SMART goal? If not, which component is missing? Restate each goal that's missing something to make it SMART.

1. "I want to increase my productivity at work by 10%."
2. "I want to set aside time each week to get good at playing the piano so I can perform at the conference in June."
3. "By January 15 I want to get my kids to spend 50% more time communicating with their parents than they are now."
4. "In the next year I want to become a man of God who is really in the word and walking in the power of the Spirit."

Chapter 10 Exercise Answers

10.1 *It's a much simpler task to coach the second goal than the first. The coaching funnel is better defined, so you'll know exactly where to start, and you'll spend less time on side issues or irrelevant bunny trails. With clear, specific goals it is much easier provide to accountability (you know what to ask) and to develop effective action steps. Encouraging and celebrating progress also works much better, because with a clear goal you know exactly what you've accomplished.*

10.2 ***Goal #1*** *is not SMART—there is no deadline, so it is not time-specific; and although you have a figure you are shooting for (10% gain), it would be hard to know when you are ten percent more productive with a way to measure your productivity. Here's one example of rewriting this goal to make it SMART:*

> "I want to increase my productivity (as measured by my total case load) ten percent by March first."

Goal #2 *needs to be made measurable—how much time will you set aside each week? As a SMART goal, it might be:*

> *"I want to set aside two hours each week to practice playing the piano so I can perform at the conference in June."*

Goal #3 *is not attainable—you are setting out to get another person to do something which isn't really under your control. Rewritten, this might be:*

> "I want to identify the things we as a family want to do together and plan ahead so we are spending 50% family time together by January 15."

This at least makes the kids part of the decision-making process!

Goal #4 *is not measurable—what does it mean to be "really in the word" and "walking in the power of the Spirit"? Depending on how that last phrase is defined, this may not be attainable, either, since it is God that gives the growth. A better SMART goal might be:*

> "I want to become more of a man of God by identifying God's top three growth priorities for me this year, then developing and walking out a strategic plan to move me to excellence in each of those areas."

Chapter 11

Listening: Curiosity vs. Diagnosis

> *"During coach training, my homework was...to listen while someone talks about something valuable in his or her life, and then do an evaluation. I did this exercise with my wife... After 23 years of marriage, she really started for the first time to tell me her mind. She told me about her past life, youth, her bad father, private things. She was very honest—it was like the first time I met with her spiritually. It felt like two jars of water being poured into each other. It was such a great experience—she was so happy. I realized that through 23 years of marriage I had never listened to her... [Learning to listen] is a gift from God!"* Pastor

Recently a friend of mine related a conversation he'd overhead at a coffee shop between a father and daughter seated at the next table. "He was lecturing her on the classic father-daughter stuff, Mark recalls. 'You're spending too much money, you aren't focused on your education, etc, etc.' It was so painful. All she wanted was for him to ask her, 'What are *your* goals? What do *you* want out of life?' He was raising his voice with her, she was in tears—it was really ugly. I believe that father genuinely wanted the best for his daughter, but he didn't know how to get there."

If you had asked this father what needed to happen, he would probably have said something like this: "If she would just *listen* to me things would work out so much better!" And if you asked the daughter what ought to change, no doubt she'd say, "Why doesn't he ever *listen* to what I want?" They're having a conversation, but nobody is really listening.

In our culture it's easy to go through life stating our own ideas or exchanging impersonal information while rarely having a real, intimate dialogue with anyone. Many of our conversations are simply two monologues; ships passing in the night (or maybe ICBMs passing in the stratosphere) as each person tries to get their point across. The father in this example carried on a monologue because he felt like his way was the right one. By focusing on his agenda instead of on his daughter, he lost the chance to be really heard—and may eventually lose the relationship as well.

All of us want to be heard. We long to be accepted, to be known, to be valued for who we are. That human desire is so powerful that we find it very difficult to receive a critique from someone we feel doesn't accept us. We react to the person instead of responding to the facts that are presented. Have you ever rejected out of hand a criticism from one person and then shortly thereafter accepted the same rebuke from another, when the only difference was that the second person was a friend and the first wasn't? Our ability to hear depends on who is speaking. Likewise, our ability to change and to operate at our maximum creativity and productivity is highly dependent on being in a supportive environment. This leads to an interesting insight about human beings:

Expressing acceptance and belief in a person often brings about faster growth than pointing out what is wrong.

The daughter in the story above is probably not going to pay attention to her father until she feels accepted by him for who she is. If she continues to receive critique without acceptance, their family relationship may be irreparably damaged—ironically, by her father's misdirected good intentions.

Listening communicates value and acceptance. People are most open to being influenced by those who accept and value them. Therefore, learning to listen deeply, intently and intuitively is absolutely vital to influencing others. Listening is a powerful tool for changing lives, because the acceptance it communicates frees people to grapple with the message instead of getting hung up on their relationship with the messenger.

The Power of Listening

Listening is the first of the four key elements of the coaching conversation. Every coaching relationship starts with listening, because it is only when we listen that we learn who our clients are and what is on their hearts. The act of listening creates a great environment for change.

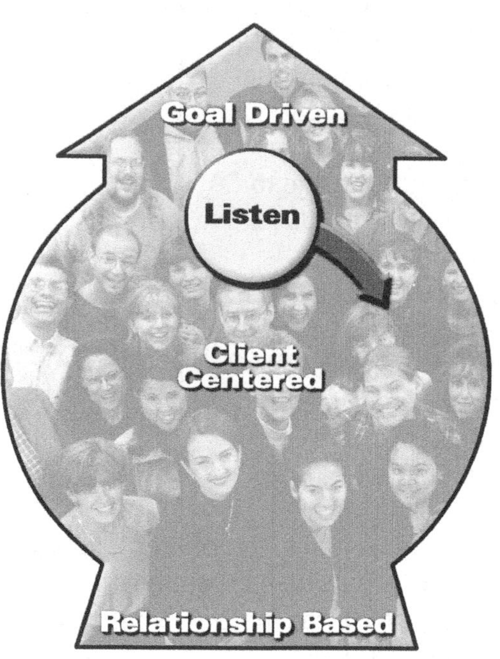

Julie began going through a coaching certification program several months ago, and one day she shared an amazing story about the impact of listening. Each Thursday she and Ashley, one of her co-workers, did the evening shift together at the coffee shop they worked at. That evening, Ashley was distraught about what was going on her life. She was so discouraged and afraid her doctor had put her on medication. A single mom, she was unable to make ends meet, the bills were piling up and her youngest daughter was constantly in trouble for acting up at school.

"She didn't know what to do—she felt like she was losing her mind and she didn't have any hope," Julie remembers. "Ashley had been a Christian, but she was not walking with God anymore. She told me, 'I don't think God wants me around. I'm not talking to Him, because I don't think He wants to hear from me, either.'"

"We'd been talking about the coaching approach in class," Julie recalls, "So I'm standing there thinking, 'This coaching thing—how do you do it?' I had advice coming into my mind and I had to resist the temptation to say it because I wanted to try this new coaching idea... I'd been giving her advice for months from things in the Bible but nothing had changed."

As Julie and Ashley cleaned up the expresso machines, Ashley talked for some time about her situation while Julie simply listened. Once Ashley had spoken her mind, a quiet calm descended. "I didn't know what to do at first, but I finally said to her, 'I know that God wants to speak to you, and when He does, you'll be able to hear His voice.'" Julie remembers. "Then I was quiet, too—I didn't know what else to say."

> *"Before [becoming a coach], when pastors would come to me with a problem, I used to listen a little and point out the problem as tactfully as I could, then I'd pray with them... there was compassion there, but I didn't go further with them because I didn't know how, and because I was afraid of the time commitment... Now I have the tools to help them... I can't just pray with someone and walk away like I used to."*
>
> Denominational Executive

"When I was just listening and wasn't giving advice I felt so inadequate—I felt like I wasn't giving her anything. It felt kind of dumb to just trust that God would do something. But the atmosphere was different when I wasn't giving advice. Ashley was more open, more receptive, calmer—it seemed like her walls were down. Before, when I'd try to talk to her about God, I didn't see that—she was more argumentative."

Ashley didn't mention anything about their conversation for a week. But the next Thursday when they were alone she brought it up. "Julie, I ought to tell you: you know the last time we talked, how awful I felt like life was? Well, the next morning I climbed up to the top of the hill behind our condo and I said, 'God, I'm sorry I've been afraid to talk to you, but I just need you so bad'—and He spoke to me! From then on everything's been totally different!"

Ashley is smiling now. There's been a change in her relationship with her kids, a total transformation in her attitude, even a significant improvement in her work performance. Julie even heard her sharing about Christ with their other co-workers . All this happened because someone listened to her and believed in her.

Imitating God

Is God a listener or a teller? Think about it: when you are communicating with God in prayer, what is He doing most of the time? Is He constantly talking, filling every quiet moment with sage advice and cosmic ideas? Or is He mostly listening? God, who knows our every need before we ask and the answers to all our problems, takes the time to listen to each one of us. To listen is to imitate God.

Years ago I did a prayer exercise with a group of seekers that had a huge impact on them. Our house had a second floor balcony that overlooked the living room. In the role-play, we sent one individual upstairs to "play God," while another got the opportunity to pose the question he had always wanted to ask God. Some questions were simple and some were profound. But, most of the time, God said nothing.

When we debriefed afterward, some of the most thoughtful comments came from people after they had played the part of God: "Now I know why God doesn't always answer my questions!" Several had profound encounters with God through that exercise. I don't know if we were able to fully explain what happened, but somehow afterward they understood God in a new way. He's not silent, He's not ignoring us: He's listening.

> *"...Jesus raised his eyes to heaven and prayed, "Father, I'm grateful that you have listened to me. I know you always do listen..."* John 11:41-42; MSG

Thinking Things Through

Becoming a great coach requires developing an extraordinary ability to listen. I often find myself telling trainees, "Don't try to figure out the client's problem—just listen! The client will tell you the answer. You just need to be listening intently enough to pick up on it." When trainees do focus in on listening instead of trying to think up an awesome question or reply, they are always amazed at how well it works. People really can solve their own problems.

At first glance, listening may seem passive, but it is actually a powerful tool for solving problems. What often holds people back is not a lack of insight, but a lack of confidence in their own ideas or an inability to put them into words. The act of listening affirms and empowers people to express themselves with confidence. When you listen consistently and intently, the message you are sending is, "You are important! What you are saying is important. You are a person of great worth and what you are saying is worth listening to. I believe you can figure this out." When you express confidence in your clients' abilities by listening, they will start believing in themselves, too. That alone is often enough to get someone unstuck.

Because I'm Listening...

Years ago, when I was selling furniture for a living, I had just wrapped up a five-figure deal on some display cases for a retailer. It was after hours, so we sat down in Terry's executive office to fill out the paperwork. As he cut me a check, Terry began to talk about how he'd gotten started in business. He told the story of opening his first store, and then began to reminisce about the health difficulties he'd overcome as a child and how he used to be teased for a speech impediment. He began to share about his concern over one of his grown children—his son's marriage was on the rocks and as a father he was discouraged and deeply concerned—when suddenly he stopped short.

"Why am I telling you all this?" he said, puzzled.

I thought for a moment and then replied, "Because I'm listening."

But listening does even more. One of our biggest weaknesses in problem solving is that we aren't very rational when it comes to our own lives. When someone else is on God's operating table, I can sit back and examine it dispassionately. When a friend has lost a job, it's easy to say, "Don't worry! God will provide for you!" When you are out on the street yourself, it's a little more of a challenge to believe God has everything under control! When we are trying to think through our own problems, our emotions, perceived limitations or past disappointments cloud the picture and we easily get stuck.

Our rational abilities play tug-of-war with our emotions until we're mentally exhausted.

But when I sit down with a friend who is really listening, something magical happens. As he listens patiently, asks me questions and helps me to look at my situation from other angles, the truth comes into focus. My objective and subjective insights begin to mesh. I push through the fog of emotions or preconceptions until suddenly I break out of the box I'm in and see the solution clearly. When we verbalize our thoughts to someone else who is listening, we think more clearly and confidently than we do alone.

What a Coach Has to Give

In Julie's story, her first attempts at listening instead of giving advice made her feel foolish and inadequate. That's a common experience. I once worked with a trainee named Nic who had extensive experience mentoring and discipling younger Christians. As a practice exercise, he was coaching a client through a programming challenge in his computer business—an area Nick knew nothing about. The practice session worked out great—the client came up with a number of good options, solved the problem and ended with a solid set of action steps. Nic's reflections from the debriefing afterward offer an insightful look at how it felt to move from a telling to a coaching mode:

> *"I felt sidelined—like I was standing on the outside of the conversation watching. You [the client] were doing all the talking and the problem-solving—and I was sitting there thinking, 'Why does he need me?' I felt I wasn't really contributing to the process because I wasn't giving you any answers. I just asked questions and you came up with all the answers and options, and I felt like I was sitting there humming the Jeopardy theme and waiting for something to happen... In fact, there were a whole lot of things happening and coming from your side, but nothing was coming from my side.*
>
> *"I get my value from what I can contribute. In mentoring and discipling the value of the relationship is what you as the mentor can contribute to it. We think*

that the value of our help is what we contribute to the conversation—answers, knowledge, ideas, the wealth of our past experience. [But in coaching] what you contribute is to get the client talking about what is going on so the client can come up with the answers.

"I realized that in the coaching process you don't have to know anything about what the person is trying to accomplish—you just have to create an atmosphere or arena where they can process and come up with the options. My past experiences and knowledge were not helpful because I didn't know anything about the topic—and if I can't contribute from my knowledge or past experiences, what is my value? But I've learned that my value is not what I can contribute, but the atmosphere I can create where people can be creative... and think things through themselves."

Exercise 11.1: Extraordinary Listening

We've all listened and asked questions since we were toddlers. It's just that most of us have never approached listening and asking as disciplines, to be systematically learned, practiced and refined. Let's take a practical look at what makes for great listening and how we can take our skills to the next level.

There are many listening techniques which communicate to another person that you are paying attention—leaning forward, having an open posture and making eye contact. But instead of focusing on the outward techniques, we're going to examine what is going on inside our heads when someone else is talking. If you learn to think like a coach on the inside, the techniques will come naturally to you.

Here's a fun challenge. Get out a pen and paper or sit down at your computer keyboard. Next, pick a favorite song that you know pretty well. Now, here's the challenge: Sing the song out loud, and while you are singing, simultaneously write or type out the words to the pledge of allegiance. Go ahead—you may be surprised at what happens!

How'd it go? I always get stuck after a few lines. I start writing random words from the song into the pledge of allegiance, or I stop singing to write, or I alternate singing and writing. Even though the lines of the pledge are burned into my brain from saying them over and over in grade school, I can still completely forget them while I am saying something else. Here's the moral of this story: as human beings, there are some things we can and can't multitask at. We can dance and sing at the same time, or walk and talk, or stir the soup while we're adding up the cost of a remodeling project in our heads. But it's tough for our brains to do two different things with words at one time.

The Conversation in Your Head

This inability to multitask with words is the fundamental challenge to listening well. The other person is talking (that's one thing involving words), and meanwhile we have a second, hidden monologue going on inside our heads where we're trying to figure

Common Distractions

What starts the conversation inside your head?

- I see your problem and I'm figuring out how to solve it while I'm listening.
- I'm already composing my reply (or my next question) while you are still talking.
- I was in a conflict today and I can't get it out of my mind.
- I really want to get back to work (or whatever I was doing before we started talking).
- "Not *that* issue again!"
- I'm personally frustrated by something in the conversation and I start thinking about my emotions instead of what I'm hearing.
- What you said reminded me of a task I need to do.
- Something you said sent my imagination roaming off into the stratosphere.
- Something in my environment (like my e-mail) gets me thinking about what I'm seeing instead of what I'm hearing.

out what to say next (which makes two things). Our brain can't do both at once, so we slip in and out between the conversation with the other person and the conversation in our heads. Every time we switch gears we lose a few words, a sentence, or a whole paragraph. At its worst, this leaves us nodding and saying, "Uh-huh" without a very clear idea of what the other person is talking about. (I have a friend who is quite prone to this, and now whenever his wife catches him nodding absently she asks him to repeat back her last sentence!) In order to listen well, we must turn off the conversation in our heads and give our full, undivided attention to what the other person is saying.

Here's a coaching challenge: can you carry on a half-hour conversation without losing a single word? (Try the "Listening Skills Test" exercise at right.) If you want to be a great coach, that's where to set the bar. This kind of high standard can greatly increase the impact you have with others. I call it "being all there." One of my personal commitments to my clients is that when I am in a coaching appointment, that person is the only individual in the world. All my attention is focused within the appointment.

Exercise 11.2: Listening Skills Test

Sit down with a friend for 15 to 30 minutes and have a conversation where you are asking questions and doing most of the listening. Immediately afterward, take another five or 10 minutes to reflect:

- What other things did I think about during this conversation?
- What started the conversation in my head? What distracted me?
- How often did I problem-solve or compose my replies while my friend was talking?

Making the Commitment

That's harder than it sounds! But I believe that making a commitment to be all there is one of the most important things you can do to improve your listening skills. Covenant with yourself that when you are listening, you won't tolerate any distractions or thoughts that get in the way of hearing what the other person is saying. Remember, when you set a concrete goal as an act of faith, it unleashes the power of God to help you meet it. If you'd like to take that step, you can do it right here, right now. Fill in the sentence below and sign after it:

> *Today, ________________ (date), I sacrificially commit myself to be "all there" for the people I'm coaching. I will treat our conversations as sacred and I won't let anything distract me from giving my full, undivided attention.*
>
> ______________________________________
>
> *Signed*

The first step in change is setting a goal. Set the bar high for yourself so you are striving for something that is really worth achieving.

Exercise 11.3: Tuning In

Just to make sure you're tuning into what I mean by "the conversation in your head," let's do another exercise. It's easiest to see how this works by looking at an example. First, get a pencil and paper handy and then read through this story about David and his coach:

"How are you doin' today, David?"

"Actually, not very good."

"Want to tell me about it?"

"OK, sure. One of my action steps was to launch my small group, right? Well, I had already set a date and talked to about 20 different people, and then out of the blue my pastor came up and said I was doing it all wrong and I needed to, quote, 'submit to the process' for developing a group. I had to cancel the first group meeting, I was embarrassed in front of my friends and right now I'm pretty steamed."

"Tell me a little more. What exactly did your pastor say?"

"Well, the whole reason I'm starting this is because a lot of people in our church are having a hard time fitting in to a small group. They aren't getting the spiritual influence they need to really

live righteous and leave the world behind. The last group I was in—one night we actually watched a secular movie during small group! The leader tried to make it look spiritual by having a discussion about what it meant afterward, but it's really just a sign of the kind of spiritual apathy I see around here all the time.

"There are a lot of people in these other groups that aren't getting fed, but Pastor Jeff didn't want me to talk to any of them! He says I'm only supposed to approach people that aren't already in a group—that I'm just taking people out from under the other leaders. Frankly, the people who are in our church who are in a small group are just as needy as those who aren't."

> *"A fool takes no pleasure in understanding, but only in expressing his opinion."*
>
> Proverbs 18:2

"David, if I'm hearing you right, your plan was to recruit people in other groups whose needs weren't being met, but your pastor didn't approve of that strategy. Is that the gist of it?"

"You've got it."

"And what do you think of your pastor's response?"

"He's missing the whole point!" David burst out in frustration. "Those leaders aren't doing their job—I'm just trying to give people what they need to grow in the Lord. But when I told him that, he just smiled and walked away like he didn't care."

"What did he say to you at that point?"

"Oh, he gave me some drivel about how he really appreciates my heart and everything I'm trying to do, and to just trust that God can take care of the people in the other groups. That's all well and good, but it doesn't solve the problem. A lot of folks in this church need leadership and he's just standing in the way."

Now, before we go any further, stop and jot down what you where thinking about while you read this story (that's the conversation in your head)—your responses to the story, distracting thoughts, etc. Try to only put down what you thought while you were actually reading.

If you can't recall what was going through your mind, the questions below might jog your memory:

- Was there a point when you thought the pastor had a problem? What did you think it was?
- Was there a point when you thought the problem was David? What did you think was the solution to David's problem?
- Did you start thinking about how you would respond if you were working with David? What did you want to say to him?
- Did something in this story remind you of someone you knew or something you experienced? What was it?

Make sure you've finished jotting down your notes before you read further!

Curiosity vs. Diagnosis

When we hear a story like David's, there's often a predictable pattern to the conversation that gets triggered in our heads. It has four steps:

1. Something makes us curious;
2. We identify the problem;
3. We develop a potential solution;
4. We develop a strategy to get the person to see our solution.

Here's what this pattern looks like in detail. First, something we hear makes us curious. For instance, when David says his pastor wants him to "submit to the process," it sets off a bell in our heads. Maybe it reminds us of a similar experience, a leadership principle we've learned, or maybe it just doesn't seem to fit. Our intuition picks up on something interesting in the conversation and we register it.

> *"Let every man be quick to hear, slow to speak, slow to anger..."*
>
> James 1:19

Now that our ears are pricked up, we start assembling clues to what is going on. It might be that when David shares his shock at watching a movie in small group, we begin to wonder if he is a little too religious. Or when he mentions that his pastor only wanted him to approach people who aren't already in a group, we realize what the pastor sees—in his naivety David is sheep stealing! We begin to think we see the problem.

If the dialogue goes on long enough, our next tendency is to develop a solution for the problem we identified. We might think, "David just needs to let go of the things he isn't responsible for," or "Lighten up, David! You don't need to make a federal case out of this!" Our natural instinct when we see a problem is to turn on our advice generator and try to solve it for the person.

Finally, we start trying to come up with ways to get the person to see what we see. If you catch yourself composing a reply in your head before the other person has finished talking, you've made it all the way to step four. (This is often where interrupting comes from as well!) By step four we've stopped listening for new information, because we've already made a conclusion about what needs to happen. At this point we are mainly listening for ammunition we can use to get our pre-conceived point across.

Making a Change

Can you identify this pattern in your notes from the dialog about David? It's amazing how much we can think about in so little time, especially when we are supposed to be listening to somebody else. Changing this pattern is simple—it just takes a lot of hard work! The key is that the first step, curiosity, is where the coaching approach starts, too. Your first instinct (curiosity) is right. *You just have to do something different with it.* Instead of using your intuition to identify problems and solutions, stop at step one, with the thing that made you curious and ask the client to tell you what it means. The key to listening well is to stop trying to fix people while you are listening and instead make it your job to just be curious. Coaching is curiosity-driven, not diagnosis-driven.

> **Work Backwards**
>
> To turn off the conversation in your head, practice working backwards to your first instinct, to what originally made you curious, and ask about that.

Whenever you are trying to change a mental habit, at first you'll always catch yourself too late. You'll already be in step four (or the words will be half-way out of your mouth) when it dawns on you that you aren't listening. But because the coaching approach and the advice-giving approach both start at the same place, no matter where you catch yourself, you can always work back to the start. If you are coaching and you find yourself wanting to give a piece of advice, ask yourself, "What problem am I trying to solve with this advice? What was it that first made me wonder if there was a problem here?" Then ask your next coaching question about the thing that originally made you curious.

For instance, if you wanted to tell David to quit trying to do the pastor's job, ask yourself, "What problem am I solving by telling him that?" Maybe the problem you saw was David taking responsibility for things that weren't his to bear. So reflect: "What gave me that impression?" The answer to that question will take you back to what made you curious in the first place—for instance, David's decision to recruit people for his group from under other leaders.

So, now you can ask a real coaching question: "David, it sounds like you set out to recruit your people from the other groups. Talk about how that fits into your understanding of how small groups work." Or, "David, you mentioned you were recruiting people who were under other leaders. Talk about how that works from an authority perspective." Or, ask a perspective changer: "David, let's say one of the other leaders got half the people in your group to switch to theirs. How would you feel about that?"

The key to listening well is to stop identifying and solving other's problems. Follow your curiosity, not your diagnosis. Register the important things the client says, pay attention to your intuition, but don't try and figure everything out. Let the client do the work of solving the problem. When you stop the conversation in your head, your listening will go to a whole new level.

Turning Off the Conversation in Your Head

Ultimately, turning off the conversation in your head means changing ministry paradigms. Here's the key: in discipling, counseling or prophetic ministry, your discernment drives the process. You are attempting to discern what is going on and then communicate your insights to the person you are working with.

Coaching is exactly the opposite. In coaching, you are attempting to draw out the client's own insight about what is going on. The client's discernment drives the process. You don't have to expend any energy trying to figure out what the client's problem is or how to solve it. God initiates the changes He wants and the Holy Spirit brings those things to the surface through teachable moments. The transformation of the client happens through experience and relationship, not the information you bring to the table. So let go of the need to fix the client and allow room for the client to deal with God.

Here's another way of saying the same thing. People only do what they want to do anyway. Push people where they don't want to be pushed and you'll only get resistance. So it doesn't matter at all what you see, or what great insights you have—the only thing that matters is what the client sees. Turn off the part of you that wants to fix people, and in its place, develop the ability to believe that your clients can solve their own problems without being told what to do. When you really start believing in your clients, you'll be willing to still your own thoughts to listen, because what they have to say will be much more important to you.

Exercise 11.4: Diagnostic Thinking

Ask a friend to share a challenge, problem, major decision or unrealized dream with you. Coach the individual for 10 to 20 minutes. Try to be aware of the conversation in your head—when you realize you are diagnosing or solving problems in your head, go back to the thing that made you curious and ask the client to expound on what it means. Immediately afterward, take five minutes to self-evaluate:

1. What do you remember thinking about while the other person was talking?
2. Identify the places in the conversation where you missed a few words (or a sentence or paragraph) because of the conversation in your head.
3. How often did you catch yourself solving the problem in your head? Was it difficult not to go there?

Exercise 11.5: Eliminating Distractions

Another important way to improve your listening is to identify and eliminate the things that distract you. You can have great listening skills, but if your phone line is full of static or you are constantly interrupted you'll still find it very difficult to listen well. Listening intently is hard work. Often simple changes like taking a few minutes before the appointment to get centered, purchasing a headset or turning off your computer monitor while you are coaching can make a big difference.

Below is a two-part tool designed to help you identify distractions in your environment. When taking the assessment, score yourself based on your last coaching appointment (if you are a professional coach, use your appointments from the past week). Circle the statements that apply to you.

Distracting Environment

- -1 Your e-mail or IM program is open in front of you.
- -1 Your to-do list is sitting out in front of you where you can read it.
- -5 You do e-mail, IM or work on other projects while you are coaching.
- -1 You are sitting at your main work desk.
- -1 You can hear a noticeable amount of background noise (others talking, a phone ringing, etc).
- -2 Your door is open, the place you are coaching in has no door, or you are in a public place.
- -2 You finished another meeting, project or deadline within 10 minutes before this appointment.
- -2 You rushed in or worked on other tasks right up to the moment the appointment started.
- -2 There is a fair amount of stress and conflict in your life, or you are emotionally needy.
- -1 You are hungry, thirsty, tired or otherwise in a state of physical discomfort.

-5 **Total**

(Continued on next page)

Supportive Environment

+1 Your notes for this client are organized and easily accessible.
+3 You took at least 10 minutes before this appointment to get centered and review your notes.
+2 You've made a serious personal commitment to be all there while you are coaching.
+3 Your desk and screen are clear, or you have a separate place to coach away from daily work.
+1 You have a phone headset.
+1 You have a comfortable environment to coach in (correct temperature, good chair, etc.).
+1 You've prayed for this client this week.
+3 You don't have any calls, walk-ins or interruptions while you coach. Call waiting is disabled.
+2 Your appointments are scheduled at a time of day when you are alert and well rested.
+1 Your connection is clear and totally reliable. You aren't using a cell phone or voice chat.
Total

Now, add up your total points. If your score is negative, change your environment. If you are coaching professionally, the bar should be higher: if your score is less than +7, make some changes.

Chapter 12

Master Class: Intuitive Listening

> *"He who restrains his words has knowledge,*
> *And he who has a cool spirit is a man of understanding.*
> *Even a fool who keeps silent is considered wise;*
> *When he closes his lips, he is deemed intelligent."*
>
> Proverbs 17:27-28

Larry was speaking to a gathering of 100 pastors in his district about listening skills. He opened with a short personal story about what had happened in his life that week, then started explaining the difference between self-centered listening (tuning in only to what pertains to you) and listening at a deeper level. After a few minutes of teaching, Larry stopped and created a powerful teachable moment for his audience.

"I walked up to a guy in the second row at random, and asked, 'How are you today?'"

"Fine," was the automatic response.

"So then I asked him, 'Tell me what's fine in your life right now. What makes today a fine day?'"

The man hesitated and then looked up at Larry. "Actually, nothing is fine in my life," he replied. Then he went on to describe a painful struggle he was having with a family member and several difficult situations he was facing at his church.

"The entire room suddenly got what I was talking about—that often we are conversing but we aren't really listening. I said, 'Several of you were probably wishing I had asked you that question.' I had those who felt like things weren't fine stand up and then we prayed for each other. It took everybody's sensitivity up two or three notches—we got beyond 'fine' to being real."

What's Intuition?

The last chapter focused on improving our listening ability by turning off the conversation in our heads and eliminating distractions that prevent us from hearing what others are saying. Now that we are (hopefully!) hearing every word the client says, the next step is to refine what we're listening *for*. In all that is being shared, how do you pick out what is most significant? How does a coach decide what to ask about next?

Learning to be attentive to meaning and significance in what a client is saying is called *intuitive listening.* Meaning isn't conveyed only in words: voice tone, body language, the context of the conversation and even our own gut responses to what we're hearing all combine with the words to create meaning. In Larry's story, the word this man chose to portray how he was doing ("fine") didn't describe at all how he really felt. Intuition helps a coach sort through the words to get to the heart of the matter.

Intuition is the combination of conscious, unconscious and spirit-generated responses to what we hear (See box on next page). Another word we might use for it is *discernment*[1]. Maybe two facts in a story don't quite line up, or the person responded in an unusual way given the circumstances, or something was said that didn't make sense. You may not even be conscious of exactly what got your attention, but your intuition assured you that something was there. Curiosity and intuition tend to go hand it hand. When something makes you curious, it's usually a sign you are picking something up with your intuition.

[1] The way we commonly use the word "discernment" puts more emphasis on the spiritual side of the equation. Coaching is not about hearing God for others—it's about helping them hear God for themselves. So I've chosen to use the word "intuition" to describe the process.

When I'm in advice-giving mode, I register what my intuition says, draw conclusions from it and act on my intuition by advising the person. My intuition drives and directs the process. But when I'm coaching, I register what my intuition says without trying to figure out what it all means. My curiosity points me to interesting places that I then ask the client to explain and explore. By using my intuition to ask instead of tell, I keep the client in charge while still offering a valuable, active contribution to the process.

A big part of that contribution is the feedback you offer to the client in the form of your questions. By asking about what made you curious, about what seems most important, you rapidly focus people on the point of greatest significance and meaning *in their own thoughts and words*. Your curiosity brings focus, but

How Intuition Works

What is your intuitive response to this statement?

> *"Our small group realized that this is where we're really connected and where we get ministered to, so we decided to pay our tithes to the small group instead of to the church."*

Sounds like something is rotten in Denmark, doesn't it? How do you know this isn't biblical? Here are several different types of intuitive responses:

1. ***Conscious:*** You know this violates a specific biblical principle. For instance, you don't tithe to meet your own needs, but the needs of those in ministry.
2. ***Unconscious:*** This just doesn't sound right. You know something is wrong, even if you can't quote chapter and verse or explain why.
3. ***Spiritual:*** God may speak directly to you, or you may have a witness in your spirit that says, "Don't go there!"
4. ***Cultural:*** We've never seen it done this way. Intuition based on cultural norms can easily be unbiblical or inappropriate for the situation.

the insights, conclusions and solutions you're focusing on are the client's, not yours. The client is still in charge of the conversation. Your contribution as a coach is employing your intuition to help the client process more effectively.

Exercise 12.1: Intuition in Action

A sample dialogue is the best way to see how a coach uses intuition. While reading through this client's statement, try to pick out and underline the most important thing(s) the client says:

> *"I don't know what to think about my job. On the one hand, working for the city gives me great benefits, job security, and a comfortable living. I'm not stressed out or anything, but some days I come home and my conscience really bothers me. The work rules say I can't do certain things, and if we have to call in an inspector I can end up sitting out on the job site for two or three hours drinking coffee while we wait for him to show. At 1:30 last Friday we ran into another snag, and the boss just gave up and sent everybody home. I got paid for the whole day—the kids thought it was great—but I sure didn't put in a full day's work. I've asked the boss about it, and he just says this is the way the system works and you can't fight it. But just conforming to the system still doesn't sound ethical to me."*

What did *you* underline as being most significant? I chose the client's mention of his conscience bothering him and the comment about conforming to the system. Now, what does it look like to follow your curiosity instead of your diagnosis? Below are five possible questions. Which two do you think best reflect how coaches use their intuition? Caution: this one is challenging!

1. *"What could you do to let go of responsibility for things that are beyond your control?"*
2. *"What does your conscience say to you about this situation?"*
3. *"Since God gave you that little 'paid vacation', couldn't you just receive it as a gift?"*
4. *"How could you help your boss see that his response is wrong?"*

5. *"Given the chance, what would you change about the system?"*

Got your answers ready? First, I'll tell you about the three questions I wouldn't ask. The first sample isn't a badly constructed question, but here it is based on diagnosis, not curiosity. The coach has assumed that the problem is letting go of things you aren't responsible for, so the question is about solving that problem. The coach has diagnosed the issue instead of allowing the client to identify and solve the problem.

Question three is an easy one—not only is it diagnostic, but it's patronizing. The wording ("couldn't you just") infers that the client has foolishly missed a blessing from God. Question four is also diagnostic—here the assumption is that the boss has a problem. In both of these examples, the coach has employed intuition to diagnose the issue instead of using it to help the client reflect more deeply and discover what is going on.

So, our winners are questions two and five. Both ask the client to reflect on the significant comments identified by our intuition. Both make no assumptions and allow the client to identify the problem. When the client answers these questions, the process repeats itself. We listen again for what makes us curious and use the next question to push the client's thinking one step further.

What to Listen for

Intuition is by definition an intuitive process, more art than science. But we can become more cognizant of the clues that cause us to sit up and take notice. A first step is to identify and name the types of phenomena that activate our intuition. The more we make intuition a conscious process, the more adept we will be at it.

Below are the five most important categories of intuition items I listen for when I'm coaching:

1. ***The Person's Own Discernment*** or insight about the situation
2. ***Turning Points*** or key actions and events
3. ***Strong Emotion*** or reaction
4. ***Red Flags***: things that don't seem to fit or don't sit right
5. ***Patterns***: Cause and effect relationships or repeated outcomes in the client's actions or thinking

These *intuition indicators* are what most consistently point to meaning or significance in what's being said. In the following story, the indicators are underlined, with the type of indicator given in the right hand column:

"So, as I understand it, Chad, you want to work on improving your relationship with your wife. Say more about what you want."	
"Alright. It just feels like we aren't on the	Person's own
same page anymore when it comes to our	discernment
future. Nothing's been the same since we	
moved to a new apartment two years ago.	Turning point
The new place is a little smaller and not in the nicest part of town, but it cut our rent almost in half. Our budget had been pretty tight up	
to that point, which added a lot of stress to	Strong emotion
our marriage. So I was really looking forward	Strong emotion
to going out more, having a little extra pocket money for hobbies, taking a cruise every so often, that kind of thing.	
"Keep going."	
"But even though life has gotten a lot more	Person's own
fun, she still isn't happy. We're getting into more	discernment
fights than we used to, and it always seems to	Pattern
be about trivial stuff. The other day I came home with four or five new DVDs and a new preamp	
and she just flew off the handle."	Strong emotion
"What did she say?"	
"Oh, every so often she'll get on this kick	Pattern
about owning a house. The minute she saw the box she snapped, "There's my house. The whole	
down payment for my house is wrapped up in	Red flag
your movie collection." Then I snapped back at her, and she stormed into the bedroom and	
started crying. Later she comes out like always,	Strong emotion
and admits, "Honey, all I really need to be	
happy is you." That's nice, but I'm getting really	Strong emotion
frustrated with her mood swings. I wish I knew	Red flag
what was really bugging her."	

The Indicators Defined

Most of us are accustomed to using our intuition already—what's new is putting a name to what we're picking up on. The story above should give you a feel for what these indicators look like. Now let's give each one a definition.

In coaching, the most common and important indicator is the *person's own discernment*. The client is the person who has the most information about and responsibility for his or her own life. If God is going to speak to a person, He speaks "the firstest and the mostest" directly to that individual. That's why we follow the client's insight.

In this situation, the client identifies what he feels is the root problem: "We aren't on the same page anymore when it comes to our future." Even though the issue is right there on the table, it's still easy to blow right by it and try to figure out the problem on our own. At some point in the conversation, the client will almost always point out what the key issue is. The coach just needs to be listening for it.

Often you'll hear your clients say, "I'm good at this," or "I'm not sure that will work," or "Here's what I think the solution is". These are all examples of clients voicing their own discernment. Learning to consciously register the client's own insights is a powerful tool a coach can use to make conversations transformational.

Once I did an intuition indicators exercise with a group of ministry leaders. After listening to a life story, we compared notes and discovered together they had not recorded a single incidence of the person's own discernment! As we discussed it, they began to realize that they'd been trained to tune into their own discernment, but not the insights of the people they were working with. It was a humbling experience.

Turning points are significant moments or transitional events in a person's life. In the example above, a turning point in the client's marriage was the move to a new apartment. While the client couldn't identify exactly what had happened to the marriage in that transition, he knew something was different. That makes me curious—what happened there? Turning points can be important insights, victories, job changes, reverses, relocations, or they can be smaller: a conversation, a project or a decision can be a turning point. Look for any event that spawned a change of course.

Strong emotion indicates that our situation is affecting us deeply or touching on something important to us (we don't get upset or overjoyed about something we don't care about). While many people discount their feelings, to a coach *emotions contain information* about what is going on inside.

Recently I ran into a former trainee in a parking lot and stopped to chat. She was visibly upset, but when I asked her how she was doing, the response was, "Fine. Everything is wonderful." When I asked about what she'd been up to that day, she mentioned an important meeting she'd just come from with a supervisor. Tears began rolling down her cheeks. So I asked how the meeting went.

"Great, really good," she choked out, struggling to control herself. "Things are going well and we really made a lot of progress."

Her words and her emotions were saying two entirely different things. The more she talked the more curious I became. Finally, I gently (but directly) inquired, "What's making you cry?" That finally opened the door to an authentic conversation.

It's not always easy to talk about our feelings. Like many clients, Chad is experiencing strong emotions—he is frustrated, his wife is in tears—without stopping to reflect on what they really mean. An interesting coaching question here might be, "Say more about how your wife feels about your movie collection," or, "You said you were really looking forward to having some extra money to spend after the move. What was your wife looking forward to?"

Red flags are when the client's statement doesn't make sense, doesn't seem to align with universal principles or simply strikes you wrong. When Chad's wife says, "My whole house is wrapped up in your movie collection," a red flag goes up—that's a very interesting statement. Something here is out of joint—what exactly is it? I want to know, so I'll ask the client to explain. The priority of house versus movie collection also gets my attention. I might ask Chad to talk about the relative importance of those two things. The last line of the story, when Chad says, "I wish I knew what was really bugging her," is a red flag for me as well: didn't she just tell him what was bugging her? What's going on there?

Here's an important principle about intuition:

Intuition indicators don't tell you there is a problem; they show you where to ask.

It would be easy in Chad's situation to diagnose the problem and say he is wasting his money and damaging his marriage with his video collection. But, who knows—maybe he is a screenwriter and this is much more than a hobby for him. You'll often be tempted as a coach to pass judgment on an intuition indicator. Instead, ask questions, gather more information and give the client a chance to explain what is going on.

Patterns are cause and effect relationships or repeating events in the client's life. You reap what you sow—and if you keep right on sowing, you'll keep right on reaping! Chad identifies a pattern when he mentions that every so often his wife's longing for a house comes out. That gets my attention—something significant must be going on to make this come up more than once. I might ask, "Tell me about some of the times this has surfaced in the past," or "You mentioned that this has happened several times. What makes a house important to your wife?"

Intuition indicators don't tell you there is a problem; they show you where to ask.

Patterns can also show up over multiple coaching appointments. I once had a client who ranked herself very high in relational skills, but every time we met she told me another story of a broken relationship in her life. That intrigued me. Her stories did not coincide at all with her self-concept. What was going on there? Why were her relationships breaking down?

If there is a pattern, there is a reason behind it. People have a good reason for what they do. Discover the reason and usually you've also found the key to changing the pattern.

Practice Time

As we've discussed Chad's story, I've tried to give you a window into the mind of a coach. Each time an intuition indicator comes up, the coach is intrigued and wants to know more. The coach uses intuition to pick up on what is most significant and then asks about it. By asking at the point of significance (instead of diagnosing), the coach keeps the client in charge and pushes the client's thinking to a deeper level. Now it's your turn.

Exercise 12.2: Intuition Indicators

In the following story, look for examples of intuition indicators. Underline each indicator and then note in the right-hand margin what kind of indicator it is. While you are reading, try to turn off the conversation in your head and tune into what makes you curious (the indicator itself).

> **Intuition Indicators**
>
> 1. *The Person's Own Discernment*
> 2. *Turning Points*
> 3. *Strong Emotion*
> 4. *Red Flags*
> 5. *Patterns*

"...College for me was a chance to finally get away from home and be out on my own. But it was hard being in such a big place. I was from a little farm town in Iowa where everybody knew everybody, and at school there were 8000 students. I was a basketball star and been in all the plays back in high school, but there I was a nobody. No one noticed if I got a 'C' instead of an 'A'—so why not go out and play Frisbee instead of studying? I think that was part of what got me so messed up—I felt very alone and irrelevant.

In the fall of my sophomore year I met Jennifer. She was the first person I really got close to. She liked me for who I was and stuck with me. By the second semester, we were going out several times a week and I was in love with her. The first time she talked about getting married, I was petrified. I wanted to be with her, but I'd seen my mom and dad live like they were at war for years and I didn't want any part of that.

Jennifer's faith bothered me sometimes, too. She was really into God and church, but I was sort of cynical. I was in this stage where I thought religion should be kept in moderation—I guess I wanted God on my own terms and not on His. She kept talking to me about getting serious with God. I knew that at some point I was going to have to face facts, but I kept putting it off.

Over the summer she went on a short-term mission trip and wrote to me that she'd really had an experience with God. I came back in the fall wanting to pick things up where we'd left off, but she told me she'd realized she could never spend her life with someone as lukewarm as me.

(3) *I was devastated. I spent the next few days in a fog—I remember showing up for calculus one morning and no one was there. I finally realized that I was a day late for class. That night I went for a walk out on the athletic field all by myself, and said, "God, my life isn't working. I can't keep playing this game with you—I'm miserable. If you're real, make yourself real to me, because I don't know who you are."*

Nothing magical happened at that moment, but I started reading my Bible and praying seriously again. And then these amazing coincidences started to take place..."

Once you've identified the indicators, turn the page to check your responses.

"...College for me was a chance to finally get away from home and be out on my own. But it was hard being in such a big place. I was from a little farm town in Iowa where everybody knew everybody, and at school there were 8000 students. I was a basketball star and been in all the plays back in high school, but there I was a nobody. No one noticed if I got a 'C' instead of an 'A'—so why not go out and play Frisbee instead of studying? I think that was part of what got me so messed up—I felt very alone and irrelevant.

In the fall of my sophomore year I met Jennifer. She was the first person I really got close to. She liked me for who I was and stuck with me. By the second semester, we were going out several times a week and I was in love with her. The first time she talked about getting married, I was petrified. I wanted to be with her, but I'd seen my mom and dad live like they were at war for years and I didn't want any part of that.

Jennifer's faith bothered me sometimes, too. She was really into God and church, but I was sort of cynical. I was in this stage where I thought religion should be kept in moderation—I guess I wanted God on my own terms and not on His. She kept talking to me about getting serious with God. I knew that at some point I was going to have to face facts, but I kept putting it off.

Over the summer she went on a short-term mission trip and wrote to me that she'd really had an experience with God. I came back in the fall wanting to pick things up where we'd left off, but she told me she'd realized she could never spend her life with someone as lukewarm as me.

I was devastated. I spent the next few days in a fog—I remember showing up for calculus one morning and no one was there. I finally

Strong emotion

Person's own discernment

Strong emotion

Turning point

Strong emotion

Red flag

Red flag

Person's own discernment

Pattern

Turning point

Strong emotion

realized that I was a day late for class. That night I went for a walk out on the athletic field all by myself, and said, "God, my life isn't working. I can't keep playing this game with you—I'm miserable. If you're real, make yourself real to me, because I don't know who you are."	Person's own discernment Strong Emotion
Nothing magical happened at that moment, but I started reading my Bible and praying seriously again. And then these amazing coincidences started to take place..."	Turning Point

By the way, don't get too hung up on getting the name of the indicator exactly right—some of these examples could fall under multiple categories. It's more important that you learn to listen to what your intuition is saying. And be aware that this story is written to have a lot of indicators—they usually won't be packed so closely together in real life.

Exercise 12.3: Real-World Intuition Practice

Ask a friend to tell you their life story: childhood, career, relationships, spiritual journey, etc. While you are listening, note the major intuition indicators that you hear. After you are done listening, pick several indicators that stood out to you, share the indicator itself ("You mentioned that your parents divorced when you were nine..."), and ask your friend to comment on its significance.

Remember: it's not the coach's job to interpret the indicator. Simply share what made you curious and ask your friend to explain what that statement means.

Chapter 13

Asking Powerful Questions

> *"The purpose in a man's mind is like deep waters, but a man of understanding will draw it out."*
>
> Proverbs 20:5

The other day my son came home with a new girlfriend, Beth. They'd gone out several times and he wanted her to meet his parents. Since it was the beginning of the school year, I asked her, "What's going on in your life right now? Are you going back to school, or what?"

She rolled her eyes. "I don't know. I can't decide whether to go back to school or keep my job or what," she replied.

"'Well,' I asked, 'Tell me a little about what you enjoy doing.'"

Beth shared a number of things she enjoyed—working with her youth group, music, playing piano. While she liked her church, it was a small, declining ethnic congregation, and she felt stuck in a place with no future.

Beth must have mentioned the word "piano" about ten times in ten minutes of conversation, so I said, "It sounds like you really enjoy piano. Tell me more about that."

Her eyes lit up as she began talking about how much she loved playing and going to concerts. Clearly this was something she was really passionate about.

"Would there be an opportunity for you to pursue piano seriously—to really go after it?"

"Well, I really ought to go to school and get a career, and I need to keep my part-time job," she temporized.

I knew nothing about her background or her abilities, so I asked, "What about your piano teacher? What does she think of your potential?"

"She gave me a great opportunity," Beth responded, eyes sparkling. "She's willing to recommend me to the top conservatory teacher in the whole city, if I'd commit to working on it—I'd have to practice five or six hours a day. I'd love to pursue that, but I couldn't do it and keep my job."

"So what would it cost to pursue that?"

"Maybe $75.00 a week for the lessons."

"What would your folks think?"

"Well, if I really focused I think they'd support me..."

About that time my son came back in the room, and he and Beth took off for the evening. A week later I found out that she had made some big decisions. She kept her job at the clothing store, but she devoted the rest of her life to piano. Now, when they have a date, she'll stop over at our house and practice for two hours before they go out! She approached the conservatory teacher, was accepted, and that became the stepping-stone for her to get into a great university piano program. She is living her dream. Her long-term goal is to teach piano—she loves to see other kids learn and have the opportunity to do what she enjoys so much."

This was a life-changing conversation for Beth, and one of the most remarkable things was that it took place at all. How many teenagers would be willing to talk about their deepest hopes and aspirations with a boyfriend's parents? Questions made this conversation happen. Beth met someone who was genuinely interested in her, who took her ideas and her dreams seriously, who believed in her, who wanted to know more—and she naturally opened up. That one conversation could change the course of her whole life.

The Power of Questions

Questions are the second element of the coaching conversation:

the bread and butter tools of a coach (See diagram). They are the main tools a coach uses to focus a conversation, foster exploration, push the client to dig deeper and reach higher, and ensure commitment. Much of what a coach says in a coaching conversation is in the form of questions.

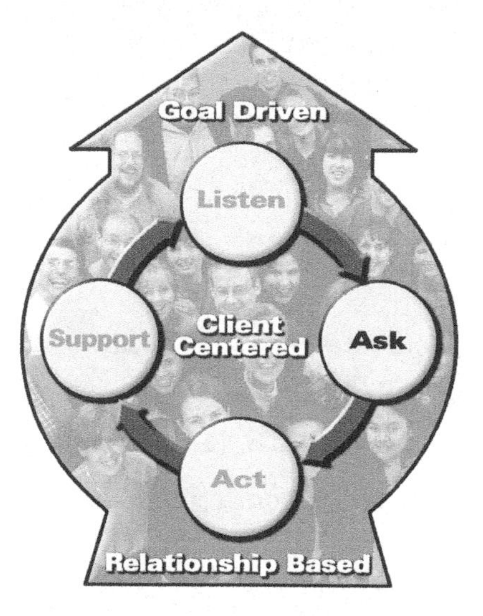

Let's debrief on the conversation with Beth to see what the coach did. There were several places where powerful questions led to breakthroughs. Beth didn't know what she wanted to do next in life, so the coach asked her to talk about what she enjoyed. He believed that if she could discover her passion, she'd be motivated to pursue it. As the coach listened intuitively to Beth, he noticed an intuition indicator: a pattern. The word "piano" came up frequently. So he made an observation ("It sounds like you really enjoy piano"), which summarized what he heard, and then asked her a probing question about the indicator: "Tell me more about that."

Notice that there's nothing awe-inspiring about the question itself–it's very simple. What makes this question powerful is that it communicates belief in what Beth is passionate about. His next question challenged Beth to take her own dreams seriously: "Would there be an opportunity for you to pursue piano?" So often in life all we hear are negative challenges–"Why did you do *that?*" or "You need to improve your performance to get a raise." Even in challenging Beth, the coach communicated belief: "What if you would dare to live your dreams?"

In response, Beth voiced the standard, dream-killing obstacles she saw: I need a career, I need to keep my job and I need money. The conversation could have stopped right there. Up to this point, that's where Beth had stopped in her own thinking. But the coach didn't give up so easily. As he continued to ask about her potential and the possibilities, Beth began to think new thoughts and see a

Jesus' Powerful Questions

"After three days they found him in the temple, sitting among the teachers, listening to them and asking them questions..." (*The boy Jesus in the temple, Luke 2:46)*

- ***"But who do you say that I am?"***
  Peter's great confession, Luke 9:20
- ***"What do you seek?"***
  To the disciples of John who followed him, John 1:38
- ***"What do you want me to do for you?"***
  To the blind man beside the road, Luke 18:41
- ***"Woman, where are they? Has no one condemned you?"***
  To the woman caught in adultery, John 8:10
- ***"What's this you're discussing so intently as you walk along?"***
  Jesus on the road to Emmaus, Luke 24:17; MSG
- ***"What is written in the law? How do you read?"***
  Jesus replies to a lawyer who puts him to the test, Luke 10:26
- ***"Show me a coin. Whose likeness and inscription has it?"***
  Render to Caesar what is Caesar's, Luke 20:24
- ***"Which is easier to say, 'Your sins are forgiven you,' or to say, 'Rise and walk?'"***
  At the healing of the paralytic, Luke 5:23
- ***"Which of these three, do you think, proved neighbor to the man...?"***
  The Good Samaritan, Luke 10:36
- ***"I ask you, is it lawful on the sabbath to do good or to do harm, to save life or to destroy it?"***
  Healing on the Sabbath, Luke 6:9

way to make her dream a reality.

The beauty of this type of approach is that the direction and the motivation came from Beth, not the coach. She went out and made her dream happen because she cared enough about it to actually do it. If the coach had given her advice and suggested the career path he thought was best for her, even if he was on the right track ("I really think you ought to purse this piano thing"), probably nothing would have changed. But by asking questions, the coach activated Beth's own energies and motivation to reach the end that she wanted.

Exercise 13.1: Types of Questions

There's an art to asking questions that make people think. Read through the following dialogue and see if you can put your finger on what's not working in the kind of questions that are being utilized:

> *"So, John, are you doing well today?"*
> *"Yeah, pretty good."*
> *"Did you do your action steps this week?"*
> *"Uh, yes, most of them."*
> *"Was there one that was harder than the others?"*
> *"Well, I had a tougher time with the journaling."*
> *"So that was the hardest. Were you able to journal two days a week?"*
> *"I probably did it once or twice."*
> *"Was there something in particular that made that a hard step to take?"*
> *"I suppose—it was just hard to get to it. I wanted to do it but it just didn't seem to happen."*
> *"So—do you want to try that step again this week?"*
> *"I guess so."*

Not much of a flow to this conversation, is there? The coach is directing the agenda in the conversation by the way he asks questions. Feeling out of control, the client is giving short answers that feel almost sullen or resistant. Because of this, the coach has to work hard to come up with question after question. He's actually talking more than the client—many of the questions are longer than the answers. What's making this conversation so strained?

The problem is simple: every question being asked is a *closed question*. Closed questions are ones that can be answered with a "yes" or "no". They don't ask for in-depth analysis—you only have two predetermined options for answers you can give. In this situation it's even worse. Every one of the questions in the example practically begs for a "yes" answer. Unfortunately, the client can't or doesn't always want to answer "yes," and to answer "no" would make him look bad ("Did you do your action steps this week?" "No"). So the client evades the questions and becomes increasingly resistant to the process. A string of closed questions tends to shut down a coaching conversation.

Open Questions

The opposite of a closed question is an open question. Open questions can be defined in two different ways:

1. They are questions that can't be answered with a "yes" or "no".
2. Open questions allow clients to answer in whatever way they want.

Open questions keep the client in charge. There is no right or wrong answer, so they don't put people on the defensive. Since

Exercise 13.2: See the Difference

The difference between open and closed questions in a conversation can be very striking. In ten minutes you can observe it for yourself. Ask a friend to share a challenge or problem with you and ask only closed questions for five minutes. Then stop (if the conversation hasn't already ground to a halt!) and try it again with open questions.

Bonus

Men, take your spouse out for a date, and just listen and ask open questions. She doesn't want you to solve her problem—she just wants to be listened to! This is good for at least the same impact as getting her flowers.

they can be answered in many different ways, they let the client's discernment lead you to what's important. Open questions also make coaching a lot less taxing! If you find yourself working hard to come up with enough things to ask, it's likely that your questions are closed.

Converting closed questions to open ones is easy. Let's rework the story about John to see how the process works. I've crossed out some words and added new ones (in bold face) to make these closed questions open:

> *"So, John, **how** are you doing ~~well~~ today?"*
>
> *"Pretty good. I had a fun week at work and our church league softball team got second in the tournament."*
>
> *"**What** did you do **on** your action steps this week?"*
>
> *"Well, I managed to exercise three times a week, so that went pretty well. I think I'm getting in a rhythm there. I tried to call my uncle three times, but I never caught him and he hasn't returned my call yet. I'll have to try again next week if he doesn't get back to me. I only did the journaling once or twice instead of the four times I was shooting for."*
>
> *"~~Was there one that~~ **Which one was** harder than the others?"*

See the difference? Not only is there a flow to the conversation, but two open questions got more of a response out of the client than six closed questions—meaning the coach doesn't have to work nearly as hard. Almost any closed question can be made open by adding "how," "what," "which," or "who" at the beginning.

Exercise 13.3: Converting Closed Questions

Change a few words in each of the following closed questions to make them open. Sample answers are at the end of the chapter:

Closed	Open
"Did the call to your uncle go well?	"How did the call to your uncle go?"
"Is there something you could do about that?"	

"Isn't there a step you could take?" ______________________________

"Did that make you feel hurt?" ______________________________

"Do you want to take action on this option?" ______________________________

"Is there a timeline for that project?" ______________________________

"Could you talk to someone about that?" ______________________________

"Will that take long?" ______________________________

Getting Outside the Box

I once did a short coaching session where the client's goal was to decide which of two different degree programs (at that time he was pursuing a joint degree) would best prepare him for his career. I began asking him some basic open questions:

- What kind of job do you want?
- What did you love about your prior jobs in that field?
- What are you best at?
- What would each of these programs enable you to do?

Once I got some background information, I was going to begin posing some questions to help him evaluate his options.

However, five minutes into the session he had an epiphany: he was studying for a pastoral career, but he enjoyed his current managerial job (which he'd taken solely to pay for his schooling) much more than his previous pastoral positions. After ten minutes, he was thinking about scrapping one degree program and changing the other in order to pursue a completely different career.

In this situation, the client supplied a simple mandate: help me choose between two options. If I had asked problem-solving questions based on the kinds of answers I expected, we would have missed a wonderful breakthrough. Instead, two of my favorite asking techniques opened the door for us to go in an unanticipated direction.

The first is to take plenty of time (even in a short session) to *gather more information* before solving the problem. Most of us jump into problem-solving mode far too quickly. The more information you have out on the table, the more you have to work with when you attack the problem.

People often come to a coach when they're stuck. They've looked at the situation to a certain depth, but with that level of information they can't come up with a workable solution. They're thinking inside a box: the set of information they already have considered. My job as a coach is to help them out of the box where their creativity can solve the problem. One of the simplest, most effective ways to do that is to ask people to talk through the situation out loud. They'll be going along, rehearsing all the information that's inside their box, and eureka! A new idea pops into their heads.

That's what happened with this client. The open questions I posed for background sparked some new, creative thinking. Instead of trying to choose between two existing options, the answer he found was outside the box: a new career. So, in summary, here's the technique: when a client is stuck and can't solve a problem, start by simply asking them to talk through it. Here are some examples of

Exercise 13.3: Gathering More Information

To use your intuition, you have to let the client talk. Most of us don't get enough information out on the table before we go into problem solving mode—and so we often lose the opportunity for our intuition to take us to the place of transformation. Here's a way to practice gathering more information.

This week, anytime someone comes to you looking for help or counsel, discipline yourself to simple probing questions and gather information *for at least five minutes* before you do any problem solving. You may need to give yourself a reminder (like putting a sign on your desk) to prompt yourself to do the exercise.

the kind of questions you might ask:

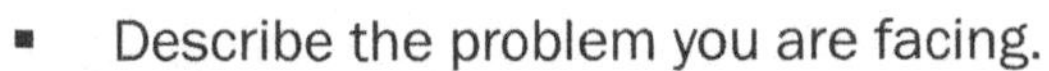

- Describe the problem you are facing.
- Give me the history of how you got to this point.
- What are the parameters you have to work within?
- What options have you considered?
- What have you tried so far and what were the results?
- What kind of outcome are you shooting for?

Getting more information on the table will make it much easier for you and your client to think outside the box.

Asking Bigger Questions

The second technique I used in this career-coaching situation was what I call *asking bigger questions*. An open question is one the client can answer in a variety of ways. The bigger the question, the more ways it can be answered. In the example given, I could have asked, "Which career fits you best: pastoring or teaching?" A good question, but a small one: there are only two possible answers. Instead, I inquired, "What kind of job do you want?" That's a much bigger question—you can answer in an infinite number of ways. The smaller question would have actually kept the client from considering a new career, while the bigger one invited it.

Let me share a little secret with you—I still catch myself solving the client's problems in my head sometimes. Probably all coaches do. But when I realize I'm doing it, I use the technique of asking a bigger question to keep myself from giving advice.

Here's an example. Let's say the client is thinking about buying a second home and has a question about how rentals would be treated from a tax standpoint. While you're listening, it occurs to you that the client's realtor might have the answer. A small question would be, "Could you talk to your realtor about that?" But before you get the words out of your mouth, you catch yourself: you're solving the problem for the client.

So how do you make that question bigger? Start by thinking backward: what problem were you trying to solve with that small question? Answer: the client needs some tax information. Are there other ways the client could get that info? Sure—from a CPA, a friend with rental properties, or maybe from a rental agency. Now you

have four possible answers. The bigger question is one that could be answered by any of these options. So, instead of asking if the client could talk to a certain person, ask, "Who could you talk to that would know the answer to your question?" Now the client is in charge of thinking up the solutions again.

Exercise 13.4: Bonus

Here's a challenge: that last question could be even bigger—it assumes the information will come in a certain way. Can you identify the assumption and craft an even bigger question? (Sample answers are at the end of the chapter.)

Exercise 13.5: Bigger Questions

Your chance of remembering this concept will greatly increase if you spend a few minutes practicing it. Below are four more small questions. See if you can come up with a bigger question for each (Answers at the end of the chapter):

1. The client's administrative assistant is upset with him.
   Small question: *"Would sending her some flowers help?"*
   Big question: HOW COULD YOU HELP/RESPOND?
   WHAT DO YOU THINK SHE NEEDS FROM YOU?
2. The client needs to talk through a conflict with a co-worker.
   Small question: *"Do you need some time to cool off before you talk to him about it?"*
   Big question: WHAT DO YOU NEED RIGHT NOW?
3. Your daughter wants to learn to play guitar, but doesn't have one.
   Small question: *"Could you borrow one for a while?"*
   Big question: WHAT COULD YOU DO ABOUT THAT?
4. Your client wants to spend more time with family, but it's hard to find the time.
   Small question: *"How about if we reexamine your priorities?"*
   Big question: WHAT DO YOU REALLY WANT?
   YOU MENTION TIME CONSTRAINTS - TELL ME MORE. ~~WHAT~~

Solution-Oriented Questions

When you first start coaching, it's hard to sit back and allow the client time to explore. One sign that you're pushing too hard is when you begin to ask *Solution-Oriented Questions* (SOCs). Here are a few examples:

1. Could you find that information on the Internet?
2. How about if you took a class in that?
3. Would it work if you gave both options and let her choose?

SOCs are solutions developed by the coach and offered in the form of a question. We know we aren't supposed to tell, so we cleverly pose our advice with a question mark on the end. Again, the way to change this habit is to work backwards: identify the problem that you originally solved in your head and ask the client to solve it instead of giving the answer. Here are three questions that could replace the SOCs above:

> **How to Recognize a Solution-Oriented Question**
>
> - It is a closed question.
> - The coach is proposing a solution in the form of a question.
> - It asks for agreement with a proposition—would you, could you, shouldn't you, how about if you.
> - You can subtract a few words from the front and get a statement.

1. ***Where*** could you find that information?
2. ***How*** could you educate yourself in that area?
3. ***What*** kind of process would lead to a decision that you both feel good about?

These questions are much bigger: they allow clients to find their own answers instead of being spoon-fed. Solutions developed by your clients have higher buy-in, increasing the likelihood that they'll be implemented. They'll also be more likely to work, since your clients' own ideas are based on greater information about the situation and about their own capabilities.

Exercise 13.6: Solution-Oriented Questions

First, underline the advice being given in each SOC. Then, rewrite the question so it is bigger and more open:

S.O.C.	Open Question
1. *"Have you thought about sending her a card or some flowers to get back on her good side?"*	1. *"What could you do to get back on her good side?"*
2. *"Would it work to take a day off and finish that project up?"*	2. WHAT WOULD HELP IN FINISHING THE PROJECT?
3. *"Couldn't you sell the car and be done with it?"*	3. WHAT ELSE COULD YOU DO?
4. *"If you'd take a continuing ed class, would that get you started?"*	4. ~~WHAT CAN~~ HOW COULD YOU GET STARTED?

Master Class: Crafting Great Probing Questions

A coaching conversation usually moves through a progression from goal to exploration to options, evaluation and then action—the coaching funnel (See diagram). *Probing questions* are employed to open up the funnel when the client is exploring an issue. These queries flow naturally out of intuitive listening and intuition indicators. Usually big, open questions, they broaden the discussion to increase the amount of information and range of potential solutions the client has to work with. Probing questions are used to explore and gather information, not to set

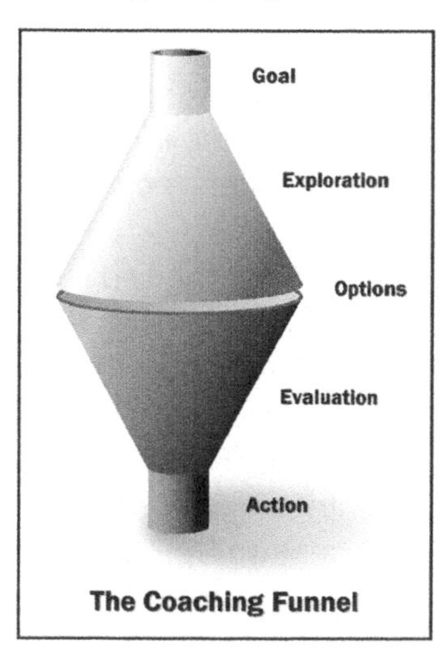

The Coaching Funnel

goals, solve problems or decide what actions to take (more on those questions in the next chapter). When you are probing, you aren't problem solving. The objective is to help the client think more deeply and creatively about the issue at hand

The basic strategy for deploying probing questions is to pick out the most important thing the client said—the thing that most made you curious—and offer a question that asks the client to expand on that point. Following your intuition helps clients zero in on what is most important in their own thoughts and words. The probing question takes them deeper than they have gone before.

Let's look at what makes a great probing question. First, read the following statement from a client who is trying to balance work and family. Underline the intuition indicators that seem most interesting or significant to you:

> *"I feel like I'm doing my new job well and meeting expectations—actually, exceeding expectations. Just last week my boss complimented my on my work and gave me a little bonus. I really love being recognized for who I am and how much I can produce, instead of just plugging along with no one noticing.*
>
> *"The only downside is the commute. It's half an hour longer than what I had before, and the workday here is a little longer, too, so I'm out about an hour a day. Every so often, I feel robbed of my personal time and I get angry about it. Some nights I come home and the kids are waiting to hang out with me, then Brenda wants attention, and by the time I'm done all I want to do is collapse into bed and go to sleep."*

What are the two most important words or phrases (intuition indicators) here? I choose one positive and one negative statement. The most significant positive indicator (client's own discernment) is this man's joy in being recognized for who he is and what he can produce. The words used to describe the experience (exceeding expectations, bonus, love, who I am) are powerful ones and represent an experience that connected with this person at a deep level. The strongest word is "love".

The most significant negative indicator is "I feel robbed". It's the strongest emotion expressed in what this individual shared. He gets angry about it. Emotions contain valuable information about what is going on inside a person and are a good way to identify what is important.

> **Airtime**
>
> *In a coaching conversation, the client should get around 80% of the airtime and the coach 20%.*

Notice that I gave a rationale for why these two statements are important, but I haven't attempted to explain what these indicators mean. That's a result of turning off the conversation in my head. You are listening intuitively and registering the indicators you hear, but you aren't trying to figure out what they mean. That's the client's job. Intuition indicators spawn questions, not diagnosis.

In this scenario, a coach might ask one of these probing questions:

- *"Tell me more about what you love about being recognized."*
- *"You mentioned you felt 'robbed' of your personal time. Describe what you feel would be a healthy amount of personal time.*

- *"You said feeling 'robbed' of your personal time was something that made you angry. Say more about what personal time means to you."*
- *"It sounds like you love everything about your new job except for how it affects your time. Could you expand on that?"*

This technique isn't hard to do—you just have to listen intently so you don't miss it when the client says something important. One of the easiest ways to probe is the *observation and question* technique. The observation is when you repeat what the client just said. For instance, "You mentioned that you love being recognized for who you are," is an observation. Simply restate the comment from the client that caught your attention. Then add a simple probing question about the observation, such as, "Say more about that," or "What does that mean to you?" The final three examples in the bullet list on page 189 illustrate this method. You can have an entire conversation using only this technique!

Characteristics of Great Probing Questions

The questions listed on this list proceed directly out of what the client shares, producing a conversational flow that naturally moves the client forward to new clarity and insight. Probing questions like these help clients explore, think new thoughts or escape from a box. In order to foster free exploration, the client must not feel threatened, misunderstood or forced in a certain direction. If he does, he'll start defending himself instead of reflecting and that will ruin the whole process.

When you're probing, your objective is to extend the client's own thinking process, not to insert your own thoughts or ideas into the picture. Ask short, open questions that generate long answers. Aim to get more information out on the table, not to develop solutions. That happens later. You want to create an opportunity for the client

Exercise 13.7: The Observation and Question Technique

Here are two scenarios to let you practice probing. Create an observation and question based on this statement (Sample answers are at the end of the chapter):

Scenario I

The client says, "I wish I could work in a place where I got something out of my job. This drudgery is just killing me."

Scenario II

"It's been a tough week. I guess I'll just have to push through the disappointment again."

Practice

Find a friend to talk with for 10 minutes or so. Ask this person to share a challenge he or she faces and have a whole conversation using just the observation-and-question technique. You'll both be surprised at what comes out of it!

to "boldly go where he's never gone before."

Your questions must be carefully constructed to create a climate for free exploration. Below are three characteristics of great probing questions:

- They use the client's own words
- They are succinct
- They are neutral

Reread the scenario (it's given again below) and we'll look at each principle in turn.

> *"I feel like I'm doing my new job well and meeting expectations—actually, exceeding expectations. Just last week my boss complimented my on my work and gave me a little bonus. I really love being recognized for who I am and how much I can produce, instead of just plugging along with no one noticing.*
>
> *"The only downside is the commute. It's half an hour longer than what I had before, and the workday here is a little longer, too, so I'm out about an hour a day. Every so often, I feel robbed of my personal time and I get angry about it. Some nights I come home and the kids are waiting to hang out with me, then Brenda wants attention, and by the time I'm done all I want to do is collapse into bed and go to sleep."*

1. Great Probing Questions Use the Client's Own Words.

Consider these three questions:

- *"You mentioned you felt 'robbed' of your personal time. Describe what you feel would be a healthy amount of personal time."*
- *"You said that your job was making it tough to get enough time alone. How much time would be enough?"*
- *"You said you got angry and felt robbed when your family took over your personal time. How much time do you need alone?"*

Although these three questions touch on the same issue, one might get a well-reasoned reply and another a defensive reaction. The difference is that the second and third questions employ words the client didn't use. While the second statement is a fairly decent paraphrase of what the client said, it loses the impact of the strong word "robbed". By paraphrasing you also take the risk that there might be some connotation of the word "tough" that the client would object to. This person chose the word "robbed" because it accurately described how he felt. Why not stick with it?

The problem with the third question is that the coach's wording makes assumptions about the client's situation. The client didn't say he was angry *at* his family, or that it was his family that was taking his personal time—he just said he felt robbed and got angry. Changing the words could cause the client to stop exploring in order to defend what he's done. "I didn't say my family made me angry! I just said I wish I had more time to myself!"

In this example the assumptions are pretty obvious and it may seem easy to avoid this kind of faux pas. But the truth is that we interpret everything we hear. No statement is perfectly clear, or conveys the exact meaning that the speaker intended to the listener. Because words are by nature imprecise, it's a serious challenge to accurately translate another person's statements into different language.

Several years ago, some training materials I'd written were translated into a foreign language and then back into English again. Every place where I'd used the phrase "powerful questions" came back as "strong questions". It pulled me up short whenever I saw it. When we talk about "powerful words" we mean ones that have a deep impact on the hearers. When we talk about using "strong words," we mean getting in someone's face. The connotations weren't quite the same.

Paraphrasing someone's language is extra work for you as the coach. So make it easy on yourself: just listen intently and repeat the exact trigger word or phrase that made you curious in your question. The observation and question technique works perfectly for this.

2. Great Probing Questions Are Succinct.

New coaches often get caught up in striving to ask the ultimate question, believing that a wonderfully nuanced query is the key to having a breakthrough. By the time they're finished conveying every shade of meaning, the client may have no idea what the actual question is. Here's a sample:

> *"You were talking about how much you love your job and the recognition you get out of it, and I was just sort of wondering, since that was something that you mentioned, if there were maybe some other ways that they had recognized you or rewarded you for your performance in the past, and if those things had the same kind of impact on you that the boss's compliment did—or if maybe there was something unique about the boss complementing you that really stands out and you respond particularly well to. What do you think?"*

If I were the client, I'd be going, "Huh?" Basically, what the coach wants to know is:

> *"Have other kinds of recognition had a similar impact on you?"*

If your questions sound like the bloated version above, you're trying *way* too hard to be brilliant. Athletes talk about "letting the game come to you" instead of forcing a shot or overplaying your position to make something happen. When you overplay your position, the team's overall strategy breaks down. Being out of place affects everyone else's assignments.

Asking bloated questions is like

Exercise 13.8: Succinct Questions

Want to evaluate whether your questions are succinct? Here's how. Set up a short coaching conversation with a friend, peer or family member. Your job is to ask probing questions. Give yourself *one short sentence only* for each question.

Bonus

Tell the person you are coaching what you're trying to accomplish and ask them to make you restate whenever your question is too long.

overplaying your position. The complexity of the question comes from trying to take the client to a specific solution you have in your head, instead of letting him lead. Let go and let the conversation come to you; don't try so hard to shape it. Instead of directing things, take the direction your client is already going and push it a little further. The client's assignment is to solve the problem, yours is to foster a creative environment where that can happen. If you play within this team concept, you'll be amazed at what you can accomplish together.

Here are several clear, simple queries that get at the same thing:

- *"What else gives you great satisfaction at work?"*
- *'What kind of recognition is most important to you?"*
- *"What motivates you most at work?"*

3. Great Probing Questions Are Neutral.

The previous two characteristics are basic skills that you can practice and become proficient at. This technique may require a change of heart! Take a look at these three questions. If you aren't sure at first what is wrong with them, think about how you would respond if they were asked of you:

- *"Why did you ever take that job in the first place?"*
- *"Tell me about how you've allowed your job to rob you of your personal time."*
- *"You mentioned that you loved being recognized. How has your need for recognition at work affected your family life?"*

The problem here is that these questions aren't neutral. For instance, the clear implication of the first question is, "You never should have taken that job in the first place!" The coach is not asking the client to think, or even asking for more information. The purpose of the question is to bring the client around to the coach's predetermined conclusion about the situation. That's not probing, it's telling.

The use of the word "why" is also problematic. "Why" questions touch on our motives for what we do. The trouble with asking "Why?" is that no matter how careful you are it always come out sounding like you believe the person's motives are impure. Because it's difficult to make "why" questions neutral, many coaches avoid them altogether.

Here's how to rephrase the first question to make it neutral: "Tell me a little about what led you to take that position."

The second question is (*"Tell me about how you've allowed your job to rob you of your personal time"*) is more subtle. Here again, the coach has made a judgment: the client has allowed something untoward to happen to him. The question says, "The way you are feeling is your own fault." On the one hand, it is true that the client chose this position. On the other hand, taking this job may have been a decision God Himself orchestrated, for any number of reasons. The point is, the coach has taken it upon himself to decide what's right or wrong. Instead, let the client make that call by asking a neutral question: "What led up to your being in this place where you're feeling robbed of your personal time?"

Great Probing Questions

Questions that let your clients lead by allowing them to answer any way they choose.

1) "Tell me a little more about that."
2) "Give me some background–what led up to this situation?"
3) "When you think about that [issue, relationship, event], what kind of feelings do you have?"
4) "You mentioned that ________. Say more about that."
5) "What did you mean when you said ________?"
6) "What was most significant to you in this experience?"
7) "What would be most important for us to focus on?"
8) "How did that happen?"

On the surface, the third example (*"You mentioned that you loved being recognized. How has your need for recognition at work affected your family life?"*) appears to be an honest, neutral query. But on closer examination, it too is skewed: the phrase "need for recognition" gives it away. The client never talked about needing recognition. Probably what's happened is that the coach has decided that neediness has compromised the client's home life. This is not a neutral request for information; it's a fishing expedition trolling for evidence to support the coach's theory about what the problem is. A great probing question doesn't have any judgment or pre-existing conclusion in it.

The Heart/Mouth Connection

In all these examples, the question wasn't neutral because the coach stopped withholding judgment. When the coach quit being neutral inside, what he said ceased to be neutral, too. The reason neutrality is so challenging is that "out of the abundance of the heart the mouth speaks" (Luke 6:45). According to Jesus, whatever is in your heart is going to come out of your mouth, no matter how carefully you try to control it. You can know all the techniques and offer the most skillfully crafted questions, but if you've decided internally that the client doesn't have a clue, you won't be able to hide it.

The terrible (in the sense that God's holiness is terrible) implication of this verse for a coach is that *the only way to coach with excellence is to never judge your client in your heart*. Not only can you not speak your judgments, you can't even *think* them. Coaching calls you to a whole new plane in how you look at people.

This is the kind of thing Jesus was talking about in Matthew, chapter five: that to look on a woman with lust in your heart is the same as going to bed with her; or to call someone a fool (the Aramaic word would probably translate well as "airhead") carries the same penalty as murder. Sin starts in your heart, your thoughts and your intentions. When it is full-grown it comes out in words and actions, but the seed germinated and took root within. Becoming a great coach requires a fundamental change on the inside. You'll need to be transformed into a person who can listen to another's story and not think, "Boy, I never would have done that," or "What was she thinking?" or even "I see your problem." Coaches withhold judgment (consistently believe in the other person) so that every question they voice is truly neutral.

The thing that has most helped me change in this area is being wrong so often. Just today I was conversing with a client who is launching a consulting business and starting a doctoral program simultaneously. When I first heard about this plan, all the alarm bells in my head went off. I've started several businesses and I know the kind of maximum effort it takes to succeed. Having two major, unrelated projects seemed like a stressful distraction—why not put off the degree until the business was up and running? So I asked him about it. However, he assured me that the time to do the degree was now. I wasn't sure it would work, but "when in doubt, listen to the client." So I chose to believe that he knew what he was doing and wait and see what happened.

I turned out to be wrong again. After several conversations with his thesis advisor, the client chose to do a major industry survey for his doctoral project. Doing the survey has energized him, given him new confidence as a consultant, opened doors to new business and added pizzazz to his presentations. I can easily see how this project could be the key to his future success as a consultant. It would have been a sad mistake if I had talked him out of what his heart told him was the right decision.

Many times I've thought a client was overreaching, taking a wrong step, violating a principle or simply being shortsighted. There are times when I'm right, but my batting average is well below .500. It is much easier than it used to be for me to believe in my clients, because I discovered that my judgment isn't always so hot. Coach for a while and you'll discover that truth for yourself.

Chapter 13 Exercise Answers

13.3: Converting Closed Questions

Closed	Open
"Did the call to your uncle go well?	*"How did the call to your uncle go?"*
"Is there something you could do about that?"	*"What could you do about that?"*
"Isn't there a step you could take?"	*"What step could you take?"*
"Did that make you feel hurt?"	*"How did that make you feel?"*
"Do you want to take action on this option?"	*"What do you want to do about this?"*
"Is there a timeline for that project?"	*"When do you want to finish this?"*
"Could you talk to someone about that?"	*"Who could you talk to about that?"*
"Will that take long?"	*"How long will that take?"*

13.4: Bonus

The assumption is that the answer has to come from talking to someone. The information could be in a book, on the IRS web site, at a real estate seminar, etc. A bigger question is, *"What could you do to get the tax information you need?"*

13.5: Bigger Questions

1. There are many other ways to smooth over a conflict—apologize, write a note, make a change to eliminate the point of conflict altogether, etc. A bigger question might be, *"What could you do to make things better between the two of you?"*
2. Bigger question: *"What do you need to do to get yourself ready for a constructive conversation with him?"*
3. There are many ways to find an instrument: buy one, rent it,

borrow from a friend or hit the garage sales. A big question would be, *"What could you do to get an instrument to play?"*

4. It might be hard to find time because priorities are out of whack. The obstacle could also be a heightened load at work, a long commute made longer by road work, need to work two jobs to get out of debt, etc. A big question would be, *"What could you do that would give you the time with family that you want?"*

Exercise 13.6: Solution-Oriented Questions

S.O.C.	Open Question
1. *"Have you thought about sending her a card or some flowers to get back on her good side?"*	1. *"What could you do to get back on her good side?"*
2. *"Would it work to take a day off and finish that project up?"*	2. *"What would help you get that project finished up?"*
3. *"Couldn't you sell the car and be done with it?"*	3. *"What do you think the solution is with your car?"*
4. *"If you'd take a continuing ed class, would that get you started?"*	4. *"What's the best way for you to get moving toward this goal?"*

Exercise 13.7: The Observation and Question Technique

Scenario I:
"You said that you wanted to get something out of your job. Tell me some things you like and don't like about your current position." Or, "You said that the drudgery at your job is killing you. What in your job feels like drudgery?"

Scenario II:
"You mentioned that it's been a tough week. What made it tough?" Or, "You talked about pushing through your disappointment again. Say more about what's going on there."

Chapter 14

Master Class: Deconstructing Questions

> *"Whoever asks questions will never get lost."*
>
> Senegalese Proverb

Up to this point we've focused on how to employ open, probing questions. Next we'll examine three other important categories of questions and how to use them effectively:

- **Direct Questions** cut to the heart of the issue.
- **Revealing Questions** change perspective and help a person get out of a box.
- **Ownership Questions** push the client to take responsibility and be proactive.

Probing questions are broad and indirect. They allow the client to explore and take the conversation in many directions to open up the coaching funnel. By contrast, direct questions are focused, pointed and often closed. While probing questions open up options, direct questions narrow them by challenging, asking for decisions or nailing down actions. While open questions are commonly used on the top half of the funnel, direct and ownership questions are most often found toward the bottom. Revealing questions populate the center.

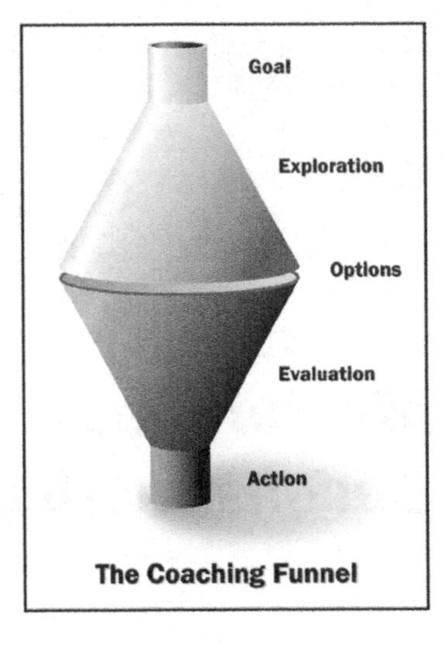

The Coaching Funnel

Direct Questions

Coaching is not only about being indirect. Coaches also challenge clients to live up to their values, ask for steps to be chosen and taken, and aren't afraid to be clear enough to nail a decision down. Direct questions are an important coaching tool. However, they are also the most easily misused type of question. A misplaced word or two can make the difference between a great coaching question and one that causes a defensive reaction. Let's focus in on the wording of several direct coaching questions to isolate the principles that separate a good direct question from a poor one.

Exercise 14.1: Constructing Direct Questions

Read through the following scenario and jot down two direct questions (questions that cut to the heart of the issue) you'd like to ask this person. Then (this is the fun part), jot down two "fleshly" direct questions you'd just love to blurt out—the kind that social conventions and self-control ensure would never see the light of

Use Direct Questions to:

- Ask for action or for a decision: *"What will you do?"*
- Challenge the client: *"How does that decision align with your values?"*
- Provide accountability: *"Did you exercise three times for 20 minutes this week?"*
- Focus the discussion: *"Do you want to focus on finding a job or making a budget?"*

day. (For example, "Have you lost your mind?!?") We can learn as much by looking at the "bad" questions as the good ones.

"Mark, what's the most interesting thing that happened in your life in the last week?"

"That's easy! You know how I've been praying that God would help me get out of debt so I can start my own business? Well you wouldn't believe what happened! I had just been asking for a miracle, and that very morning a friend of mine called me up out of the blue and told me about this international financial ministry he's gotten involved with. I think this is the answer I've been looking for!"

"Sounds interesting. How does it work?"

"Well, they invest in the international gold markets. They've made arrangements with the Bundesbank in Germany and central banks in other countries, so when a nation wants to buy or sell gold for its reserves it goes through them. It's one of those backroom things that the big players have tried to keep secret because there's so much money in it. Since they're dealing in precious metals, there's virtually no risk and the returns are fantastic! My friend said I could probably double or triple my money in three months."

"What's the name of this ministry?"

"It's called Higher Power Ministries—'helping Christians fulfill their destiny.' My friend said they call it Higher Power because God is behind it, and because your investments multiply exponentially—to a 'higher power.' I don't have much cash on hand, but my friend suggested that I could tap my retirement account. That was a great idea! You have to pay a penalty for withdrawing your money early, but I figure I can make that back in a month. If I invest all of it—I've got about $60,000—by the end of the year I'd be able to pay off our credit card debt, put the $60,000 back in our IRA and have the seed money I need to start the business. What an answer to prayer!

"I'd have jumped on this already except for my wife—she's been a total stick-in-the-mud about it. She keeps saying, 'Honey, it just doesn't feel right.' But when I ask for a rational explanation, she doesn't have any. Frankly, I think she's just operating out of fear. I only hope she'll come around before the opportunity goes away."

Now that you've finished the story, make sure you have two "good" and two "bad" questions jotted down before you go on—

you'll need them later.

The Good, the Bad and the Ugly

I hope that scenario was lurid enough to give you plenty of things to ask about! Let's compare some sample direct questions to see what separates the good, the bad and the ugly:

Direct Question	Alternative Version
1. "Don't you have any idea what Scripture says about 'wealth hastily gotten?'"	1. "What does Scripture say about this kind of investment?"
2. "How could you possibly fall for a scheme like that?"	2. "Since this is an important decision, what would you need to do to ensure that you make a well-informed decision?"
3. "Why don't you ever listen to your wife? It sounds like she's on to something."	3. "Let's say your wife is picking up on something important. What might it be?"

Now step back for a moment and imagine that someone was asking you these questions. How would your internal, gut-level responses to the questions in column I be different from the way you'd respond to the alternative versions in column II? Which column would be more likely to get reasoned responses and which would tend to elicit visceral reactions?

Most of us would react to the questions in column I. They back us into a corner, use pejorative language or express frustration at our apparent stupidity. The questions in column II express belief in us even while they challenge our thinking. Therefore, we're much more likely to think them through instead of reacting. These two groups of questions demonstrate what to avoid when constructing direct questions.

The problem with the first example is that it is a *rhetorical question*. According to Webster, a rhetorical question is "a question asked merely for effect with no answer expected." It isn't a request for a response or an attempt to gather more information. The purpose of the question is to communicate disgust with the other individual's conduct. What we're really declaring is, "You're an idiot!" Instead of focusing on the client's growth, the dialogue now revolves around the coach's issue (frustration with the client). When the coaching conversation starts to center on the coach's emotions, it is no longer client-centered and one of the key principles of coaching has been violated.

Great direct questions elicit a rational response instead of an emotional reaction.

Great direct questions are about the client's growth, not the coach's emotional agenda.

There are several ways to improve this question. First, the phrase, "*Don't you have any idea* what Scripture says..." serves no purpose except to communicate frustration. Replacing it with, "*Do you know* what Scripture says..." is more positive; although it leaves us with a closed question with a strong implicit answer within it (what we're saying is, "No, you don't know what Scripture says..."). Questions with an implied right answer tend to get people's hackles up. There's a second principle:

Great direct questions don't accuse, they inquire.

When we open the question up, like this: "*What does* Scripture say about 'wealth hastily gotten?'" it is transformed from an accusation into an inquiry. Now what we're communicating is that we honestly want to know what the client thinks, instead of that we've written him off.

Our question is still a little awkward, though. The phrase 'wealth hastily gotten' is out of Scripture, but the way we are using it implies that the person has failed. A last alteration will make the question *neutral*: "What does Scripture say about *this kind of short-term investment?*" That phrase doesn't have negative connotations, so it is more likely to elicit a thoughtful response instead of a reaction.

Effective direct questions are neutral.

The question we ended up with has its rough edges knocked off, but it is also less direct than the one we started with. In some situations, you'll want to preserve the direct impact of referring to a specific Scripture passage. If so, you might ask this way: "Proverbs says that, 'Wealth hastily gotten will dwindle.' Talk to me about what that verse means in your situation." By stating the verse and following up with an honest question, you challenge the client to deal with God instead of reacting to your delivery of the challenge.

The second sample question ("How could you possibly fall for a scheme like that?") is a good example of *inflammatory language*. Imagine the voice tone that would be used to ask a question like this. It sounds like the proverbial nun who's going to rap you across the knuckles with a steel ruler. This kind of language is a crude attempt to influence the client's behavior by making him feel stupid or guilty. "Fall for" and "scheme" aren't much better—those words communicate that this investment deal is so obviously a scam that anyone with half a brain would have caught on by now.

Examples: Effective Direct Questions

- "How have you prayed about this? What has God said to you?"
- "What do you do when you and your wife disagree on a big decision?"
- "This sounds too good to be true. What facts do you have that say it isn't?"
- "Just for the sake of argument, let's say you lose all the money you put into this. How would that affect your financial future? Your marriage?"
- "Let me play devil's advocate for a moment. What concrete evidence do you have that you'll get that much return on your investment?"
- "What do you know about this ministry's track record?"
- "How does this investment fit with you and your wife's financial values and principles?"

Great direct questions avoid inflammatory language.

It may be that this thing *is* a scam and that it would be a poor judgment on the client's part to get involved with it. However, your shock and dismay are not going to help the client reevaluate. If you over-react and start dropping emotional guilt-bombs, the client will start reacting to you and the message will be lost. The focus moves from the issue at hand to your frustration with each other. When that happens, any chance to influence the client's behavior is lost. Reactions breed reactions. Your job as a coach is to maintain enough detachment from the situation (remember, you are not responsible for the client's outcome) that you can help the client think things through. Great coaches keep their cool.

If you find yourself reacting, stop and go back to the thing that originally got your attention. You probably started wondering at some point if this whole investment deal wasn't a scam. So, if that's the question that needs answering, how could the client discover that answer for himself? These questions might work better:

- "What research have you done on this ministry?"
- "Have you seen a prospectus or any other literature on this investment?"
- "Since this is an important decision, what would you need to do to ensure that you make a great one?"
- "What steps would you have to take to be certain that this thing is on the up-and-up?"

You can be very direct with your clients as long as you honor them and allow them to make the decisions about their own lives. Being a coach does not mean being a softie or a pushover. A coach knows how to challenge clients while keeping responsibility with them.

Great direct questions challenge without using guilt, shame or intimidation.

What do you think is wrong with the third question? ("Why don't you ever listen to your wife? It looks like she's on to something!") One problem is the word why. "Why?" asks the client to justify what he's done. No matter how careful you are, with "why" there's always an implication that there's a wrong motive. That risks an unwanted reaction. So, let's replace it: "What's your rationale for not listening to your wife?" That comes across as less threatening.

Great direct questions avoid the word "Why".

But we can do better. Coaching is about moving toward a positive future, not fixing problems. And a positive, proactive question is more likely to be received as an inquiry instead of an accusation. We are always drawn more to a positive outcome than to a failure.

Great direct questions point toward a positive outcome.

So, let's change the question around to make it positive: "How might it benefit you to pay attention to your wife's perspective on this?" or "Let's say your wife is picking up on something important. What might it be?"

To sum up, great direct questions:

- *Are about the client's growth goals, not the coach's emotional agenda*
- *Don't accuse, they inquire*
- *Are neutral*
- *Avoid inflammatory language*
- *Challenge without using guilt or intimidation*
- *Avoid the word 'why'*
- *Point toward a positive outcome*

Exercise 14.2: Direct Questions

Step One: Take the two "good" questions that you came up with and run them through the principles we developed. Reword them where you need to.

Step Two: Now take your two "bad" questions and rework them using the principles listed above.

Revealing Questions

In the last chapter, we discussed the idea of thinking inside a box. If we've considered all the options we can think of and there are no workable solutions, we get stuck. When a problem like this has stopped a client, coaches use revealing questions to break the person out of the box and open up a new world of opportunities.

Exercise 14.3: Deconstructing Questions Worksheet

Take the examples below and revise them into more effective questions using the principles outlined so far (answers are at the end of the chapter).

Rhetorical Questions	Honest Inquiries
1. "When are you going to realize that you can't do everything at once?"	1. "How many of those things can you realistically do at once?"
2. "Why can't you just do your action steps every week like a normal client?"	2.
3. "Didn't we talk about that last week?"	3.
Inflammatory Language	**Neutral Language**
4. "Why did you get mad and lose control over that?"	4. "What caused you to get upset?"
5. "Why in the world did you take that job?"	5.
6. "What were you thinking when you told him off like that?"	6.
Questions that Use Guilt	**Questions that Honor the Client**
7. "Should you be spending your Sunday mornings on the golf course or at church?"	7. "Where do you think would be the best place to spend your Sunday mornings?"
8. "Do you think that more money is going to make your marriage work?"	8.
9. "Are you sure it's a good idea to kiss a girl on the second date?"	9.

The first step in getting out of a box is to identify it. In any situation, the walls of the box are *the parameters we're using to make the decision*: the circumstances, beliefs or rules that we've accepted as unchangeable. They may be:

- **Physical limitations** such as time, money or resources
- **Beliefs**—personal standards, values, strongholds, conceptual frameworks
- **Priorities** or lifestyle choices, such as how much time I need with friends, my standard of living, etc.
- **Lack of information**—we may not know the solution exists
- **Blind spots** that are obvious to others but for various reasons we don't see

Exercise 14.4: Identify the Box

Your intuition will help you tune into when a person is in a box. Read the following dialog and see if you can jot down at least one box this client might be in.

"Janet, you mentioned that you wanted to talk about your ministry involvement. Say more about that."

"Well, I'd really like to get more involved in ministry. I'm doing some stuff, but I think I'm capable of a lot more. There just doesn't seem to be a way to make it happen."

"OK. Tell me what you are doing now: how are you currently involved at church?"

"I've been an usher for a year or so. That doesn't take much time—I just have to be at church half an hour early because we pray together before the service. I'm also the assistant leader for the Senior High Sunday school class. We're working out of a lesson book and I don't do much unless the leader is out of town, so that's easy. The pastor suggested I get involved there, and I'm being faithful at it. I just feel like I could be bearing a lot more fruit."

"What's standing in the way of that additional fruit?"

"I've got two problems. The main one is time. My job is second shift and takes about 20 hours a week. Between work, taking care of the kids and my marriage, I just don't have any evenings during the week when I could get involved. I'm pretty maxed out. That means whatever I do would need to happen on Sunday morning."

"What's the other obstacle?"

"There just doesn't seem to be any opportunity. Like I said, the pastor asked me to be an assistant in this class, but I haven't talked to him in a while and he hasn't asked for anything else. I offered to preach at one point but he never got back to me."

"If you had the opportunity to do anything, what would it be?"

"My gifts are teaching and encouraging. I feel like I'd be good at bringing the Word and helping people grow and stuff, so I'd like to get involved in something that gives me a chance to do that. The roles I'm in are OK, but I don't really get to teach or do much one-on-one ministry with people."

"What kind of roles would allow you to do those things?"

"Well, I was thinking of something like leading a Bible study group or a small group, or maybe preaching sometimes. I could teach a Sunday school class, too, if it was more of an expository thing instead of just discussion-leading. Those are the only things I can think of that fit into my schedule."

> **Silence is Golden**
>
> You'll know you've asked a great question when it is followed with silence—the longer the better. If the client has to stop and think before answering, the conversation has gone to a place the person hasn't been before. Silence isn't bad; it's a sign of success.

If you haven't done so yet, take a moment and jot down the boxes this client may be in. Push yourself a little—what are the parameters this client is thinking within that she believes can't change?

Several possibilities are illustrated in this story. One is, "I don't have time." There may be a creative way to free up time for what she wants to accomplish. Another is, "Ministry is something that happens in church." What if Janet began to brainstorm about places outside the church where she could teach and encourage people? A third box might be, "There are no opportunities within my church's existing structures." Could she do something inside her church yet outside its existing structures that might fit within her time constraints? You may even have come up with a box that I missed!

It takes practice to learn to listen for boxes people are in. One way is to listen for the parameters the person is using to develop solutions. In this example, the client is only considering Sunday morning involvements because of her schedule—which she sees as a given. I begin to ask, "Could that schedule change?"

Sometimes intuition indicators tip me off to the presence of a box. When I listen to this individual talk, I see a *pattern*: when she thinks about ministry, she always places it within the four walls of the church. That may be part of her conceptual framework about ministry, or it may be a blind spot, but either way it makes me curious. Another way I become aware of boxes is that occasionally potential solutions pop into my head, and I ask myself, "I wonder why he didn't think of that?" For instance, in this situation I think, "Why couldn't you invest in someone at work?" The reason why that idea didn't occur to her could be a box.

Using Revealing Questions

Once you've identified a box, name it and then ask a question that pushes the client to think outside it or reexamine whether it could be changed. Below are several examples.

- *"It sounds like your work and your kids are a given and you're trying to fit ministry around them. Could you change that? What if you started with family and ministry, and changed your work to fit around that?*
- *"It sounds like your church doesn't have any existing opportunities that fit what you want to do. What if you thought outside your church's existing structures?*
- *"What could change about your work or family time that would free up the time you need to do ministry?"*
- *"It seems like you don't have time to get involved in anything else. So think creatively: where are people in your life now who need what you have to give? Who are you already around that needs teaching and encouragement?"*

In this situation, the question I actually asked was the last one: "Where are the people in your life that need what you have to give?"

The client thought for a few moments, and then said, "You know, there's a gal at work—another one of the managers—and she is really searching for some meaning in life. We get together at least once a week already for lunch to shoot the breeze. She's somebody who really needs encouragement… and I could help her without adding anything new to my schedule. That's a great idea!"

When she thought outside her box, this client was able to solve her own problem in a creative way, even though she initially felt stuck.

Exercise 14.5: Crafting Revealing Questions

Take one of the boxes you identified in the scenario above and develop a revealing question that pushes the client to think outside that box. It's easy to read someone else's questions—and a lot more challenging to think of your own!

Walk Around the Block

Another technique for helping people think outside the box is to imagine that the parameter that is blocking them has been eliminated. You don't need to come up with an actual strategy to remove the block—just ask the person to imagine as an exercise that it is gone. Then ask the person to envision their ideal future without that obstacle in the way.

For instance, in the example above you might ask, "Let's say your job only took 10 hours a week and you didn't work evenings. What would you do in ministry then?" Give the client permission to "walk around the block" and envision an ideal life without the obstacle. Once you've established what the client really wants, work backwards from the ideal future toward reality and see how much of that ideal life you can keep.

Below are examples of questions that might help this client walk around the block:

- "If you had all the time you needed, what would you do in your church?"
- "If God said to you, 'I want your ministry to be at work,'

or 'I want you to focus on using your gifts at school,' then what would you do?"

- "If you knew you couldn't fail, what would you try?"
- "If your church had the perfect opportunity for you to serve, what would it look like?"

If we asked this client the last question, she might have replied, "It would be ideal if I could lead a Sunday morning class that studied a book of the Bible—since you've asked what would be perfect, we'd study Daniel. That's my all-time favorite book. I'd have about 20 people who were really engaged with the study—maybe we'd be reading a book together, too. And in class I'd have a chance to teach for 15 minutes each week and then discuss what the passage means and how to apply it."

Walk Around the Block

- If you knew you couldn't fail, what would you attempt?
- If you had unlimited resources, how would that change your approach?
- If your hurt went away, how would you respond?
- If you had four more hours in a day, what would you do?
- If you knew everything would turn out all right, what course of action would you take?

Now that we've got her ideal future out on the table, the next step is to work backward to the present. A great question to start with would be, "What would it take to make this dream happen now?" It might lead the client to consider starting a group of her own. Or she may get inspired enough about her vision to make a sacrifice she wouldn't have been willing to before. Or she might realize that in three months her circumstances will change, and if she starts laying the groundwork now her dream can happen in full then. Visualizing an ideal tends to get clients thinking in new, creative ways, and can motivate them to make radical changes they weren't previously considering.

Some boxes are very common—like time, confidence, networks, responsibilities or money. The reason I hear most frequently for why people can't follow their call is because they don't have the cash. But they may be in a lifestyle box. What could you change about your lifestyle that would free up that money? Is it more important to you to have cable and DSL or to follow your dream? What could you do that would cut your entertainment expenses in half? It's amazing what you can do without when you are caught up in pursuing your destiny.

Debt is another money box. "I can't go to the mission field until I pay off my debts and that will take six years." A great way to work with a box like that is to ask, "What would it take for you to get there in half that time?" It may not actually be possible to do it in three, but by pushing a client to stretch and really think creatively, you might come up with a solution that shaves a year off what you thought was the best case. And my experience is, when we begin to make a real, sacrificial commitment to fulfill our destiny, no matter what it costs, God intervenes and we find ourselves doing the impossible.

Exercise 14.6: Working with Boxes

Now you try it. For the following real-life scenario, read the first paragraph and identify at least one of the boxes this pastor might be in. Then come up with at least two questions you could ask to help him think outside the box. Finally, read the rest of the story to see how this person actually got out of his box (some examples of boxes in the story are at the end of the chapter).

"Once, during the Lenten season, I was feeling overwhelmed with pastoral responsibilities. The tasks could not wait! The load felt oppressive and I saw no relief. I would just have to slog through the work for eight weeks and pray that God would not send me anything else to do.

"I was not expecting that my coach could give me any help. But he asked me a question that I decided to adopt as an action step: "What would reduce your stress by 50%?" As I discussed that question with the Lord and journaled about it, I found that just thinking about the question made me smile... I realized that part of the strain came not from the tasks themselves but from a fear of failure: a fear of disappointing people, of disappointing myself and of disappointing God. I discovered that I could reduce my stress by

not taking responsibility for things that God had not called me to take responsibility for.

"I gave up being self-defensive. It helped me to turn away from the thinking that "life would be good and restful if only such and such would happen." I discovered that joy and rest were something that already existed in the present and I could experience them now rather than resigning the present to distress.

"My coach did not tell me all these things. I'm not sure I could have heard them if he had. Rather, my coach asked me a question. I took the question to God in prayer, thought it over and found an answer."

Exercise: 14.7: Get Outside the Box

Sit down for 15 minutes with a friend and ask that person to share a current leadership challenge, a place they are stuck or an issue that has been difficult to work through. Use probing questions to get the story out on the table. When you have a good idea what the situation is, try to help the person identify a box they are in, then craft a question or two to help them think outside that box.

Ownership Questions

Dave was a youth pastor from a local church whom I'd been coaching for several months. One day he began to share his frustrations with Mike, one of the adults on his leadership team. Mike had been a member of the team before Dave was hired, and his ideas of what youth ministry ought to be were aligned more with the previous youth pastor's approach than they were to Dave's. As Dave settled into his role and began to carry out the mandate he'd been hired to accomplish, Mike got more and more upset.

The week before our appointment, things came to a head. Dave discovered that Mike had showed up at the previous elders' meeting, presented a one-sided view of what was happening with the youth and tried to get Dave fired. Unfortunately, his tactic boomeranged when the senior pastor sided with Dave. Even more upset, Mike came to the youth group and dropped a bomb. He angrily repeated his frustrations with Dave, and told the youth he was leaving the church because he felt that what Dave was doing was controlling and unbiblical. Dave came to our coaching appointment outraged about how he'd been treated, alarmed about the effect of Mike's outburst on the youth and pretty convinced that he was completely in the right. Hadn't the senior pastor sided with him?

I saw something different—an opportunity for growth. On other occasions when things had gone wrong, I'd witnessed Dave's tendency to blame others and justify his own actions. This seemed like a great teachable moment.

"Dave," I inquired, "There are always two sides to a conflict. Can you identify anything you might have done that contributed to the breakdown?"

"Well..." he replied, "I suppose I got frustrated at him when he was acting up. He's just not very self-aware. He'd get all emotional about some peripheral issue, and instead of talking to me first he'd dump it all out in the group meetings in inappropriate ways. A couple of times the kids were getting upset and I had to cut him off to save the meeting. I don't know—maybe I could have anticipated more when he was upset and tried to take him aside. But frankly, the senior pastor agreed that this is his issue, not mine."

"If you were going to keep something like this from happening again, what would you do?"

"A lot of it comes down to the fact that he wasn't part of my team. The last youth pastor brought him on, not me. If I were doing this over I'd make sure that I had my own team in place. When you've got the wrong people, things always go wrong."

"Let me rephrase that question a little. What could change about *you*, so that if God put you in the same situation again with a person just like Mike, that things wouldn't break down?"

"Even if I changed, only like 5% of the issue is me. The person who needs to deal with God in this situation is Mike. I mean, the senior pastor backed me, the elders backed me—I'm the one that is in the right here and he's the one that screwed things up."

"OK, let's assume for a minute that Mike is 95% of the problem. Let me challenge you on that last 5%. You could say you are in the right and this is Mike's problem and leave it at that, and you'd be perfectly justified in doing so. Or you could take this as an opportunity and say, "God, I want *everything* you have for me—don't hold anything back! Even if I'm only one percent responsible, I want to change it. Which way do you want to handle this?"

Types of Ownership Questions

In this story, the coach is asking Dave *ownership questions.* Ownership questions challenge the client to take responsibility and change the situation. There are three types of ownership questions:

- The challenge to take ***responsibility***: "What have you done that has contributed to the problem?"
- The challenge to be ***proactive***: "What could you do to make things better?"
- The challenge to ***deal with God:*** "What does God want to form in your character through this situation?"

In the story, the coach asked all three types of ownership questions. The first, "Can you identify anything you might have done that contributed to the breakdown?" is a challenge to take responsibility for what happened. The second question, "If you were going to keep something like this from happening again, what would you do?" asks Dave to be proactive. What can he do to ensure better results in the future? The final question challenges him to deal with God. Even if only a tiny fraction of this is your problem, God can still use that part to refine you. A coach believes that every problem, conflict or circumstance in life holds the potential for character growth, if only we engage it in terms of God's purposes. "All things work together for good..." (Rom. 8:28) means that God can use anything to refine us and make us more like Christ.

One of the dynamics that makes coaching so effective at change is that it encourages people to take ownership for their circumstances and their future. The only sure way to produce change in our situation is to take responsibility for it and do something pro-active. As long as we are blaming others or waiting for the organization to change or the boss to retire or the denomination to fix things, very little happens.

Daniel or Couch Potato?

A great example of ownership in Scripture is in the book of Daniel. Daniel was not personally responsible for the sins that led the Jewish people into exile. But when he perceived what had happened, he took responsibility for them and repented; he became proactive and fasted and prayed for God's answer; and he allowed God to deal with his own character. Daniel could have waited for the people to repent, for the priests to come up with a solution or for the princes to deal with God. If he had, he wouldn't be in the Bible. Daniel took ownership of his situation, and when he did God's power was unleashed and a radical, nation-changing transformation took place.

Christians today face the same choice: whether to be passive or to act like Daniel. Passivity can be wrapped up in spiritual lingo that makes it sound really great to do nothing:

- "I'm just waiting for God to open a door."
- "If God wants me to go, He'll give me an opportunity."
- "I'm still seeking God for what He wants me to do."
- "If I'm supposed to do that, God will make it clear."

By all means, pray! By all means, seek God! But as the saying goes, God can direct a moving object. When you're sitting still, it's much harder for Him to intervene. Often what happens is, we're afraid of making a mistake, so we don't want to move until it is so abundantly clear that God has spoken that our course of action is risk-free. That's being afraid to take responsibility for our lives. God is waiting to move until, like Daniel, we take ownership and step up to the plate. Even though God could do everything for us without our help, He's chosen to work in partnership with us for the sake of our relationship with Him. Too often, we're sitting around waiting for God to do something *for us*, and meanwhile, God isn't doing it because His objective is to do it *with us*.

Take Responsibility

God wants to work with Daniels who will take responsibility and co-labor with him, not with spiritual couch potatoes who sit back and wait for Him to put on a show all by himself.

God wants to partner with us. And because He's given us free will, He needs our assent to use us in His program. He's not going to run over us or do everything for us. We need to take ownership of our destiny and co-labor with Him to accomplish it. Ownership questions are a key way coaches help people move from a passive mode to an aggressive posture of responsibility.

Uses of Ownership Questions

While ownership questions are often used in conflict situations, they are also commonly used when asking for action steps:

- "What do you want to do about that?"
- "What step do you want to take?"
- "How do you want to go about that?"
- "What do you think the answer is?"

When coaches ask for a step, they are requesting that clients take ownership, be proactive and solve their own problems. Coaches also use ownership questions to help clients move from a "doing" into a "being" (or transformational) mode:

- "What does that response say about who you are and what you believe?"
- "What do you think God wants to do through this situation?"
- "Assume for a moment that your circumstances have been custom designed by God for your growth. If that's true, what is He trying to do in you?"

Exercise 14.7: Ownership Questions

Think of a conflict or difficult interpersonal situation you are in currently or were in recently. Develop three ownership questions a coach might ask a person in your situation. Try to come up with one from each of the categories (responsible, proactive and dealing with God). Now that you've developed three questions for yourself, how would you answer them?

Finally, ownership questions are a great tool for helping a client progress from blaming or venting to solving the problem:

- "Let's say that Doris never gets it—that she never changes. So unless you do something, nothing is going to get any better. What would you do?"
- "Visualize the best possible outcome for this situation—what it would look like if everything turned out great. What could you do to give yourself the best possible chance of seeing that outcome?"
- "Can I make an observation? So far I've heard you talk about what needs to change about Jerry, but I haven't heard what needs to change about you. Could you talk about that a little?"

Whenever the focus needs to shift to taking responsibility, being proactive or engaging God's purposes, use an ownership question.

Chapter 14 Exercise Answers

Exercise 14.3: Deconstructing Questions Worksheet

Rhetorical Questions	Honest Inquiries
1. "When are you going to realize that you can't do everything at once?"	1. "How many of those things can you realistically do at once?"
2. "Why can't you just do your action steps every week like a normal client?"	2. "You finished one out of five action steps—can I ask you to reflect on that a bit?"
3. "Didn't we talk about that last week?"	3. "What progress have you made since we talked about this last week?"

Inflammatory Language	Neutral Language
4. "Why did you get mad and lose control over that?"	4. "What caused you to get upset?"
5. "Why in the world did you take that job?"	5. "Talk through your rationale for taking that job."
6. "What were you thinking when you told him off like that?"	6. "What do you think you did that contributed to the situation?"
Questions that Use Guilt	**Questions that Honor the Client**
7. "Should you be spending your Sunday mornings on the golf course or at church?"	7. "Where do you think would be the best place to spend your Sunday mornings?"
8. "Do you think that more money is going to make your marriage work?"	8. "Of the things you could do to improve your marriage, where would you rank increased income?"
9. "Are you sure it's a good idea to kiss a girl on the second date?"	9. "What are your standards for physical touch in a dating relationship?"

Exercise 14.6: Working with Boxes

Possible boxes:

- I must do all these tasks myself
- I must do all these tasks to this standard of excellence
- The work before me is bound to be joyless and stressful

Powerful Questions Examples

Open/Probing Questions

Questions that let your clients lead by allowing them to answer in any way they choose.

1. "Tell me a little more about that."
2. "Give me some background—what led up to this situation?"
3. "What feelings do you have when you think about that situation?"
4. "You mentioned that __________. Say more about that."
5. "What did you mean when you said __________?"
6. "What was most significant to you in this experience?"
7. "What would be most important for us to focus on?"
8. "How did that happen?"

Revealing Questions

Questions that change viewpoint or help the person get out of a box and think creatively.

1. "What does your [spouse, peer, coach, friend] think about that?"
2. "If you removed that limitation, then what would you do?"
3. "If [money, time, resources, energy] wasn't an issue, what would you do?"
4. "Put yourself in the other person's shoes—what can you see from their perspective?"
5. "What does Scripture say that you could apply to your situation?"
6. "What worked for you in similar situations in the past?"
7. "What would be the best possible outcome?"
8. "If the perfect opportunity came along, what would it look like?"

Ownership Questions

Questions that focus on taking responsibility and being proactive in order to make things better.

1. "How might your actions have contributed to the breakdown?"
2. "Let's say God is using this situation to get your attention on something. What do you think that something could be?"
3. "Let's say this person never changes or 'gets it.' What do you need to do to move on in life even if he doesn't?"
4. "What could you do that would turn this into a positive experience?"
5. "What do you think God is trying to form in your character through this?"
6. "If you were going to respond in the best possible way to your circumstances, to do something you'd really be proud of in the future, what would you do?"
7. "Since we can't change the other person, what could change about *you* that would make things better?"
8. "If you were still in this situation three years from now, what would that be like? What would you be willing to do to prevent that from happening?"

Direct Questions

Questions that cut to the heart of the issue.

1. "Are you being true to your own values?"
2. "What are the implications of that choice for your [marriage, family, job, relationship]?"
3. "What has God said to you about this?"
4. "Is this the way you want to live?"
5. "Who benefits most from that course of action?"
6. "How does your response line up with Scripture?"
7. "Are you comfortable with your decision?"
8. "What are you going to do about that?"

Asking Permission

Opens the door to entering a new area or broaching a sensitive subject.

1. "Would it be OK if we probe that area a little?"
2. "That statement caught my attention—would you mind talking a little more about it?"
3. "Would it be helpful if we talked through that a little together?"
4. "Can I challenge you on that?"
5. "Can I ask you to look at that from another angle?"
6. "Would you be open to hearing another perspective on the situation?"
7. "Can I make a request? (You may choose to do this, to not do it or to modify this request.)"
8. "Would you like to talk about that?"

Choosing an Agenda

What to ask when starting a new coaching relationship or a new change goal.

1. "If you could change any two things about your life right now, what would they be?"
2. "What are the top three things God has been speaking to you about?"
3. "What would it take to cut your stress by half?"
4. "How would you like your life to be different in this area?"
5. "What's the most important step you could take right now to move toward your destiny?"
6. "What areas of life are your circumstances forcing you to address?"
7. "What are you most motivated to change?"
8. "What one obstacle would most transform your life if you overcame it?"

Decision-Making

Questions to ask in a decision-making process.

1. "What do you need that you don't have now to make a great decision?"
2. "Who could you tap to help you make a great decision?"
3. "If you had unlimited resources and couldn't fail, what would you do?"
4. "If you saw someone else in your situation, what would you tell him/her?"
5. "On a scale of one to ten, how sure are you that this is the right decision? What would it take to make that 'six' into an 'eight'?"
6. "What has God spoken to you about this decision?"
7. "What's the worst-case scenario if you take this course? Can you live with that if it happens?"
8. "What would it cost you if you *didn't* move forward with this?"

Life Purpose

Questions that help people identify and pursue their destiny.

1. "What do you most want to be or accomplish before you die?"
2. "Think of a situation that really fit you—where you felt like you were doing what you were born to do. Describe it."
3. "Who are the people you are most drawn to help?"
4. "What is stopping you from pursuing your dreams now? What could you do about that?"
5. "What did you want to be when you were a kid? Why?"
6. "What are you passionate about? What kind of career would make you leap out of bed in the morning?"
7. "Where do you want to be in a year? In five years? What do you see yourself doing?"
8. "What have you done in your life that was deeply fulfilling, that you'd like to do more of?"

Taking Action

Questions that turn ideas into committed action steps.

1. "Make an action step out of that—what do you want to do?"
2. "What *will* you do? When will you do it?"
3. "On a scale of one to ten, how sure are you that you'll carry that step out? What would it take to make that 'six' into an 'eight' or a 'nine'?"
4. "Is that a step you want to take?"
5. "You said you [might, ought to, could] do that. Nail it down: what *will* you commit yourself to doing?"
6. "Is this step important enough to take? Will it move you toward your goal?"
7. "What kind of support do you need from me or others to make sure this gets done?"
8. "What obstacles do you need to overcome to reach your goal?"

Chapter 15
Taking Action

"Hell is full of the talented; but heaven of the energetic."
Ste. Jeanne Francoise De Chantal

When a client comes to us with a growth issue, the first step is to convert that intention into a goal. Then we use intuitive listening and powerful questions to open up the conversation, exploring new thoughts and ideas and pushing clients to reflect more deeply than they've done before. Those steps complete the top, exploratory half of the conversational funnel, where the conversation goes from very specific (the goal statement) to very broad. Once plenty of information is out on the table, the coach begins to narrow the conversation back down again toward a specific solution. At the conclusion of the conversation, the client has developed a strategy and committed to take specific actions to accomplish the goal.

Action is one of the four fundamentals of the coaching conversation, along with listening, asking and support. The role of the coach is to manage the coaching conversation, walking the client through each step of the process to ensure that the client comes out the other end committed to concrete action steps.

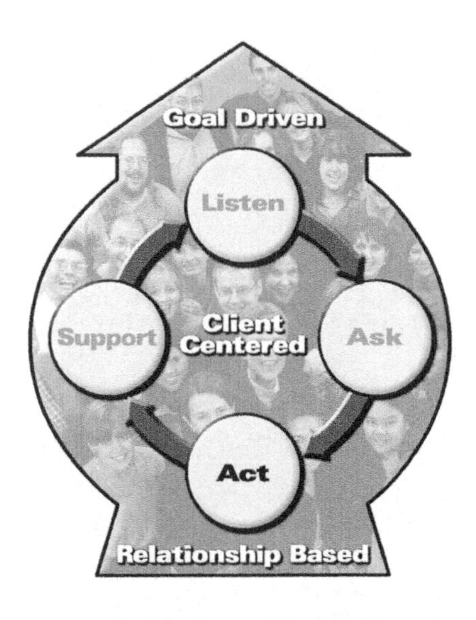

Listening and asking are used to explore the situation and develop a strategy for change. Action and support are where that strategy is implemented. The action component of coaching is so important that we say, "If you aren't taking action, you're not coaching."

In this chapter, we'll look at how you move the coaching conversation from exploration through problem solving to action. We'll examine a problem-solving model (G.E.T.) used to generate options and convert potential solutions into concrete steps of action that get into the client's date book. We'll also look at how to develop action steps within a larger coaching conversation. The main methodology for developing solutions and actions in a coaching context is listening and asking questions; so we'll use the asking techniques from the previous two chapters and learn a few new ones.

Problem-Solving with the G.E.T. Model

A coaching conversation isn't usually a nice, clean, linear dialogue that lasts 45 minutes and ends up with a single, all-encompassing solution. For instance, if the goal is to get the house organized, you'll probably end up with different action steps for each room of the house; with issues that have to be addressed with family or housemates (Billy never picks up after himself and Sally's taken over the whole hall closet with her projects); side issues (what about organizing the car?), and changes you'll have to make to your personal habits. Every one of those things is a separate problem to be examined, solved and acted on.

These smaller side issues don't usually need to be processed through the whole coaching funnel. Often you can dive right into the G.E.T. model and solve them one by one. Since this same process also works as part of the coaching funnel for bigger issues, it's a very useful tool. The G.E.T. model is:

- Generate Options
- Establish Solution
- Take Action

To use GET, first help the client generate multiple potential options for solving the problem. Second, help the client evaluate those options and establish the best solution. Third, develop and commit to the action steps needed to implement that solution.

Exercise 15.1: Using G.E.T.

Here's an example. We're talking with Connie, a client who wants to get organized around the house. As we discuss cleaning out the garage, a new thought occurs to her. As you read the story, underline the points where the coach introduces each step of the GET model (the answers are at the end of the chapter):

"You know, talking about the garage gets me thinking about the car. That's another bit of chaos in my life that really bugs me. The trunk is full of stuff that was being taken somewhere and we forgot, or we brought back from the beach and never took out. It hasn't been washed since the Reagan administration, and the floor is covered with the reminders of every trip to McDonalds my husband has ever taken."

What if the Client Just Wants to Talk?

I've been involved in coaching relationships where I discovered that the client just wanted to get together and talk every week, and I've decided that I won't do that. To meet for fellowship or to shoot the breeze is friendship, not coaching.

If your clients want the assistance of a professional coach to act—to accomplish an important goal or move toward their destiny—I think that's great. If they want to pay someone be a friend, I think that's fundamentally unhealthy. I'd much rather coach that person to develop healthy friendships than be a mercenary friend.

"So what could you do that would make a lasting difference with the car?"

"Well, I could just clean it out—but that would last about a week. Or I could have the kids do it regularly as part of their chores. That would work."

"What else could you do?"

"To be honest, the two biggest offenders are Bob and I. If Bob would quit throwing his trash on the floor, that would make a big difference."

"What would it take to make that happen?"

"I could always nag him about it," Connie laughed. "Or I could fine him for every piece of litter. If I could just get him to commit to throwing stuff out... He just doesn't think about it. He needs some kind of reminder—maybe a sign on the dashboard would help."

"OK. You mentioned that you were part of the problem, too..."

"Yeah," Connie sighed. "The junk in the trunk is mine. I've got bags of clothes in there just in case I happen to drive by the Salvation Army, but I never do. Bob keeps telling me to just toss it all out, but that seems wasteful. I guess I need to fish or cut bait on that one."

"Connie, it sounds like you've got a lot of good options. You mentioned cleaning the car yourself, having the kids do it as a chore, fines for car litter, putting up a reminder for Bob, and throwing out what's in the trunk. Which of those options do you think will make the most difference?"

"Well, somebody's got to clean the car, and I think that somebody is going to be Billy. I'm going to quit putting stuff in the car and I'll figure out some way to remind Bob to throw away his trash."

"Sounds like you have a solution. Let's nail that down. You mentioned you are going to have Billy clean the car. Make an action step out of that."

"Alright. By Wednesday, I'll talk to Billy and have this on his chore list. He can clean it for the first time this Saturday."

"What are you going to do about the trunk?"

"OK," Connie groaned. "I'll commit to take that stuff to Salvation Army this week."

"You don't sound too energized. What would help you get that step done?"

"Well...I'll tell Bob I'm either going to take it in by Friday or he can pitch it. He'll be out there at 7:00 am Saturday morning to gleefully heave it in the dumpster if I forget."

"OK—and what about Bob?"

"I need to get him to remember, but I don't think a note on the dashboard would work. He could forget his children's names when he's driving the car. You know," Connie brightened, "If I stuck a little trash bag in there that might do it. It would give him a place to put stuff instead of on the floor, and Billy could dump it whenever he cleans the car."

"Is that a step you want to take?"

"Yes! I'll talk to Bob about it tonight."

Debriefing

In this coaching conversation, a side issue developed around cleaning out the car. Since it was a smaller challenge that already fit within the client's main goal (getting the house organized), the coach chose to skip the top half of the coaching funnel and move directly into developing actions with the GET model.

Notice that the coach used a listening-and-asking methodology throughout. The coaching approach to problem solving taps the client's insight and ability to develop effective solutions. All the options and the steps in this conversation came from the client. While the coach's questions helped the client analyze the situation in an orderly way and arrive at a concrete action plan, the client did all the thinking. Notice too that the coach had very little information about the situation, but still helped the client develop a great solution. The coaching approach depends on the coach believing in the client's ability and trusting the client's insight. Because the coach didn't need to elicit all the details, the problem was addressed quickly and efficiently.

> *Even when you are problem-solving, a coach's primary tools are listening and asking questions.*

This scenario is also a good example of the kind of creativity clients generate when problem-solving. Solutions were developed which the coach probably wouldn't have thought of, because the client had more information and experience with the problem.

These client-generated solutions fit Bob's personality, the chore structure in Connie's home, her kids' ages and capabilities and the relational dynamics between Connie and her husband. Generally, a solution developed by the client will be most effective, because:

- It naturally fits the client's personality and capabilities
- It draws on a greater depth of information about the situation
- Clients have higher buy-in for their own solutions

Problem-Solving Strategies

Here are some tips for helping the client generate options in the GET model instead of falling into the trap of solving the problem for the client:

1. ***"What could you do?"***
   Simply asking the client to solve the problem is the place to start. Most people think they can't think of a solution until they stop to think.
2. ***"What have you done so far?"***
   Find out what the client has already tried. Often solutions come from looking at what hasn't worked or has only solved part of the problem.
3. ***"What has worked for you in similar situations in the past?"***
   This is a great technique—a solution that worked once for this client will likely work again. And since it has worked before, the client will be more willing to risk trying it.

For a simple problem like the one Connie faced, these types of questions will usually be enough to generate multiple options. With larger issues, and especially in places the client has been stuck, you may need to go farther. Here are some techniques to employ when the client's solution-well has (temporarily) run dry:

1. ***"What else could you do?"***
   The first time you ask for options, your clients will tell you what they've already thought of. Ask again, and they'll

have to dig deeper. Not long ago I was modeling GET in a training session, and afterward one of the observers offered this comment: "You asked the client what he could do, and after he answered I was surprised to hear you repeat the same question twice more. I thought, 'He's already answered that—he won't know what to say!' But every time you asked, he came up with new options."

2. ***"Give me five options."*** Challenge the client to come up with a certain number of options. Don't stop working until you reach the target. My clients and I almost never fail to reach the number of possibilities we shoot for.

> **Note Taking**
>
> It can be extremely helpful for the coach to take notes when the client is generating options. When it comes time to choose which one to pursue, I like to be able to recount all the options we've discussed. Otherwise, if we get four or five choices out on the table we're liable to forget some.

3. ***"Are you serious about that? What if you were?"*** Sometimes when you are pushing for options, the client may throw out a semi-humorous idea. For instance, in our example Connie joked, "I could always nag him about it!" If you take that idea seriously, it might contain the seed of an idea. "How could you get his attention on this without making him feeling nagged?" I once had a client who joked, "I could always quit my job!" He was surprised that I took him seriously—but the eventual solution to the problem was a job change that came out of that blow-off comment.

4. ***"What if money (or time, energy, or any other limitation) wasn't an issue?*** Identify the box and ask a revealing question that helps clients think outside it (See chapter 14). Name the box and push the client outside it, or eliminate the parameter

that is the obstacle and "walk around the block".

5. ***"What would be the best possible outcome?"***
   Ask the client to define the ideal future, then work backwards to see how it can be realized in the present. This works well when a client has come up against a persistent obstacle and gotten discouraged. Reconnecting them with the possibility of a great future can help restore the motivation to be proactive and work at change.

Making Suggestions

A final way to generate options is for the coach to make suggestions. This is not your first option in a coaching context, but sometimes it can be very valuable. The coach may have access to resources or have information about potential solutions that the client doesn't have.

For instance, years ago I made my living as an Internet marketing consultant, helping small businesses develop and implement profitable Internet strategies. Recently, one of my clients came to me for help when his web designer dropped the ball. He needed to find another developer, rework the site and start promoting it. I suggested the name of a designer that I'd worked with in the past and walked him through the basics of search engine promotion.

Referral Ethics

When you make referrals, maintain a sterling reputation by doing the following:

- Refer clients to those who are experts in their field and can provide the service needed.
- Only recommend those who have a track record of integrity and honesty.
- Offer no guarantees—remind clients that they should check out any referrals to their own satisfaction.
- Remember to tell the clients that they are under no obligation to use those that you suggest.

In this situation, I had information and expertise that was valuable to my client and it was appropriate to share it. However, too much suggesting will turn your relationship into consulting or mentoring instead of coaching. Below are some tips on how to make suggestions without turning yourself back into a teller:

1. ***Ask a question instead.***
   It is always preferable from a buy-in standpoint to have the client develop the solutions. Could you ask a question that would help the client go down this road without being told? Employ the same thinking-backward technique that we used to develop bigger questions (See chapter 13). For instance, if the solution to the dirty car problem you're tempted to propose is to take the car to an auto detailer, instead ask, "So far you've thought about cleaning the car yourself. If money were no object, what would you do?"
2. ***Offer your ideas last.***
   Proposing a solution right off the bat makes it too easy for the client to be passive and let you do the work. Push the client to think things through, and wait to offer your ideas until the client has put several options on the table.
3. ***Make multiple suggestions instead of only one.***
   One temptation for the client is to treat you as an authority figure (which you aren't) and choose the option you offered because it's the one the coach suggested. That's abdicating their responsibility to make a decision. An elegant way to get around this is to offer several possibilities instead of just one. Then the client has to make a real choice.
4. ***Ask the client to choose.***
   Whenever you make a suggestion, follow it up with a choice: "Here's an option—this might or might not work. What do *you* think?" As much as possible, you want clients to freely choose the course of action that they think is best and then verbalize their own choice. By being tentative ("this might or might not work") and asking for their opinion, you ensure that the clients maintain responsibility for the decision.

Exercise 15.2: Ask, Don't Tell

A client who is a realtor aims to increase his sales by 50% in six months. Below are four options a coach might suggest for reaching that goal. Can you think of a big question for each that might result in the client coming up with a similar option? Try to avoid solution-oriented questions! (Answers are at the end of the chapter.)

1. You could hire an assistant.
2. You could increase your advertising.
3. You could target employees of the new corporate headquarters that is coming to town.
4. You could develop a better follow-up system for contacts.

Establish the Solution

Once you've generated multiple options, it's time for your clients to make a choice. Which course of action do they want to pursue? Most of the time, the answer will come naturally: the client will be evaluating each option as it is developed, and by the time several options are on the table one or two will clearly stand out above the rest. To complete this step, recount the options that the client generated from your notes, and then ask a question like this:

- "Which option(s) do you want to take?"
- "Out of all those options, which do you think is the best?"
- "What do you think the solution is?"

Having the client verbalize the choice is important. When we say something out loud instead of just thinking it, it becomes more real and concrete to us and we are more committed to it. The same principle is at work when we have new believers give a testimony about their salvation experience. When we verbalize what happened inside, we solidify it and give it new credence. Scripture attests to this principle as well: "For man believes with his heart and so is justified, and he confesses with his lips and so is saved" (Rom 10: 10). I often ask, "Is that the solution?" or "Is that a step you want to take?" because I want to hear the client say, "Yes!"

There will be times when the client can't decide what course to take. It may be that several options could work, or maybe the client isn't happy with any of them. There are many ways to sort options. For instance, you might list the pluses and minuses of each one, or talk through how each would be implemented to identify their strengths and weaknesses. My favorite approach is an extension of the GET model. Identify the top two or three choices and the major negative outcomes or obstacles to implementing each one. Then use the GET model to develop options to overcome each obstacle. A particular option becomes workable if you can find ways to alleviate the client's major concerns about that option.

For instance, let's take our realtor client who wants to increase his sales. One option is to hire an assistant. That might help, but the client is afraid that managing the assistant and doing the paperwork for taxes and workman's comp would be more hassle than it is worth. A new contact management system might also solve the problem, but the client once had a system like this and never got it set up right, so he's afraid of wasting his time.

> **Exercise 15.3: Problem Solving Skills**
>
> Get together with a friend and have the individual share a practical, concrete problem—a challenge they face as a leader, an obstacle, or a change that needs to be made. After you've used several probing questions to get some information out on the table, help the person generate and evaluate at least four options. Can you help your friend arrive at a great solution without giving advice?

Faced with these obstacles, the coach might ask, "Give me four options: how could you hire someone without getting stuck with the paperwork?" or "What would it take to make sure you could computerize your contact management without wasting your time?" Once the client has generated several options for each obstacle, evaluate them and see if you can make either the new hire or the contact management system work.

Taking Action

The final step in the GET model (and the coaching funnel) is to

Sample Action Steps

Here's a list of action steps from a recent appointment with my own coach. My goal is to renew several basic disciplines after a particularly stressful period of life. Before our next appointment, I will:

- Continue my TV fast. Only movies with my wife after 9:00 pm when the kids go to bed.
- Continue computer game fast.
- Take a 15-minute work break every morning and afternoon: get a snack, read a book or enjoy nature to relax.
- Exercise: This weekend I will open up the pool for the summer. Starting next week I'll exercise in the pool three times per week, for 20 minutes each time.
- Finding a new small group: I will visit the youth group again, and schedule a meeting with the youth pastor to talk about getting involved.

develop concrete action steps to implement the chosen solution. Here's an example.

Jeannie was a client of mine with an independent consulting business. Her personality type is strong at exploring options, adapting to change and trying new things, but not as adept at concrete strategies and firm commitments. I noticed early on in our coaching relationship that we seemed to dance around each other when it came to action steps. Whenever we approached the point of commitment, Jeannie would equivocate. I'd say, "What do you want to do?" and she'd respond by rehearsing several options. So I'd ask which she wanted to choose. She'd tentatively pick one, but then point out several obstacles or get distracted into a side issue. It was clearly difficult for her to commit to a definite course of action.

After seeing this pattern several times, I started pushing a little harder. That day we were talking about a frustrating client she wanted to drop.

"Jeannie, what step do you want to take on this?"

"Well, I really would like to let go of that client—I mean, I'm not enjoying the relationship and he hasn't paid me for the last contract. But maybe next time will be different—I mean, who knows? Tomorrow he might bring me a big contract. So I'm not sure I want to cut off that possibility."

"So nail yourself down—what step are you going to take before our next meeting?"

"Um... I guess I ought to talk to him—but I don't want to come across real negative. Maybe if I wait a little longer a good opportunity to say something will present itself."

"Jeannie, you said you wanted to make a change in this relationship, but you still haven't committed yourself to any concrete steps. What exactly are you going to do and when will you do it?"

It took another five minutes for Jeannie to finally make the decision and verbalize it clearly. It was like extracting a tooth without anesthesia—a painful process. I wasn't sure if I hadn't been a little too aggressive with the pliers, so I asked her about it (when in doubt, ask the client). "Jeannie, I pushed you pretty hard there to pin yourself down. Is that what you want from a coach?"

"Oh, yes, definitely!" she affirmed. "That's exactly what I need. I know it's hard for me to make decisions, especially if it involves conflict, and having you push me to choose was very helpful."

Most of us have a lot of great ideas in our heads, or know exactly what we could change to make life better—the problem is acting on our insights. One of the great services coaches do for their clients is to help them commit to getting something concrete done. I often hear comments like this: "I knew what I wanted to accomplish, but I guess I'd never really broken it down into steps. Because I wasn't clear on what to do first, it never got into my schedule." Or, "In the past, I would decide to do a project and just throw myself into it without developing any kind of strategic plan. I'm much more successful when I think it through and come up with definite action steps." It sounds so simple, you'll wonder if helping someone turn a goal into an action step is that big a deal. But it is!

The Four Tests

What exactly makes an effective action step? Take a look at the following statements and pick the one you think is the best example:

1. *"I'll do something about that next week."*
2. *"I'll figure out which college I want to attend by the end of the month."*
3. *"I guess I probably ought to call her this week and make things right."*
4. *"On Tuesday I'll set aside time to clean out that entire drawer and put everything away."*
5. *"I will phone my top five job opportunities and send them my resume."*

Creating action steps is the process of turning a goal into clear, committed action items you can put in your date book. Here are four simple tests you can use to evaluate an action step:

1. The **Clarity** test: I know exactly what I need to do
2. The **Commitment** test: I definitely *will* do this
3. The **Date Book** test: I've broken this down to where I can put it in my date book
4. The **Deadline** test: I know when I've committed to have this done

So let's go back and evaluate our five sample action steps and see how they hold up. Number four (*"On Tuesday I'll set aside time to clean out that entire drawer and put everything away"*) is the example that passes all four tests. It is clear, committed, can be scheduled in a date book and has a timed deadline. By contrast, the first step (*"I'll do something about that next week"*) fails the clarity test. What exactly are you going to do? Without naming a specific solution, it is too easy to temporize. It's also pretty tough to hold a person accountable if you don't know what is supposed to be done! Action steps must be clear, concrete and precise. To clarify a vague action step, ask: "Flesh that out: what exactly are you planning to do?"

"I'll figure out which college I want to attend by the end of the month" fails the date book test. Figuring out which college to attend is a *project* that involves multiple action steps. To complete the project you might research a number of schools on the Internet,

call your top five and get a catalog, and maybe take a weekend and make an on-campus visit. Each of those sub-items is an action step because it passes the date book test (*"Friday night: research five schools from my list on the Internet"*). However, the original example is a project. Action steps are individual tasks you can schedule on your calendar. For many clients, working the project down to the level of actual steps is very empowering.

The third example (*"I guess I probably ought to call her this week and make things right"*) fails the commitment test. The words "guess" and "probably" give it away. The client is considering taking this action, but has not yet made an internal commitment to do so. Don't allow the client to equivocate on an action step! The person should either be able to say, "I will definitely do this," or the action step should be modified so that the client can make that statement. Action steps are hard work. If we've not made and verbalized a clear commitment to the step, the chance that we'll do it is not very high.

> **Asking for an Action Step**
>
> Here are some direct questions to ask when it is time to move from options to action steps:
>
> - Make an action step out of that—what do you want to do?
> - Is that a step you want to take?
> - What *will* you do?
> - Give me a date: when will you have that done?

Sometimes a person will hesitate to commit because the action step depends on another person. For instance, if a client's step is to "have a conversation with my sister about the estate this week," he may not be able to get a hold of his sister. If you think back to the S.M.A.R.T. format (See chapter 10), you'll realize that this step is not *attainable*: the outcome is not fully under the client's control. "Set a goal that you control" by rewording the step in terms of what the client alone will do: "I'll make at least three attempts to reach my sister and talk about the estate this week."

The fifth prospective step (*"I will phone my top five job opportunities and send them my resume"*) fails the deadline test—by when will you have done this step? Address this omission by asking the client, "When will you have that done by?"

Nailing it Down

In most coaching situations, you'll be working with multiple goals or action items in one appointment. As you cover each item, go ahead and develop new action steps within the flow of the conversation instead of leaving everything for the end. (The peril of doing all the action steps at the end is that if you run out of time the client won't have any actions steps.)

For instance, every coaching appointment begins with a review of the previous set of action steps. Often new steps will be birthed out of the existing step. Here's an example:

"Jim, give me a quick progress report on your action steps."

Exercise 15.4: Nailing Down the Step

Often as you are discussing options or opportunities in the middle of an appointment, your clients will suggest potential solutions or actions. Don't miss the opportunity to convert those ideas into action! Here are five examples of suggested steps you might hear from a client. The first two include the coach's response–you supply a response for the final three.

1. Client: "I guess I ought to talk to her about how I feel."
   Coach: "Is that a step you want to take?"
2. Client: "I know I ought to do something, but I guess I've just been avoiding a confrontation."
   Coach: "So what would you like to do?"
3. Client: "Yeah, I probably ought to take care of that bill before it's late."
   Coach: ______________________________
4. Client: "The answer is probably to just go out and hire someone to do it–we're never going to do it ourselves."
   Coach: ______________________________
5. Client: "I need to stop watching so much TV."
   Coach: ______________________________

"OK. On developing a leadership team for the singles' group: I talked to the Robinsons and they are excited about coming on board. I'll need to do some training with them and help them find another couple to share the load; but having some leadership besides me is real relief."

"Great! That sounds like a breakthrough. What's your next step on that?"

"Probably to find another couple to help lead. I've got two or three names in mind."

"Do you think those people will work out?"

"Yeah, any of them could do it, if they'd be willing to make the commitment."

"So what's the step that you want to take?"

"I'll get a meeting scheduled with all three of those couples and the Robinsons to talk about the opportunity to serve the singles."

"Are you going to have the meeting in the next two weeks, or just get it scheduled?"

"Just schedule it—with five different couples it will take more than a week to get us all together."

"So state your action step."

"In the next two weeks, I'll call these four couples and schedule a meeting to present the singles group opportunity to them."

"That's excellent. OK—tell me about the other steps you were working on."

Ensuring Commitment

The single most important variable for an action step is commitment, or buy-in. Change is a function of motivation, not information. The higher the buy-in, the more likely it will be that the step gets done. You can do everything else right when helping the client develop steps, but if you settle for low buy-in the client is likely to fail. Here are six principles that foster high commitment for client action steps:

1. ***Client-Generated Steps***
   Any step that the client thinks up will automatically possess higher buy-in than one the coach suggests. People are most committed to their own ideas. Whenever possible, help the client generate the options instead of

Equivocation Red Flags

These words are red flags that the client is equivocating on an action step. Don't let your clients get by with a half-hearted commitment! Either secure a stronger commitment ("I will...") or change the step to something the client can commit to with certainty.

- "I <u>ought to</u> have regular daily devotions."
- "I really <u>should</u> have regular daily devotions."
- "I can <u>probably</u> make that happen."
- "I <u>guess</u> I'll start this week."
- "Yeah, <u>I think I can</u> do that this week."
- "I <u>might</u> be able to get that done."
- "I <u>want to</u> do that." (Change to "will")
- "<u>Maybe</u> that is the answer."
- "I'll <u>think about</u> that.

offering them yourself.

2. ***Verbalize the Action***
   Asking, "Is that a step you want to take?" is a direct, closed question that forces the client to make and verbalize a decision: "Yes, I will take that step!" Verbalization fosters high commitment.
3. ***Eliminate Equivocation***
   Don't settle for a step your client "ought to" do, "could" do, or "thinks she might" do. Equivocation indicates the decision has yet to be made. When clients prevaricate, ask, "What *will* you do?" to nail them down.
4. ***Quantify Commitment***
   A great way to ensure high commitment is to ask clients to quantify their level of motivation. Here's a favorite question: "On a scale of one to ten, how certain are you that this step will get done?" You want an answer of eight or higher—it is pretty certain that the step will be taken. If the client gives a lower number, make an adjustment to raise the number. You might ask, "What would it take to

make that 'six' into an 'eight' or a 'nine'?"

5. ***Expect Accountability***
   A vital part of high commitment is building a pattern where clients know they'll be held accountable for every step they set. If you know you are going to be asked whether you did something, you are much more serious about agreeing to it in the first place.
6. ***Write it Down***
   If steps don't get written down, they aren't taken seriously and they don't get done. The coach should note every goal and action step and require the client to write these down as well. If your clients aren't consistently recording steps, ask them to e-mail you their action step list within 24 hours after your appointment. That will provide some accountability for having the steps recorded.

Making a Request

As with options, it is generally best for action steps to come from the client. However, sometimes a coach will want to suggest a step. That's called "making a request." Here are several examples:

- *"Let me suggest three questions you can reflect on to take*

Exercise 15.5: Self-Coaching

Take an area in your own life you want to change, and create two action steps you want to take in the next two weeks to make that change. For *one* of the two steps, implement all of the six principles given above for high buy-in. For the second step, implement none of these six principles. Which of the two steps is most likely to get done?

Bonus
Make a note on your calendar in two weeks to check back to see how you did. Which of the two steps were you most motivated to take? Which step got done? Which of the six principles made the most difference for you?

this a step further..."

- *"Can I make a request? I think you'd find it beneficial to..."*
- *"Can I push you to take this a step further? Consider doing this..."*

The value of making requests is that the coach can bring insights or ideas into the process that the client may not think of. The risk in making a request is that the client might agree to do something just because you asked, without really buying into the idea. Here are two things I generally do when I request a step to make sure it's something the client really wants to do.

First, when I request a step, I always try to give the client an out:

> *"You can choose to adopt this as one of your action steps, you can modify it or you can discard it."*

If the person really isn't that excited about the step, you've provided a graceful way to say, "No" to it. This approach also allows clients to make changes to your suggestions if they have a better idea.

Second, I always ask my clients to choose the step they want and verbalize their choice by asking, "Is this a step you want to take?" or "Do you think that step would be worth the time and energy to do, or would you rather not do it?" Giving the final decision about requests back to your clients keeps them in charge and is one more way to express belief in their abilities.

Chapter 15 Exercise Answers

15.1: Using GET

Generate Options: *"So what could you do that would make a lasting difference with the car?"*

Establish Solution: *"You mentioned cleaning the car yourself, having the kids do it as a chore, fines for car litter, putting up a reminder for Bob and throwing out what's in the trunk. Which of* *those options do you think will make the most difference?"*

Take Action: *"Sounds like you have a solution. Let's nail that down. You mentioned you are going to have Billy clean the car. Make an action step out of that."*

Exercise 15.2: Ask, Don't Tell

1. *"How could you get more work done without increasing your hours?"*
2. *"What would get your name out there to more people?"*
3. *"Can you see any opportunities to get larger sales or more than one sale at a time?"*
4. "What would improve the percentage of contacts you turn into sales?"

Exercise 15.4: Nailing Down the Step

1. Client: *"I guess I ought to talk to her about how I feel."*
   Coach: *"Is that a step you want to take?"*
2. Client: *"I know I ought to do something, but I guess I've been avoiding a confrontation."*
   Coach: *"So what would you like to do?"*
3. Client: *"Yeah, I probably ought to take care of that bill before it's late."*
   Coach: *"OK, so make a decision – are you going to take care of that bill this week?"*
4. Client: *"The answer is probably to go out and hire someone to do it—we're never going to do it ourselves."*
   Coach: *"So—is hiring this out the solution?"*
5. Client: *"I need to stop watching so much TV."*
   Coach: *"What do you want to do about that?"*

Chapter 16
Support Structures

"Whoever knows what is right to do and fails to do it, for him it is sin." James 4:17

Eli had a problem: his sons were out of control. He had put them in influential ministry positions under his leadership, but they flaunted the rules and became increasingly unethical. When people came to give their offerings to God, Eli's sons would dip into the pot for their own personal use. If objections were raised, they would threaten to take whatever they wanted by force. Eli's sons acted as if the things God's people had placed sacrificially on His altar were their own. God was not pleased.

Eli made an attempt to challenge his boys, weak though it was. He'd heard reports of their sordid affairs with their female co-workers, and he remonstrated with them over their sinful behavior. "Why do you do such things?" he inquired, clearly pained by what was happening. But they wouldn't listen, and Eli could not summon up the courage to remove them.

Twice God spoke very clearly to Eli about his failure to take responsibility for the situation. He was told directly that he was putting his sons before God, and that he and his family would be severely punished for his failure to honor God first. When Eli still didn't act, God spoke prophetically again through a young boy, Eli's protégé. Even as Eli mentored the boy in how to hear God's voice, the first prophetic word the boy gave spoke of the disaster that was coming to Eli's household. While his sons were the ones who had cast off all restraint, Eli was in charge and God held him to account for failing to lead. He still had one last chance to change.

But by that time Eli had lost hope. He acknowledged that God was speaking, but in despair simply replied, "It is the Lord; let Him do what seems good to Him." Not long afterward, Eli's two sons were both killed, and the ark of God, the centerpiece of Eli's ministry, was lost. Eli himself fell over and died of a broken neck when he heard the news. All these disasters came to pass in a single day.

First, a Little Change Theory...

Eli had a problem: he knew what he needed to do, but he couldn't bring himself to do it. We're often in the same boat. We know we need to lose weight, but somehow it's always easier to eat ice cream straight from the carton instead of going to bed hungry. We've read a hundred times how regular exercise can make us happier and longer-lived, but every time we try we run out of steam after a few weeks and give up. God has been speaking to us about our devotional life, but it's so hard to find the time.

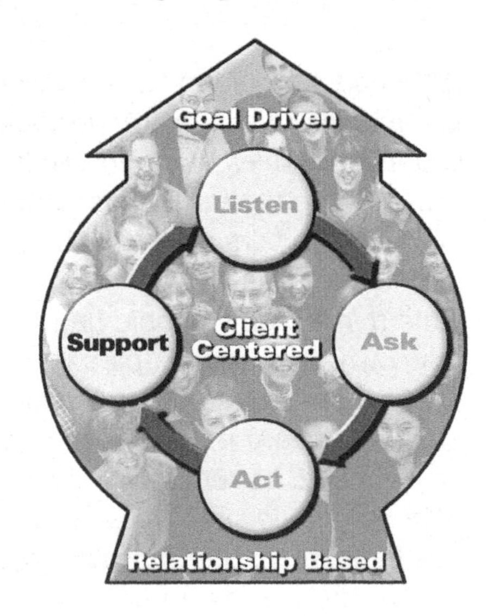

The process of habit change is not well understood by Christians, and neither are the relational resources God has given us to do it. As we've discussed before, the key factor in change is motivation, not information. It isn't knowing what to do that produces change—it's having the incentive to tackle the hard work it entails. We have to get motivated, to get energized to change, and then stay motivated and energized long enough to form a new habit. When our energy and motivation wane, we fail.

Coaching helps people change because it offers a support system that adds extra energy and motivation to the change process. Healthy support structures are the fourth element of the coaching conversation (see facing page), a key reason why clients who are coached can do more than they can on their own. To see how the coaching support structure works, let's first take a glimpse at a little change theory.

Below is a diagram that tracks how energy and motivation influence the change process. The curved line represents how we change over time, with *the slope of the curve* representing the amount of energy we expend at each point in the change process. The steeper the slope, the more energy it takes to get up it.

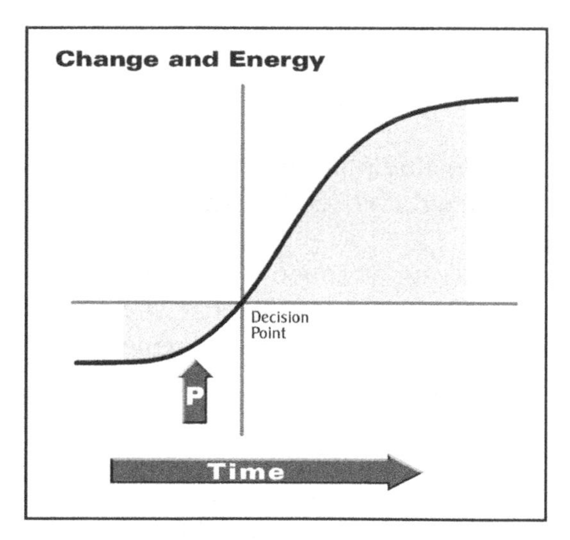

The horizontal line represents the boundary between positive and negative energy. When we are functioning below the line, we operate out of the negative pressures of guilt, discouragement and shame. Once we've decided to make a change (the decision point is where the axes cross in the diagram) we move over into positive territory: we get a surge of energy because we're finally doing something proactive about the problem.

Here's a simple way to visualize that process. Picture yourself on a bicycle riding along the change line. On the left side of the diagram, before you start thinking about making a change, the line is flat—you're coasting and expending little energy. The hard part is going up the steep hill in the center. To climb it you downshift, get up out of the saddle and pedal harder. Your heart rate goes up, the crank turns slower and slower, and soon you're gritting out the ascent. If you don't give up, the slope gradually levels out again at the top of the hill. You can let up and start coasting again. As your energy expenditure goes back down, your pulse returns to normal.

Here's what that means in terms of change. Let's say that the thing you're working on is controlling your temper. On the left side of the diagram the line is flat—you aren't expending much energy. It doesn't require any special effort to get angry. Your spouse pushes one of your buttons and you explode, like always. You didn't have to try to blow up, you didn't consciously work yourself into a lather over what she said—getting angry flows out of you naturally and effortlessly. That's what a habit is—something we do naturally. Bad habits require little energy to maintain

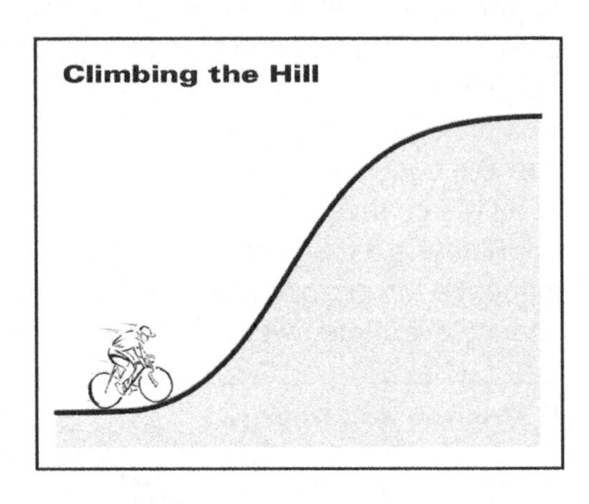

Then one day something calls your attention to your anger issue. Usually it's the pressures of life that alert us that we have a problem—that's the "P" arrow at the bottom of the diagram. "P" stands for pressure. Your short fuse at work earns you a reprimand, or maybe one of the kids walks in on a particularly caustic argument between you and your spouse and afterward asks you in tears, "Are you and Mommy going to get a divorce?" Now you aren't feeling so good about yourself, and the curve starts to slope upward: you're pedaling harder. Because you haven't yet made a decision to change, you're expending negative energy (feeling guilty or discouraged, denying you have a problem, etc.) The energy you're using up isn't accomplishing anything; it's just assuaging (or worsening!) your feelings about the issue.

Sometimes we can go on expending negative energy without dealing with an issue for years. But today, you get inspired: "I'm going to make a change!" God has leveraged the pressures of life to motivate you to act. The vertical line on the diagram represents this point of decision. Making a decisive choice to changes gives us a burst of energy, because we've also moved over the dividing line from negative emotions to positive ones. You get your second wind:

for a little while you're working hard but you've got the energy to attack the slope. You're feeling good about yourself because you're actually doing something about the problem.

However, in a few weeks you reach the steepest part of the hill. Your breathing becomes labored and your legs feel like lead. Controlling your anger is getting harder and harder. Your son just did the same thing wrong for the umpteenth time even though you told him not to, and right now you could just *SCREAM!* Out of gas, all you want to do is to stop being disciplined and vent.

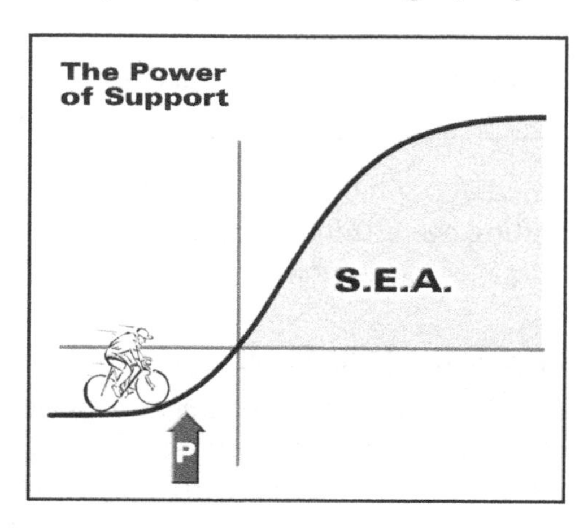

The problem is, you can't stop. Changing a habit means *doing the same thing enough times in a row so that you begin to do it instinctively.*[1] As soon as you stop practicing the new behavior ("I'll let myself eat whatever I want this weekend and go back to the diet on Monday"), you're reinforcing the old. With habit change, either you are going forward or you're going back. If you aren't pedaling up the hill, you're freewheeling back toward the bottom.

Sometimes we do make it all the way up the hill. In a few more weeks, the climb starts to ease off bit by bit. After six weeks, we're in a good rhythm: we're catching ourselves before we get upset now (instead of after we've eviscerated someone), and we have the tools to deal with frustration in a healthy way. After three months, we're hardly expending any energy at all controlling anger—we've developed a new habit. The curve has flattened back out again at the upper right of the diagram.

But for most people, most of the time, the hill is too steep. We

[1] It's often said that it takes six weeks to form a habit. While you can develop a good rhythm in that time, a habit isn't truly formed until something can break it (for instance, going to grandma's house for Thanksgiving when you've been dieting) and you instinctively go right back to the new pattern without much effort. While you can make the habit in six weeks, making it one that lasts often takes three to six months.

don't have enough strength in our legs to climb all the way to the top, and after a few weeks of effort we lose energy and slide back into the old habit. Often the guilt and discouragement from our failure leads to a binge where the old behavior actually gets worse. Our shame and frustration make our fuse even shorter than it was before and we blow our top at the slightest provocation. Or, since we've failed at our diet anyway, we try to feel better by going out and getting two dozen Krispy Kreme donuts and snorking them down all at once. This is what I call the *Energy Deficit Pattern* (See diagram).

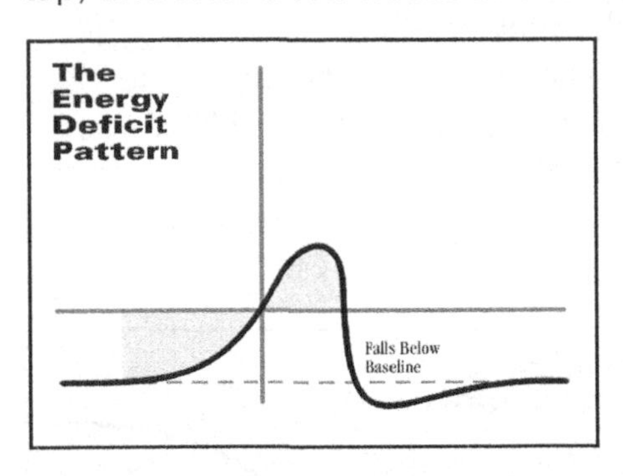

Change is a Team Sport

Here's what this diagram means to a coach. People fail to change because they run out of energy. Changing a habit takes a serious, concentrated effort over a period of weeks or months. It requires picking yourself up when you are down and trying again. Most of all it takes consistency. And right when you are starting to make progress, life comes along and throws you a curve ball. You're trying to get out of debt and the transmission goes out on the van; or you're trying to jog every week and it rains for eight days straight. People fail to change because life knocks them down and they don't have the energy to get back up. Change has to do with energy, and succeeding at change has a lot to with staying energized.

The thing that we're too often missing is the body of Christ. The reason we run out of energy, is that we were not created to overcome these obstacles all by ourselves. Change is a team sport. The fact that we are made for relationship is so deeply encoded in us that *no individual can fulfill the call of God on their life without other people.* God did not create us to be independent entities. We are specifically designed to be interdependent with God and others. This principle is evident in Scripture from the beginning. It was not healthy for Adam to be on his own—he needed a helper suitable to his needs. Jesus never sent His disciples out to minister alone—it was always two by two. The same concept is repeated in Paul's writings. We are a body, and each part needs every other part. Many of the promises of God in the New Testament, which we unwittingly claim for ourselves as individuals, are actually given to the Body of Christ as a whole organism (For instance, see Ephesians 1). It is only "the whole body, joined and knit together by every joint with which it is supplied, when each part is working properly," that "makes bodily growth and upbuilds itself in love" (Eph. 4:16).

> **Finishing Well**
>
> "In our studies of leaders, we can clearly conclude with few exceptions that those who experienced anointed ministry and finished well had a significant network of meaningful relationships that inspired, challenged, listened, pursued, developed and held one another accountable. Those that failed to reach full maturity and finish well did not have [these relationships], or cut all or part of [them] off at some point."
>
> J. Robert Clinton, *Connecting*, page 159

People fail at change because they fail to draw on the relational change resources God has provided. Coaching delivers those resources. For instance, coaches supply accountability for action steps, encouragement when we're down and a place to celebrate when we triumph. When we're out of gas and ready to give up, the knowledge that "tomorrow the coach is going to ask how I'm doing" keeps us going when our own resources wouldn't have been enough. When life knocks us down, a coach is there to help us dust ourselves off and get back in the saddle. The support, encouragement and accountability (SEA) a coach provides is so invaluable that it can transform lives all by itself.

Personally, I've reached the point where I don't even try to change a habit on my own any more—it simply wastes too much energy. Recently I asked my coach to hold me accountable to rise to a new standard in my thought life, and right now I'm kicking myself about it. Why didn't I talk to him about this months ago? I frittered away more energy feeling guilty about where I was at than it has taken to make the change! Once you get over feeling embarrassed that you can't do everything on your own (do yourself a big favor and get over this lie quickly), building support structures for change in your life is one of the most empowering things you can do for yourself.

Coaches serve their clients by offering the relational support they need to maximize growth and change. Here's how to build extraordinary support structures that help your clients succeed.

Accountability: Standing in for God

It's 11:00 pm, you just got back from another long day of ministry two time zones away from home and you're sitting alone on your hotel bed, exhausted. Tomorrow you fly back through O'Hare, but right now all you want is to crash for a half an hour or so before bed. As you're flipping through the channels trying to find ESPN Sports Center, there right in front of your eyes is a graphic, X-rated sex scene.

Temptation is always the worst in that kind of situation. Alone, tired, far from home and outside your normal routines, your defenses are down. It would be an easy place to slide back down the hill.

Of course, we aren't alone. The Holy Spirit is right there in the room. But in the seeming privacy of our thought life, it is awfully easy to rationalize away the invisible presence of God. We block Him out of our minds, or say we'll repent later, or give in on the pretense that we won't get caught. What makes it possible for us to sin like this is not that God is any more distant than usual, *but that people are*. We'd never watch that movie with our spouse, or with a buddy from church, or at home where the kids might wander into the room. The difference is that we're by ourselves.

And therein lies the cure. The way to overcome a clinging private sin is to voluntarily remove the veil of secrecy surrounding it. A besetting sin is like a mushroom that takes root and grows only in the darkness. The solution is to turn on the lights. When you're tempted to rationalize away the presence of a God whom you can't see, bring in a friend you can see.

Being accountable is voluntarily asking to be held responsible to live up to a chosen standard. In spiritual terms, *accountability is standing in for God*. The company of a brother or sister in Christ makes the invisible presence of God real and undeniable at the point where we'd most like to ignore it. For you, lust may not be the issue: it could be late night trips to the refrigerator, skipping your morning run, avoiding conflict or wasting an hour on the internet when you're supposed to be working. We all have tough hills to climb, and alone we don't have the resources to live the life God created us for. But if you're accountable, you're not alone.

When I know my coach is going to ask me next week about my conduct, I am much more successful at sticking to my standards. His presence in the situation provides the extra energy I need to make the change. The knowledge that I'm accountable keeps me focused on the goal, so I'm less likely to forget it or rationalize it away. And, when I do fail, accountability helps me quickly get back up and try again; because someone else knows I'm down and need encouragement. Accountability provides the energy I need to make it up the hill and establish a new habit.

The Power of Accountability

Here's what one client said when asked to name the most significant thing he learned through his coaching relationship:

"I became a big proponent of telling people what's going on in our lives. Most of us know things we need to change, but we never do, and we develop these stuck, staunch habits that we can't break out of. When someone comes into your life from the outside, they can help you break out of those unhealthy patterns. I don't have to hope and pray that this year I'll finally do something different—I'm doing it!"

Because accountability is standing in for God, the way you hold your clients accountable literally gives them a picture of who God is. Accountability that is gentle but firm, energizing and encouraging draws us closer to God. On the other hand, if we try to motivate people through fear, shame or guilt, we are standing in for God but acting like the devil. ("There is no fear in love, but perfect love casts out fear. For fear has to do with punishment, and he who fears is not perfected in love" I John 4:18.) Many Christians have soured on accountability due to this kind of negative modeling. Let's reexamine what makes for healthy and unhealthy accountability.

Unhealthy Accountability

Years ago my wife and I ran a small mentoring program for dating couples in our church. The congregation had been going through some major leadership changes so we ran the classes for about two years with virtually no oversight from the church. Finally, a new staff person was hired for that area, and in due course he requested a meeting.

After a few pleasantries, he began the meeting by saying, "Let's look at everything you are doing in this course, and then we'll decide what has to change and what you can keep."

That immediately got my hackles up. "Wait a minute," I thought. "We've been doing this successfully without any oversight for two whole years and now in the first meeting you want to come in and tell us what to do?" We expected to be honored for serving faithfully without any help, but instead we felt we were under suspicion before we'd even said a word.

Things went downhill from there. He kept asking pointed questions about what we were doing. We felt that he didn't know what he was talking about and got defensive, and he took our defensiveness as rebellion and used his authority

Exercise 16.1: Health Check-up

Here's a quick, simple way to test the health of any accountability relationship. Think of a place you are accountable now, and ask yourself:

Does this give me life?
Do I want this to continue?

That's all you need to know. If being accountable to this person is something you avoid, that drags you down instead of building you up, or it isn't helpful, then something needs to be adjusted (either in the way the accountability is provided or the way you receive it). If accountability is healthy, it will be encouraging, energizing, and effective, and you'll want it.

position to pin us to the wall. At the end of the meeting, I finally said, "If you want to make all the decisions about this, then you go ahead and run it yourself, because I don't have any interest in functioning this way." He replied, "Well, if that's your position, I'm going to have to take this to the elders and recommend they shut it down."

In one of those blissful surprises that the Lord manufactures every so often, his spouse received an attractive job offer and he quit and moved away before things ever came to a head. We went back to being unsupervised and continued to run the program very fruitfully for several more years.

I was a person who believed in and wanted accountability, but his approach rubbed me completely the wrong way. Instead of bringing me into greater alignment and partnership with the church, it pushed me away. Suspicious from the start, that process was more concerned that things were done "right" than it was about me as a person. Instead of energizing me for ministry it made me want to give up. That's not healthy accountability.

Healthy Accountability

When accountability is working properly, it energizes and motivates us for change instead of making us feel watched or controlled. Accountability is *not* meting out punishment for wrong

Voluntary Consequences

One way accountability works is by providing a consequence for blowing it. Being undisciplined often has no immediate consequences. Think about smoking—the pain of our wrong choices can be years away, and one more cigarette today doesn't seem to make any difference. Asking someone to hold us accountable to stop smoking provides an immediate consequence: we have to admit to our accountability partner that we failed.

Sometimes adding a significant consequence can help a client get over the hump and succeed. I once coached a student who decided that if he didn't stop procrastinating and turn in his paper by his deadline, he'd pay his girlfriend $50. She held him accountable and he succeeded.

behavior. It's not someone making you feel shamed or guilty when you blow it. In fact, the focus of accountability isn't on failure, but on success. Accountability is a pro-active, voluntary openness that is meant to preempt wrong behavior. *The purpose of accountability is to supply energy for change.*

A number of years ago I went on a diet and lost quite a bit of weight. One of the keys to my success was a friend who called me every week for six months to ask me how I was doing. There were many times when I would have given up on my own, but I knew Eric was going to call, so I stuck it out. Our accountability relationship was built around seven principles that made it tremendously life giving:

1. ***Voluntary***
   I asked to be accountable, instead of being pushed into it against my will. The person being held accountable initiates healthy accountability.
2. ***Positive***
   Eric believed I could change and he was always there to cheer me on. I drew strength from that. Trying to motivate with negative emotions like guilt or shame is counterproductive in the long run.
3. ***Preemptive***
   Eric's purpose in calling was not to reprimand me when I failed, but to help me succeed. Accountability is primarily proactive, not reactive. It is meant to preempt wrong behavior rather than punishing it.
4. ***Consistent***
   Eric and I talked every week. Consistent accountability is particularly vital in habit change, where a slip up can start you sliding back down the hill and may require starting all over again.
5. ***Honest***
   Effective accountability doesn't let you slide by. It calls for honest, authentic answers.
6. ***Specific***
   Effective accountability is specific and to the point: "Did

you stick to your diet this week? How much weight did you lose?"

7. *Energizing*
   I was more focused and motivated because I was accountable. It gave me the energy to keep going for the long haul. Eric's calls felt like a gift and not a weight.

Accountability for Coaches

To this point we've talked about how accountability works for changing habits. But the same principles work with any kind of action step. Whenever a client needs to get something done, accountability improves the chances of success. Here's an overview of how accountability is normally applied in a coaching relationship.

> **Exercise 16.2: Progress Reports**
>
> Evaluate these requests for a progress report in light of the seven principles of accountability. What's wrong with each one? (Answers are at the end of the chapter.)
>
> 1. "How did your action steps go?"
> 2. "Give me a progress report on your homework assignments."
> 3. "Did you do your action steps this week?"
> 4. "OK, let's look at your action steps. The first one was to find a book on small group leading. Did you do that?"

The most basic support structure in a coaching relationship is the *progress report.* At the beginning of each coaching appointment (after a few minutes of chit-chat), the coach asks the client to review progress on the action steps chosen in the previous session:

"Give me a brief progress report on your action steps."

This question is direct, keeps the client in charge and emphasizes the client's ownership of the process. Train your clients to quickly run through the steps on their list. Once you've determined what they did or didn't do, you can respond, ask for new action steps in a particular area or move the focus to the main agenda for the coaching appointment.

Consistently asking for progress reports creates a performance-enhancing environment which is characterized by:

- ***Responsibility***
  Clients catch on pretty quickly that you expect them to write down and keep track of each and every goal and action step. It is their list and they are responsible for it.
- ***Seriousness***
  Progress reports communicate that we are taking the steps seriously—seriously enough to follow up.
- ***Consistency***
  Clients realize that they are going to be consistently held accountable for each and every step. Therefore, if I choose a step, I'm serious about taking it.

The coach also keeps a list of every goal and action step the client develops. If the client skips a step in the progress report, the coach must ask for a report on that specific step. Maximum

How Often Should You Meet?

Some coaches meet with their clients weekly, others two or three times per month. How often should you meet?

Here's a rule of thumb: when you're working with a performance issue (i.e. making 10 more sales calls per week), or daily habit (diet, exercise, self-control), meet weekly in shorter, 30-minute appointments. More frequent accountability provides more reinforcement and gets things back on track sooner if things break down.

For clients who are working on life- or transformational coaching issues (i.e. who am I, what is my life purpose, what is God doing in me in this transitional season), I generally meet bi-weekly for 45 to 60 minute appointments. The additional time lets us delve more deeply into complex issues.

performance is generated when every step is covered and there is no sliding by.

Progress reports provide sufficient accountability for most action steps. However, if the client is working at a daily habit or a particularly thorny issue, increasing the frequency of the accountability may make a big difference. One way to do this is to increase the frequency of your coaching appointments (See previous page). Another strategy is to use e-mail or "spot calls" of a few minutes to check in with the client more often. A one-sentence e-mail every other day can be a great boost for the client. That's the beauty of accountability—it gives the client much more energy than it takes to supply it.

Peer Accountability

A third approach is to help clients enhance their own support systems. We all have people in our lives that we can tap to support our change goals. Building intentional S.E.A. (support, encouragement and accountability) into our relationships with friends, family and co-workers creates a great resource for change. I love to help my clients do this because it is such an effective long-term strategy. If I provide accountability my clients, I've helped them change one thing. If I help my clients learn to develop accountable relationships, I'll affect every change issue they undertake for their whole lives.

Since accountability is standing in for God, the most effective approach is to put the accountability where the behavior is. For instance, if your goal is to develop a daily exercise habit, having a running partner is a great way to get effective accountability. Every day, someone knows whether you ran or not. For daily habits, someone who sees you in action can be a wonderful help.

The disadvantage with this strategy is that most people don't know how to make peer accountability work. Without guidance, what will happen is this: the client will ask a person off the cuff to "hold me accountable to such-and-such." No direction will be given for what to ask, nothing will be written down and no structure will be set up to ensure that the question is consistently asked. Nine times out of ten, the client will never be asked an accountability question.

Peer accountability is a powerful tool. But for it to work for your clients, you'll have to teach them to teach their friends to provide effective accountability. Here are three keys to making peer accountability work:

1. ***Permission***
   Saying, "Please ask me about this" one time will probably not be enough. It may seem awkward, but a formal, written accountability agreement between client and accountability partner makes a huge difference. Giving permission several times verbally is also a big help. A friend who knows what to ask and is clearly empowered to ask it is an effective peer partner.
2. ***Question***
   Develop and write down the question you want your friend to ask you. This way the accountability partner feels free to be direct while knowing we won't be offended.
3. ***Structure***
   Accountability is most effective when it is consistent. Saying, "I'll ask you about it when I see you at church," doesn't cut it. Define when and how often the accountability will be provided.

Exercise 16.3: Accountability Questions

Pick an area of your life that you are currently working at changing. Craft an accountability question you'd want to be asked by using these three principles.

Crafting Accountability Questions

The actual accountability question you ask can make all the difference. Say the client's goal is to share her faith and provide an invitation to believe in Christ to at least one person a week. Most people would ask an accountability question something like this:

"How did it go with the evangelism thing this week?"

And the answer you'll usually get with that question is (cue drum roll), "Fine". The problem is that "fine" could mean anything from, "Yes, I shared the Lord with someone this week," to "I tried on several occasions to share but it didn't work out," to "I didn't actually *share* with anyone so to speak, but I thought about it a lot, and that's an improvement over where I was at." The question doesn't provide much accountability because it is so easy to evade. Below are three principles for crafting great accountability questions:

- ***Ask a Direct, Closed Question***
  "How's it going?" doesn't cut the mustard. Ask a question with a yes or no answer: "Did you speak to at least one person about your faith this week?"
- ***Let the Client Develop the Question***
  This step helps you know exactly what the client wants from you and creates buy-in for the process. "What do you want me to ask you next time we meet?"
- ***Be Positive***
  It's easy to come across like a schoolmarm: "Did you do *all* your work this week, Johnny?" If things feel a little heavy-handed, try expressing your accountability question positively: "Who did you talk to about your faith this week?" This question assumes the person has taken the step, instead of assuming they haven't.

Exercise 16.4: Peer Accountability

Now let's use that issue to practice the discipline of peer accountability. Find someone who is around you when you are working at your goal, and "put the accountability where the behavior is" by asking them to hold you accountable. Use the three steps listed on page 266 for peer accountability. Write down what you are going to do together, use the accountability question you've already developed and create a structure to make sure you are asked consistently.

Chapter 16 Exercise Answers

Exercise 16.2: Asking for a Progress Report

1. **"How did your action steps go?"** *Any time you ask, "How did it go?" the response you'll get will be, "Fine". Be more specific: "Run through your action steps and tell me what you did on each one."*
2. **"Give me a progress report on your homework assignments."** *When you use words like "homework" or "assignments" it sounds like these are involuntary duties assigned by the coach. I like the phrase "your action steps"—it keeps ownership with the client.*
3. **"Did you do your action steps this week?"** *This isn't a very positive way to ask—it almost assumes the person didn't complete the steps. A question like, "Give me a report on what you accomplished on your action steps" assumes that you accomplished something. Believing in people makes accountability energizing.*
4. **"OK, let's look at your action steps.** The first one was to find a book on small group leading. Did you do that?" *Here the coach is keeping track of the list and asking the client about each step. That takes the responsibility from the client. Keep your own list, but always ask the clients to work from their list—that puts the onus on them to keep track of what they decided to do.*

Chapter 17

Master Class: Encouragement and Expectations

Two are better than one, because they have a good reward for their toil. For if they fall, one will lift up his fellow; but woe to him who is alone when he falls and has not another to life him up." Ecclesiastes 4:9-10

Encouragement is a second important tool for keeping clients energized and motivated. Encouragement is inspiring for all of us, and for some personality types it is the single biggest factor in motivation. Therefore, coaching support structures should always include encouragement, affirmation and celebration. When you are consistently excited about your clients' progress, it helps them stay motivated and get more done.

Offering encouragement is one of the disciplines of believing in people. My son got a unicycle last year from an uncle for Christmas. He is very athletic and is not usually intimidated by new things, but riding on one wheel had him stymied. He'd mastered his pogo stick and his rock climbing techniques, but this time he was ready to quit. We didn't force him to go out and ride, but whenever he did we complimented him and when he'd forget about it we'd remind him to give it another try. It wasn't hard to stay positive and believe in him, because he really is great at those kinds of activities and we had no doubt that if he kept at it he could master it.

One day he came rushing in all excited: he'd gotten all the way to the end of the driveway! We all went out to watch and share his moment of triumph. Two days later, he rode around the block. Two weeks later he could ride that unicycle for a mile without falling off. With a little encouragement he overcame his obstacle and managed to ride the first 10 feet—and that one push was all he needed to really shine.

Exercise 17.1: Effective Encouragement

What does effective encouragement looks like? Say you've

Replacement, Removal and Rewards

Many goals—from pursuing a dream to self-discipline to overcoming sinful behaviors—involve giving up a short-term pleasure for long-term fulfillment. The "Three R's" are three simple tools a coach can use to support the change:

- ***Replace the Pleasure***
  Replace an unhealthy pleasure with a healthy one. Say a client is fasting from TV. What can she do that is fun instead? Going out with good friends is much more likely to keep her on track than sitting at home alone willing herself not to watch.
- ***Remove Temptation***
  Find a way to remove the temptation, or at least put it out of sight. If she unplugs the TV and carries it to the garage, she'll have to go out of her way to fail at the goal.
- ***Reward Progress***
  Suggest that the client establish a reward for progress. "If I make it through the week without turning on the TV, I'll treat myself to dinner at Angelo's." Even better is to have an accountability partner participate: "If you get through the week without the tube, we'll both go out to dinner at your favorite restaurant."

just completed the first stage of a major life goal—finishing the first draft of your book. You've been working on this project for a year with your coach, you've overcome many obstacles on the way and at this appointment you're enthused about reaching a significant milestone. Put yourself into that role as much as you can. Then review the four sample responses below. For each one, if your coach had actually responded this way, how would it have affected your motivation?

1. "So, we've finished phase one—that leaves two more to go. Since you're roughly two months behind schedule, what could you do to get caught back up in this next phase?"
2. "I'm glad to hear you've wrapped that up. What other steps did you have on your list for this week?"
3. "Alright! Writing a book is a big achievement! You overcame some major obstacles to do this, especially the job change—you should be proud of how you stuck it out. How are you going to celebrate?"
4. "Wow, that was super-great! You did a fantastic job! You are awesome!"

How did you react to these three statements? The way affirmation is used sends a powerful message to the client. In the first statement above, the client has just completed a major, year-long project, yet the coach's focus is on how far behind the client is. By not including any appropriate encouragement, the coach sends this message: "Even though you finished you didn't do it right. Nothing you do is good enough." That may not be what the coach intends to communicate—internally, he may be very pleased with the client's progress. But failing to verbalize his feelings and moving immediately to the next problem or obstacle is a real downer for the client.

The second response above would feel like "damning with faint praise" to many. The coach's level of excitement doesn't match the scale of the client's achievement. A good yardstick is to be as passionate or more than your clients are about what they have accomplished. When you are less animated, you tone down the client's enthusiasm when your job as coach is to raise it. If the gap between your response and the client's is wide enough, you can even come across as disapproving of their progress. So, when something good happens, celebrate it together. Some of us are instinctive encouragers and do this unconsciously. If you are by nature more reserved, you may not realize that your natural responses are putting a damper on the client.

For most people, the third response above would launch them most energetically into the next phase of the project. What makes this affirmation meaningful is that it has genuine substance. The coach references specific obstacles that were overcome, and grounds the affirmation in real evidence of the client's character and performance. He is validating and affirming the client's identity as well as his performance.

> **Celebration**
>
> Extraordinary accomplishments call for special celebrations. If I have a client interviewing for a job or doing a major training event or waiting to hear back on a big contract, I'll say, "E-mail me and let me know what happens!" For most of us, life could be moresatisfying if we'd stop more often to smell the roses along the way. So help your clients rejoice in their progress:
>
> - "How are you going to celebrate finishing that project?"
> - "Let's just stop and celebrate! How does it feel to be done?"
> - "What could you do to savor that accomplishment before you dive into the next project?"

The fourth example ("Wow, that was super great! You did a fantastic job! You are awesome!") makes me a little queasy. Besides being overdone, it's a pretty lazy affirmation. Nothing specific is mentioned—it's merely a bunch of superlatives strung together. There is no reference to what was actually achieved, the difficulties that were overcome or what the outcome says about the character and calling of the person being affirmed. Offering superlatives alone doesn't require that you listen closely or tune into who your client really is. This type of affirmation quickly loses impact and begins to feel fake when overused.

I often say, "Great!" or "Alright!" when a client completes a simple step. But when it's time to give some significant feedback, I want to say something substantial and specific, like this: "You are much more positive about life than you were two months ago—and you talk a lot less about being stressed out. You've focused in, and already you're a third of the way to your sales goal for the year—that's wonderful!"

Validating a person's identity is the most powerful kind of affirmation. It's great to hear you that you did something well: "You did a tremendous job organizing the retreat." But to have someone call forth what is great in you is even more powerful: "The way you handled the retreat shows what a tremendous organizer you are. You are really gifted in that area." A coach should be constantly tuning into what is great about a client, so that when the opportunity for some real affirmation comes along you are primed and ready to offer something significant.

Superb affirmation is:

- ***Genuine:*** You mean what you say
- ***Unequivocal:*** Affirm decisively and confidently—no maybes!
- ***Energizing:*** Your response should match the client's enthusiasm and bring the energy level up
- ***Specific:*** Tie affirmation to tangible performance and real evidence of character
- ***Substantiative:*** Strong affirmation says something important about who the person is

The acronym G.U.E.S.S. is a memory device you can used to recall those characteristics: Genuine, Unequivocal, Energizing, Specific and Substantiative. When you affirm this way, the client never

Exercise 17.2: Encouraging with G.U.E.S.S.

Here's a simple way to practice giving encouragement. Think of a friend or relative who has recently achieved a major breakthrough or accomplishment. Take a few moments and sketch out what you might say to affirm that person, using the G.U.E.S.S. model.

has to *guess* about how you feel things are going.

Maintaining Expectations

Even with regular encouragement and accountability, sometimes action steps don't get done. Let's say your client's goal is to organize her office. For two weeks running her action step has been to remove the piles on her credenza, but today you find out she still hasn't even begun. How do you respond? Read the following two options and think about what impact each approach would have on you if you were this client:

1. "You know, when we set up this relationship you agreed that you were going to take it seriously and complete the steps that you chose. It's time to step it up and stop playing around. Set up a time this week when you are going to do this and *follow through*. OK?"

Exercise 17.3: Voice Tone

If affirmation doesn't come naturally for you, working on developing an enthusiastic tone of voice can increase your effectiveness. To see the difference, sit down with the person you thought of in exercise 17.2, and deliver the encouragement that you sketched out in three different ways:

1. Using your natural manner and tone of voice.
2. Again, consciously attempting to be more enthusiastic than normal (using the same words).
3. A third time, consciously attempting to be less enthusiastic than normal.

Let your friend know beforehand that you are working on voice tone, but don't let on which of the three is "normal" for you. Now, ask for some feedback: "which of these three approaches seemed most genuine and energizing to you? How did the other two approaches come across? Why?"

2. "That's OK—don't feel bad because you didn't get it done! It happens to all of us. I've had action steps with *my* coach that I didn't get done, too. When the right time comes, you'll get to it."

Coaching works because it is a great relationship built on clear expectations about change. If either the openness in the relationship or the high expectations are eroded, you'll lose effectiveness. The first example above maintains expectations, but at the expense of the relationship. I wouldn't want to be treated like this—would you? There is no grace or understanding, which damages the climate of unconditional belief a coach tries to build.

The second example is the opposite—it sacrifices high standards to maintain relationship. The problem is, if you don't uphold expectations in the relationship, the client will lose respect for both the process and you as the coach. The coach in the second example will soon find that his clients never get anything done. This type of response supplies no consequence for failure.

So the challenge for the coach is to maintain expectations without using up the goodwill in the relationship. You can do both! Here's the principle:

Give grace but don't lower the standard.

What that means is that the coach is not there to punish wrong behavior, but to help the client get up and get back on track as quickly as possible. I call that "doing a reset"—restarting the change process without wasting energy feeling guilty or shamed. Give grace where the client has failed, identify any obstacles that are blocking the process, and immediately get the client back on track. To not lower the standard means maintaining the expectation that this step *will* get done, even if it takes a little longer than we first thought. To give grace means accepting that there may be a good reason why things didn't get done and believing that the person's actions weren't motivated by apathy or disrespect.

Years ago I had a client who couldn't get his action steps done. He was an educator in the middle of a fund-raising campaign, and phone calls, interviews and meet-and-greets were always upsetting his plans for growth. So I said to him, "I'd like us to reach the point where you succeed at every step you set out to do. What could we change to reach that standard?"

At first he was at a loss, but as he began to examine options, he realized that his best time to work on reflective action steps was at work, not at home. It was the only place in his life where someone (his secretary) could guard the door for him and leave him uninterrupted. He had a legitimate obstacle to get around and his action steps were never going to get done until we overcame it.

Here are several more examples of how to give grace and not lower the standard when doing a reset:

- "Thanks for being honest with me about that. What do we need to do to make sure that your step gets accomplished this week?"
- "OK—that happens sometimes. Let's identify the obstacle and make a plan to deal with it. What stopped you from taking that step? What do we need to do to overcome that obstacle and move the piles?"
- "Is that still a step you want to take? [If so...] When would be a realistic date you could have that done by?"

The way these statements give grace is that there is no punishment or accusation in them. But they uphold the standard by assuming that the client is going to solve the problem and take the step. Although the client has failed in the short term, the coach still believes in the person and remains focused on future success.

As a coach, I never want to give up on an action step unless the client no longer wants to take it. We may adjust the step or put it on hold while we work at an underlying obstacle, but I won't forget about it unless we clearly decide to drop it. On one occasion I asked

Exercise 17.4: Maintaining Expectations

Think of a situation at work, church or at home where someone hasn't met expectations. What would it look like in that situation to give grace but not lower the standard? Jot down three options for what you could say to that person.

a client, "Is this a step you still want to take?" After thinking for a moment, he replied, "To be perfectly honest, Tony, no, I don't. That isn't nearly as important to me as the other things we are working on." At that point, we dropped the step and moved on without a second thought. If the client is not internally motivated to take a step, it shouldn't be on the list.

The Transformational Approach

I'm not discouraged when a client has a breakdown, because over and over I've seen breakdowns be the catalyst for breakthroughs. When a person is repeatedly tripped up by a simple step, it often reveals a much deeper issue. Taking a transformational approach means stopping to uncover and address the underlying issues instead of just pushing harder on the original step.

Sharon Graham had a client who suffered from insomnia. "As I talked with my coach about getting to bed earlier, she started probing. I come from a troubled family background, and though in day-to-day life it wasn't affecting me, I wasn't at rest in my mind and I couldn't sleep. I'd have periods where I couldn't sleep at all.

"When touched base on this in our next session (I hadn't made any progress), I said, "I want to meet this goal, but I just *can't!*" We started discussing it, and the next thing you know [we were talking

Exercise 17.5: The Good Reason

Think of a person or organizational leader that is doing something that doesn't make sense (i.e. seems stupid) to you. Challenge yourself:

1. Can you think of three good reasons why they might be acting in that way? (This is a great way to train yourself to believe that there is a good reason for what people do—whenever they do something you don't understand, see if you can come up with a plausible explanation for that behavior.)
2. Come up with three neutral probing questions you could ask that would help uncover that good reason.

about] forgiving my family and letting go. My coach didn't just stick with the surface issue—she helped me deal with the underlying problems. One was feeling unworthy, that I wasn't worth taking care of. If you don't believe you are worth taking care of, you won't make those long-term changes."

Sharon believed that her client had a good reason for what she did, and it led to a much broader transformation. When clients do something that doesn't make sense or seems self-destructive, find out why. If a person wants to take a step and can't, or sets out to pursue a goal and shies away from it, there's a reason. Find the reason and you can overcome the obstacle.

Challenging a Pattern

Sometimes you'll need to challenge the client more directly to maintain expectations. Years ago one of my clients, an entrepreneur with young children, was habitually late to our appointments. I knew he was a busy man, but when I began to probe a little I found that he was extremely overworked—to the tune of 80 plus hours per week. When I pointed out his pattern of being late and asked him to comment on what it meant, the resistance was palpable. He was sorry for being late, but he was fine, thank you, and didn't see anything wrong with his life patterns. Because he was not ready to hear, I backed off.

Six weeks later I gingerly brought up his schedule again. "You know," he said ruefully, "When you asked me about showing up late and my workload a while back, it was like a doctor probing a wound. Every time you touched it, it hurt! I was going, 'Ouch!' But when I went away and thought about what you said, I realized that I needed to make a change." One of the action steps he developed in that appointment was to make a covenant with his wife that before he said "yes" to any new commitments, he'd talk it through with her first.

Because coaching is about believing in people, my first response to a breakdown is to withhold judgment and believe that there is a good reason for what happened. Often that works. But there are still times when people are simply undisciplined, live out-of-control lives or the coaching relationship is not the priority for them that it should be. If you aren't accomplishing what you set out to do together, have an honest conversation about it and make some changes. If the reason the coaching relationship isn't working is that it isn't a priority, then respect the client's choice, give the person a graceful out and wrap up the relationship.

If we do decide to end the coaching relationship, I work hard to close on a positive note. I don't want my frustrations to put any obstacle in the person's way that would keep them from reaching out to a coach or mentor in the future. Terminating the relationship by telling the person off out of frustration is doing just that. It's not my job to judge a client's motives for not wanting to be coached. Who knows—in six months the person may be back with a whole new attitude.

Getting Into Coaching

Taking the Next Step

> *"The whole reason I came here [to graduate school] may have been for this [coach training] class...I have a $45,000 coaching bill right now... and it's worth every penny."* Grad Student

> *"All said and done, I will have spent about $4,000 out of pocket on [coach training] and travel, but it was worth the investment. If I had to do it over, I would do it again in a heartbeat. Can you put a price tag on life change, like this experience?"* Parachurch Ministry Leader

Now that you've completed a book on becoming a coach, you might be wondering, "Where do I go from here? How can I use this in my everyday life, and how can I continue to improve?" If you've really gotten inspired by the coaching approach, you may be asking, "Where do I go to get some serious coach training?"

Right now, the best thing you can do to grow as a coach is to put into practice the concepts and techniques you learned in this book. You don't have to be in a formal coaching relationship with a covenant and a client—you can practice coaching with your spouse, your kids or your friends (just let them know what you are doing so they understand and have a chance to buy into the process). The basic techniques of listening and asking questions can be used to make any conversation extraordinary.

Last Sunday I was chatting with a friend in the aisle before church—he was looking to hire a business manager to free up his time for other things, and I inquired if he had found anyone yet. While we were talking, my coaching intuition began to kick in. He was in a transitional period and I wondered if there was something more that God wanted to show him during his season of change. So I asked, "If you could do anything in life, what would you do?" At first, he said he was very content running his business and looking forward to adding a new division. But as we talked, a dormant vision began to come to the surface. He'd always wanted to start a U.S.-based import/export company to market items handmade by African Christians. So, I followed up: "What's stopping you from pursuing your vision?" In ten minutes we had a great discussion and he began to think seriously again about pursuing this God-given dream.

Invest in Others

The opportunities to invest in others by coaching them are all around you. Back when I was 17, I remember desperately wanting someone to walk with me as a mentor. If only I had someone I respected to help me understand and live out the Christian life! I got through those teen years, but it was a tough and lonely time spiritually. Years later, I was sharing my story with an old friend of my father's, a retired pastor who had been in our church at the time. He replied, "You know, I felt a leading back then to reach out to you and mentor you, but I had been exposed to the shepherding movement years before and after that I was afraid to try."

What a tragic story! God heard my prayer and prompted someone to respond, but my answer never came. I didn't know why until 20 years later.

Today, you could be the answer to someone's prayer to grow faster, reach higher, or live more fully for Christ. Want to respond? Ask God to send someone to you who needs a coach. Ask God to show you who to take initiative with and offer to coach them. Don't be timid—you probably know at least five people who would love to have a coach right now.

A Daily Coaching Workout

While you are looking for a formal relationship, practice your coaching skills in informal situations. Here are ten ways to do a daily coaching workout:

1. When you meet people, practice posing significant questions instead of surface ones. Ask: "What do you want out of life?" or "Where do you want to be in five years?" instead of "Did you catch the Lakers last night?"
2. Try to listen three times as much as you talk.
3. Gather information for twice as long as you are used to before you go into problem-solving mode.
4. Give more responsibility to your kids and treat them more like adults.
5. Set a goal to have one significant, extraordinary conversation each day.
6. When people ask your opinion, turn it around and ask them what *they* think—and then affirm their insights.
7. Form an accountable, growth-centered relationship with a peer and keep it going for at least six months.
8. Set a growth goal for your own life and build the support structures you need to reach it.
9. Find someone who needs support and send them an encouraging e-mail or call every week.
10. Identify the three people around you that you most tend to take responsibility for and practice letting go.

The Limitations of Book Learning

Coaching is like basketball. Read a book about basketball and you may develop a great conceptual understanding of the game. But go out on the court the next day and you won't be any better at shooting free throws or dribbling the ball behind your back than you were before you started reading. The book can give you the *information* you need to excel, but only *practice* can change your stat line. In sports, you practice to develop the muscle memory and confidence in your shot you need to perform consistently at a high level. If you don't practice, you don't play.

Reading this book will give you a good conceptual understanding of coaching. But go to work or to church tomorrow and your actual conversations won't be much different. Understanding coaching concepts won't magically change the way you act around people. You have the conversational habits of a lifetime to contend with. To learn to coach, you're going to have to work at it. To transform others, you must first be transformed yourself.

So, start with the fundamentals: listening, asking, believing in people and keeping others responsible for their own lives. The ten steps on the previous page will give you a daily workout. Or you might tackle something bigger:

- Your son is in his 20's and giving advice is no longer a productive way to relate to him. Completely revamp your relationship using coaching principles. Listen instead of telling, stop giving advice, keep him responsible and allow him the freedom to learn from failure as well as success. Can you build a great, authentic, fun relationship with your son as a fellow adult?
- Find a young, emerging leader or two in your church and offer to invest in their lives. Set up formal coaching relationships, let them set their own goals and choose their own actions. Be an empowering influence and not a teller. Be their biggest fan and greatest advocate.
- Find a peer who is interested in coaching and go back through the book together. Try out the exercises on each other. Then set up a peer coaching relationship and practice coaching each other: I'll coach you for half an hour and then you can coach me.
- Interview everyone on a team you lead. Find out what their dreams are, what they'd like to accomplish in the next year, what they are passionate about. Listen, and get to know them at a new level. Then find a way to support or advocate for each person's dream during the next month.

Practice is hard work, but the payoff is tremendous.

Find a Coach

Every coach should have a coach (unless you want to be one of the "blind guides leading the blind"). If you want to help others grow, you must be growing yourself. You'll learn invaluable lessons about coaching by watching your coach in action, and your own progress will be an inspiration to those you are working with. Your personal testimony of the impact of coaching on your own life is a great tool for getting others interested. Plus, you'll grow faster and reach your own important life goals!

If you'd like to find a personal coach, the first step is to chat with several coaches to see which one is the best match for your needs. Many coaches offer brief complimentary sessions for serious inquiries, so you can experience working with that coach before you sign up.

Coaching Certification

In every coach training class I hear someone say, "This is me! I've been doing this all my life; I just never knew what to call it!" If you sense a calling to coach, a formal coach-training program is the next step. (If you want to coach as a vocation or as part of your job responsibilities, it's a must.) The greatest benefit of formal training is exposure to a professional coach trainer. You'll get to watch an expert model coaching techniques and debrief afterward, practice your skills with other trainees and get feedback, and explore coaching issues in much greater depth. The "Leadership Coaching Live" CD set that goes with this book provides a sampling of coach trainers in action, but there's no substitute for live interaction.

Most programs include personal coaching, workshops or tele-classes, a set of coaching resources and materials designed for use with your clients and interactive practice with other trainees. You'll also gain access to web-based resources, a community of other coaches, continuing education opportunities and more. The coaching industry provides certification standards for credentialing coaches and in most cases you'll also receive a credential with your coach training.

Consult *The Complete Guide to Christian Coach Training* by Linda Hedberg for a list of Christian coaching programs. http://www.coach22.com/guide-to-christian-coach-traingin.html

Make a Difference

Learning to coach is discovering how to make mundane conversations extraordinary. It's training yourself to show respect, honor and belief in other people. It's building the kind of relationships we all long for. It's helping others grow, fulfill their destinies and exceed even their own expectations for themselves.

What would it be worth to you to significantly improve your relationship with your spouse or your kids? What if the performance on your team at work improved by even 10%? What difference would it make if the people you minister to each had a coaching support structure to provide the follow-up they need to succeed? What if you invested significantly in just ten other people in your lifetime, so that they accomplished twice as much in the Kingdom of God as they could on their own?

Those are all things you can do with coaching. Reach for the best, lay down your life and make the difference in the world that you were born to make. Real fulfillment comes from serving others. As the apostle John said, summing up his own lifetime in ministry, "Nothing could make me happier than getting reports that my children continue diligently in the way of Truth!" (III John 1:4 MSG).

Appendix A

50 Key Coaching Principles

Goal Setting

1. Set a goal that you control.
2. Don't set any goals you aren't going to meet.
3. Success breeds success.
4. The best goal is the one you are most motivated to work on.

Listening and Asking

5. Ask, don't tell.
6. Collect more data before making a conclusion.
7. People have a good reason for what they do.
8. The See/Say Principle: just because I see something doesn't mean I'm supposed to say it.
9. It doesn't make any difference what you see; the only thing that makes any difference is what the client sees.
10. Don't try to diagnose a problem the client has lived with for 30 years in 30 seconds.

11. Listening and asking questions are the disciplines of believing in people.
12. Follow your curiosity, not your diagnosis.
13. Your intuition doesn't tell you there's a problem; it shows you where to ask.
14. Turn off the conversation in your head.

The Heart of a Coach

15. If you have the heart of a coach, the skills will come naturally.
16. What you do comes out of who you are. (Who you are is what you have to give.)
17. Out of the abundance of the heart the mouth speaks.
18. Your greatest ministry effectiveness will come in the areas God has most deeply shaped you.
19. Skills channel character.
20. Technique without heart is manipulation.
21. It's about the client, not about you.

Transformation and Change

22. Information does not produce transformation.
23. It takes six weeks to form habit; but six months to make it permanent.
24. A skill can be learned in a day; habits take time.
25. Transformation is experiential and relational, not informational.
26. Change is more a function of motivation than information.
27. Your own insight is ten times as powerful as my advice.
28. Reflection is the key to replication.

Personal Responsibility

29. Keeping people responsible builds leadership capacity.
30. Leaders take responsibility for their own growth.

31. We have the ability to steward responsibly the life that God has entrusted to us.
32. Authority and responsibility go together.
33. Healthy accountability is voluntary.
34. You can't have authenticity without integrity.

The Coach's Role

35. You aren't responsible for the client's outcome.
36. I can only do the things I see my Father doing.
37. The client sets the agenda; the coach focuses the conversation and drives it to action.
38. Follow the client's discernment, not your own.
39. The relationship comes first; then the change.
40. The line a coach never crosses is, a coach never takes away the client's responsibility to choose.
41. Build leaders, don't solve problems.
42. Problems are opportunities.
43. People can solve their own problems.
44. Let the client do the thinking.
45. Give grace but don't lower the standard.

Conflict and Relational Capital

46. You build relational capital so that it's there to spend when you need it.
47. Don't use a bigger stick than you have to. (Conserve your relational capital.)
48. If God can live with the million things that He sees wrong in my life, I ought to be able to live with the few that I see in you.

Decision Making

49. I'm more interested in seeing you become a great decision maker than make a great decision.

50. If I help you make a great decision, I've helped you today. If I help you become a great decision maker, I've impacted every decision you'll make for the rest of your life.

Destiny

51. Character is in short supply, and God doesn't waste it.
52. God is more interested in who you are becoming than in what you are doing.
53. Fulfilling your destiny is only possible in community.

My Coaching Principles

1. ______________________________
____
2. ______________________________
____
3. ______________________________
____
4. ______________________________
____
5. ______________________________
____
6. ______________________________
____
7. ______________________________
____
8. ______________________________
____

Appendix B
Coaching Resources

Sample Welcome Letter

Welcome!

Coaching is a great way to develop your self as a person, work at change or live a more focused life. I'm looking forward to working together to help you cultivate a life of greatness!

One of the things I most enjoy about coaching is that it isn't about fixing people. Instead, a coach functions as a partner and an advocate, helping you live out your own values and dreams for your life. You'll be the one setting the agenda for our relationship and taking responsibility for making the changes. I'll focus our conversations, helping you to go deeper, reach higher, and explore the strategies and support structures you need to succeed. And together we'll create a customized, systematic plan and walk it out to make your goal a reality.

Here's how we'll start. Since effective coaching is based on relationship, I'd like to begin with a double session (twice as long as normal) so that we have time to get to know one another. I want to hear your life story and tell you mine, to build trust and a context for understanding each other. Then we'll finalize the goal you want to work on, clarify expectations by filling out a coaching agreement (see attached), and create a plan of action you can start on immediately.

I've included several exercises for you to complete before our first appointment so we'll hit the ground running. The first objective is for you to clearly identify what you'd like to work on with your coach. You might choose:

- A habit or skill you want to develop.
- A dream or goal you'd like to pursue in a focused way.
- Discovering or understanding your gifts, dreams, life stage or calling.
- A practical change you want to make to your life patterns (like getting organized).

If you aren't sure where to start, the *Wheel of Life* exercise will help you evaluate your level of satisfaction in 12 different areas of life and hone in on which area you are most motivated to change. Once you've established a general objective, use the *S.M.A.R.T. Goals* format to create a clear, measurable goal. We'll use this objective as the launching point for our discussion.

I've also included two informational pages about coaching. Please take a few minutes to review them before we meet. The *What is Coaching?* flyer gives an overview of what coaching is and how it functions. I've also included a page of testimonials by my clients to give you an idea of what to expect!

You can contact me from 8 am to 5:30 pm eastern time at 333-333-3333. My e-mail address is *JohnDoe@MyDomain.com*. I'm looking forward to a great, transforming relationship!

Sincerely;

John Doe
TLC Certified Coach

Sample Coaching Covenant

(For unpaid coaching relationships)

Client

I'm excited about working together on this growth goal:

____

____

____

I will diligently complete the action steps we agree on, and be punctual for our meetings so we'll make the most of our time together. I will consistently take the initiative with you in this relationship. I'm responsible for my life, and I'll make and follow through with my choices about what actions to take and what we work on together.

I will be a trustworthy partner, honest and open with you about what is going on in my life, and handling what you share with me with respect and discretion.

Coach

I am excited about coaching you in this area. I covenant with you to be punctual and well-prepared so we can make the most of our time together. I will be a trustworthy partner, honest and open with you about what is going on in my life, and handling what you share with me with respect and discretion. I'm committed to believing in you, supporting you in your change goals and helping you live out your destiny.

Practical Expectations

1) **Meeting Frequency**:
   We'll meet ______ times per month for ____ minutes each session.
2) **Commitment**:
   We're committing to work together in a coaching relationship until ______________________ (date).
3) **Review**:

We will take time to review how our relationship is going and make any needed adjustments on ________________.

4) **Outside Perspective**:
I periodically approach ______________________ for advice and consultation on my coaching relationships in order to offer you the best coaching service that I can.

5) **Action Steps**:
Our appointments may be canceled if agreed on action steps have not been substantially completed.

6) **Schedule**:
We will respect each other's schedules by making every effort to hold rescheduling and cancellations to a minimum.

7) **Initiative**:
If I can't make a meeting or meet expectations, I will take initiative to let you know and reschedule with as much notice as possible (24 hours minimum).

I agree to maintain these expectations in our coaching relationship.

______________________ ______________________
Coach Client

The TLC Wheel of Life

For each of the sectors on the chart below, rank yourself on a scale of 1 to 10: "How satisfied am I with this area of my life?" For instance, if you are feeling great about your *Personal Development*, you might give yourself a "9". So, shade in nine tenths of the *Personal Development* segment, starting from the inside out.

Evaluation

The diagram gives you a picture of how your present life matches up with what you want it to be. If you aren't sure what this means, bring the chart to a coaching appointment and ask for help.

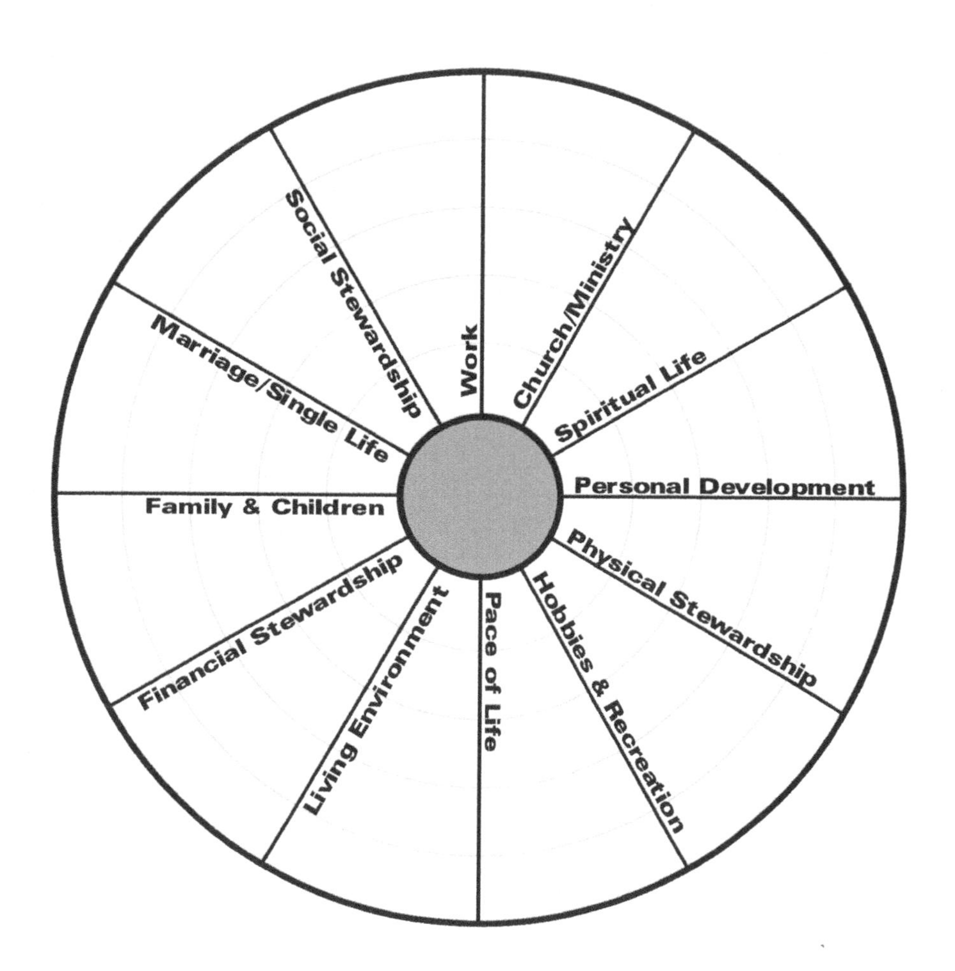

Index

Topical Index

Index of Major Topics

Made in the USA
Monee, IL
27 May 2021